How to Form Your Own "S" Corporation

and Avoid Double Taxation

(2nd Edition)

Ted Nicholas
Robert Friedman

DEARBORN™
A **Kaplan Professional** Company

This publication is designed to provide accurate and authoritative information in regard to the subject matter covered. It is sold with the understanding that the publisher is not engaged in rendering legal, accounting, or other professional service. If legal advice or other expert assistance is required, the services of a competent professional person should be sought.

Acquisitions Editor: Jean Iversen
Managing Editor: Jack Kiburz
Interior Design: Lucy Jenkins
Cover Design: The Publishing Services Group
Typesetting: Elizabeth Pitts

Published by Dearborn, a Kaplan Professional Company

Printed in the United States of America

99 00 01 10 9 8 7 6 5 4 3 2 1

Library of Congress Cataloging-in-Publication Data

Nicholas, Ted, 1934–
    How to form your own "S" Corporation and avoid double taxation /
Ted Nicholas, Robert Friedman.—2nd ed.
      p. cm.
    Includes index.
    ISBN 1-57410-126-9
    1. Subchapter S corporations—Popular works.   I. Friedman,
Robert, 1953–   . II. Title.
KF6491.Z9N53   1999
346.73'0668—dc21   99-23050
                                        CIP

Contents

1

How the "S" Corporation Works for You

More than 40 years ago, President Dwight D. Eisenhower, in his Budget Message to Congress, made the point: "Small businesses should be able to operate under whatever form of organization is desirable for their particular circumstances, without incurring unnecessary tax penalties. To secure this result, I recommend that corporations with a small number of active stockholders be given the option to be taxed as partnerships."

President Eisenhower's recommendation recognized the difficult, often irreconcilable choice facing many entrepreneurs when they embark on a new venture: whether to opt for (1) the favorable tax advantages available to individual entrepreneurs and partnerships and risk the vast potential for personal liability to which every business is exposed in our litigious society or (2) the security of the corporate form and expose the profits of their labors to the double taxation imposed on corporate profits.

Four years after President Eisenhower's recommendation, Congress finally acted: in 1958, the subchapter "S" corporation was created. While not providing everything sought by the President, the new form of corporation was responsive to his request. It required a series of amendments in the law through 1982 for President Eisenhower's request to come to life. Today, the "S" corporation, in most respects, is a corporation that is taxed as if a partnership.

As important as this measure was in the 1950s, it is even more meaningful to today's businessperson. In the past, the top rate for corporations was lower than the top rate for individuals. Then the Tax Reform Act of 1986 reversed that rule: corporations now pay a top tax rate that is 3 percent higher than the maximum rate imposed on individuals. Adding insult to injury is the fact that corporate profits remain subject to double taxation, whereas an individual or a partner is taxed once on his or her income.

Despite some early claims that the Revenue Reconciliation Act of 1993 dealt a severe blow to the "S" corporation, that simply is not the case. Most leading tax experts still recommend the "S" corporation as the single most valuable tool entrepreneurs can use to eliminate the harsh impact of the double taxation imposed on regular "C" corporations. The simple truth is that the single tax imposed on "S" corporation shareholders always leaves more money in their pockets than would the double tax imposed on their business's profits if the shareholders had selected a "C" corporation.

The Small Business Job Protection Act, which went into effect on January 1, 1997, made "S" corporations more attractive. The act permits the IRS to waive inadvertent errors in elections and terminations; eases the restrictions on the number and type of shareholders; allows sprinkling trusts, retirement plans, and tax-exempt organizations to be "S" corporation shareholders; and permits "S" corporations to own shares in a corporation or have a wholly owned "S" corporation subsidiary.

The new shareholder rules facilitate planning as follows:

1. The "S" corporation may now have 75 shareholders, instead of 35. The owners of family businesses may vest share ownership in several generations. Start-up companies can obtain capital from a larger number of shareholders.
2. The corporation may have an electing small business trust (ESBT) as a shareholder, instead of a qualified subchapter "S" trust (QSST). The owners may spread income among a class of people through a single trust.
3. Tax-exempt organizations also may qualify as shareholders. Employees can own the corporation through employee benefit plans. Shareholders can donate their stock to charity.

In order to understand just how valuable an "S" corporation can be, also consider these results of tax changes implemented in recent years:

1. If a "C" corporation has annual profits of more than $75,000 and less than $250,000, it will pay a top tax rate of at least 3 percent and as much as 11 percent higher than the tax rate imposed on individuals who form an "S" corporation—and the "C" corporation's profits will be taxed twice.
2. Even if a corporation's profits are less than $75,000 or more than $250,000, *shareholders will always pay less taxes if they form an "S" corporation.* This is because regular "C" corporation profits are taxed twice, whereas an individual's profits are taxed only once.

3. If a "C" corporation has profits that range between $100,000 and $335,000, its tax rate is 39 percent. The top tax rates for individuals in those brackets range from 31 percent to 39.6 percent.

THE CONCEPT OF DOUBLE TAXATION

When a regular corporation, (i.e., a "C" corporation) ends the year in the black, it pays a corporate income tax on its profits. If those profits will go to the corporation's owners, its shareholders, the corporation must declare a dividend. The recipients of that dividend—again, the corporation shareholders—are required to include the dividend as part of their income; and that money is taxed again. These results stem from the fact that for tax purposes, the "C" corporation is viewed as a taxable entity—that is, a person.

Assume you did not form a corporation, but instead operated your business as an individual or, together with another person, as a partnership or an LLC. The profits of the business would not be taxed. Rather, the business would file a tax return showing income, deductions, losses, and credits for the year. Those items are then passed through to the partners, who report them on their returns and either pay a personal income tax on any profit or take the benefit of the loss, if there is one. These results stem from the fact that a partnership is not viewed as a taxable entity. It is merely a conduit that pays no taxes, but shifts its profits and losses to its partners.

HOW THE "S" CORPORATION WORKS FOR YOU

The "S" corporation combines what is generally viewed as the best of all possible worlds: it provides the limitations on investor liability associated with incorporation and the "pass-through" taxation attribute of a partnership (i.e., single, not double taxation).

The tax benefits that flow from using the "S" corporation mean that any loss suffered by the corporation is not wasted and that profits made by the corporation are taxed once, not twice. Let's look at three examples of how "S" incorporation can benefit you.

Example No. 1

Assume John Investor formed a regular "C" corporation in 1998. Given high start-up costs, the business absorbs a $20,000 loss during its first year. That loss is useless to Mr. Investor. He cannot claim it on his return because it is the corporation's loss, not his personal loss. All he can do is carry the loss forward on the corporation's books and use it to offset corporate profits in 1999.

Now let's assume Mr. Investor had formed an "S" corporation. That $20,000 loss would flow through to him, and he could use it to offset other earnings. If we assume Mr. Investor is a single person with additional income of $90,000, the "S" corporation loss would reduce his other income to $70,000. In his case, the tax savings would amount to $6,200. Mr. Investor, therefore, would have kept an extra $6,200 of his hard-earned money in his pocket simply by choosing "S" incorporation over regular incorporation.

Example No. 2

Jane Businessperson, a married woman, formed a regular "C" corporation in 1998. Assume that after paying her a salary of $75,000 the corporation had $100,000 in profits. The corporation would pay $22,250 in taxes on those profits (15 percent on the first $50,000; 25 percent on the next $25,000; and 34 percent on the next $25,000). The corporation's after-tax profits will be $77,750.

Now assume she takes the $77,750 out of the business as a dividend. Also assume that she and her spouse have other income of $16,850, which brings their combined income to $91,850—the point at which the 31 percent tax rate begins. Their total income will be $169,600 (including her salary, the $77,750 dividend and their other income of $16,850). Mr. and Mrs. Businessperson will pay a total of $46,469 in personal income taxes on that $169,600. Add to that the $22,250 her corporation paid on its $100,000 in profits, and the total paid to the government is $68,719—*almost 69 percent of the corporation's profits have been lost to taxes*.

Now let's assume Mrs. Businessperson had formed an "S" corporation when she went into business. The $100,000 in profits would not have been taxed at the corporate level. Instead, it would flow through to her, and she and her husband would have had income of $175,000 from the corporation (her salary plus the $100,000 in profits) plus the $16,850 of other income. Their total income of $191,850 would be subject to $54,371 in taxes—instead of the $69,719 they would have paid if they had formed a "C" corporation. Mr. and Mrs. Businessperson will end up keeping an extra $15,348 in their pockets simply because Mrs. Businessperson had the foresight to form an "S" corporation. And she has all of the protection and benefits offered by the corporate form of business organization to boot.

Example No. 3

Let's assume that five years go by and Mrs. Businessperson (see Example No. 2) sells the business assets at a $1,000,000 gain, liquidates the corporation, and distributes the proceeds to herself. Before the Tax Reform Act of 1986, the proceeds in this example would have been taxed only once, as a capital gain to Mrs. Businessperson. Today, however, the corporation will be taxed at a 34 percent rate on its gain, and Mrs. Businessperson will be taxed on the remainder. Translated into actual dollars, $340,000 of the money paid to the corporation will be lost to taxes. Of the remaining $660,000, an additional $237,665 will be lost to taxes when the money gets into Mrs. Businessperson's hands. The bottom line is that $577,665 of the $1,000,000—more than half—will be lost to taxes.

What would have happened had Mrs. Businessperson formed an "S" corporation? She would have saved almost a quarter of a million dollars in taxes. The $1,000,000 would have been taxed once, not twice. Mrs. Businessperson would have paid $372,305 in taxes instead of $577,665—a savings of $205,360 because she chose "S" incorporation.

THE NUMBERS THAT WORK FOR YOU

You may have heard that because some personal income tax rates are higher than corporate rates, it may not pay for certain individuals to form an "S" corporation. That simply is not true. In fact, in Example No. 3 above, Mrs. Businessperson, as the shareholder of an "S" corporation, was taxed at the top rate of 39.6 percent on her profits—well above the corporate tax, which averages out to 34 percent. Nevertheless, she still had a total tax bill that was $200,000 less than it would have been had she formed a "C" corporation. This is because she paid a single tax rate that averaged out to 37.2 percent instead of a corporate tax rate that averaged out to 34 percent followed by a personal tax rate of 39.6 percent.

The reason an "S" corporation is always the better choice for most entrepreneurs is that its profits are taxed only once. Furthermore, for married taxpayers with incomes of less than $140,000 (or single taxpayers with incomes of less than $115,000), the tax rate imposed on their earnings is always lower than the corporate rate. In those cases, not only will you pay one tax instead of two taxes if you choose "S" incorporation, but you will pay a significantly lower tax rate than the corporate rate. Even in those situations where an individual's personal tax rate is higher than the corporate rate, the single tax applicable to an "S" corporation's profits always makes it the best choice.

Finally, we should note that if you reside in a state with both corporate and personal income taxes, the "S" corporation is even more attractive because states often apply their tax laws in the same manner as the federal government. That means you will enjoy comparable "single-tax" savings on your state taxes if you opt for "S" incorporation instead of "C" incorporation.

2

Choosing Your Business Organization

THE SIX CHOICES

Most professionals, if asked what choices an entrepreneur has when starting a business, list three options: the sole proprietorship, the partnership, and the corporation. More sophisticated professionals are aware of two other choices: the limited partnership and the limited liability company. But, as countless thousands of small business people know, there is a sixth choice—the "S" corporation.

The choice of business form usually involves two key issues: favorable tax treatment and protection from liability for the debts of the business. Under most options, you can get only one of those benefits, but not the other. The "S" corporation allows you to enjoy both. Let's see what each of these six choices means to the businessperson embarking on a new venture.

The Sole Proprietorship

The greatest drawback to the sole proprietorship is that it exposes its owner to complete liability for the debts of the business. That exposure can be unlimited. In effect, when an individual forms a business and operates it in his or her own name (or a trade name), that person runs the risk of having all of his or her personal assets exposed to creditors of the business. So, for example, if an employee accidentally or carelessly injures a customer or some other person, the owner of the business stands personally liable for the injury. Even if there is insurance coverage, the possibility always exists that liability may exceed the coverage provided by the policy—particularly in a society such as ours, where multimillion-dollar judgments are becoming commonplace.

Another drawback exists. If the sole proprietor becomes ill or dies, the business he or she has developed immediately loses much of its value. It becomes difficult, if not impossible, to hide the fact that the business is available under a forced sale—a situation guaranteed to bring less than the best possible selling price.

The chief benefit of the sole proprietorship is favorable tax treatment—a benefit not to be taken lightly. A sole proprietorship is not a taxable entity. In other words, any gain, loss, deduction or business credit available because of the business belongs to the sole proprietor.

Overall, however, having all of one's assets (e.g., savings, home, auto, etc.) at risk because of a business venture makes the sole proprietorship unattractive to many people.

The Partnership

The partnership form of business shares many of the benefits and drawbacks of the sole proprietorship. Each partner is personally liable for all of the business debts. The partnership relation comes to an end whenever any partner decides he or she no longer wants to be part of the business or whenever a partner dies or becomes bankrupt. This means that the continuity of the business is uncertain and can end on the whim of a partner.

Other drawbacks include the difficulty of obtaining new partners, particularly if they do not share profits on an equal basis. Would you, for example, be willing to take less than an equal share of profits as a partner if you had to expose yourself to the potential of 100 percent liability for the business debts?

As in the case of the sole proprietorship, the partnership is not a taxable entity. Its profits, gains, losses and credits pass through to its partners. Unlike the corporation, which is discussed below, a partnership's profits are taxed only once, not twice.

The Corporation

Perhaps the greatest bundle of "nontax" benefits is wrapped in the garb of the corporation.

The most significant attribute of the corporation is its ability to shield its investors from personal liability. The shareholder is not liable for the debts of the business. The corporation, in the eyes of the law, is an independent person held solely liable for its debts. The only exception to this rule occurs when courts "pierce the corporate veil" because of fraud on the part of its shareholders or with respect to penalties imposed under environmental laws. Otherwise, the shareholder's maximum risk in the corporation is measured by the amount of money he or she invests in it.

Second, the corporation has perpetual life. If one of its shareholders dies, becomes incapacitated or bankrupt or chooses to leave the business, the corporation continues its independent existence.

Next, the corporate mode of doing business makes it easier to attract additional investors and to attract them on more favorable terms than does a partnership. If a corporation with a proven track record needs additional money, it may find it possible to attract investors who will put in more money than the original shareholders and who will take back less proportionate interest. Remember, those new investors—unlike potential investors in a partnership—will not put their entire personal fortunes at risk when they invest in the corporation.

Why would an investor pay more for less? For several reasons. First, the business's proven track record indicates the nature of the expected return. Second, the business's form ensures the investor that he or she will not pick up any unanticipated liabilities.

Third, the corporate form of business makes it possible to attract passive investors who will allow those entrepreneurs who have run the business profitably to continue doing so without much interference. In a partnership, where new investors have all of their personal assets at risk, it is more likely that they will demand that they be kept up to date on all business decisions and that they have equal voices in those decisions.

Fourth, an individual can form a corporation and maintain anonymity. So, for example, a doctor who wishes to open a copying center may not want the general public to know of his involvement in the center. If he operates as a sole proprietor, he must be known openly as the owner; the same probably will be true if he joins with a second person in a partnership. If, however, he forms a corporation, his affiliation with the business need not ever become a matter of public record.

Finally, a corporation's shares are freely transferable. This means that any shareholder may sell his or her shares to any other person without ending the business (if the parties wish, this right can be restricted).

With all of these benefits, why isn't the corporation the perfect vehicle at all times for every investor? Because of the federal government's tax laws!

A corporation is a person for tax purposes. This means that if it profits, even if those earnings are not distributed to shareholders, the corporation must pay a tax on the profit. If it suffers a loss, that loss does not work to the benefit of its shareholders. At most, the loss can be saved and applied against corporate profits in a future year. Then, when profits are distributed to shareholders as dividends, they are taxed a second time as income to the recipients.

The Limited Partnership

The limited partnership was created in an attempt to gain the best attributes of the corporation and the partnership. It is a business entity that enjoys single taxation and at the same time protects most—but not all—of its investors from personal liability. Essentially, a limited partnership must have at least two limited partners and one general partner. The limited partners are passive investors who cannot be held personally liable for the debts or obligations of the business. As a general rule, a limited partner does not get a salary or other compensation for services from the limited partnership. Instead, the limited partner receives only his or her proportionate share of the company's profits, and that income is taxed only once, just as income of a partner in a general partnership is taxed only once.

A limited partner, however, cannot take part in the management of the business. He or she must be a passive investor. That is why we noted that a limited partner generally does not get a salary for services offered to the limited partnership. If a limited partner is to receive a salary or compensation for services, the services must be routine, nondiscretionary services such as secretarial work or bookkeeping.

In addition to limiting the management role of the limited partner, this form of business involves a second substantial drawback: a limited partnership must have at least one "person" who can be held liable for the debts of the business. That person is its general partner. There is a way to get around the thrust of this requirement: appoint a corporation as the general partner. However, this option requires that the corporation be a funded entity with a meaningful amount of assets or the limited partnership will not receive the favorable tax treatment its investors have in mind.

Overall, the complications involved in gaining both favorable tax treatment and limited liability make the limited partnership a questionable and expensive choice for a new business. Not only will you incur the cost of setting up a limited partnership (most lawyers charge more for setting up a limited partnership than they do to set up a corporation), but you will also pay to create a corporation to serve as the general partner. Furthermore, because most small-business owners are active managers of their businesses, the requirement that they take themselves out of management may prove highly unattractive to most entrepreneurs.

The Limited Liability Company

A rather new creation, the limited liability company (LLC), much like the limited partnership, seeks to offer entrepreneurs the best of both worlds: protection from liability for debts of the business and favorable taxation. Today, almost every state recognizes the LLC.

The structure of an LLC closely resembles the corporate structure. The owners of the company are called "members" and function like the shareholders of a corporation. Depending on how the "articles" of an LLC are drafted, the members can run the company themselves or they can elect managers who function as the directors and officers of the company.

In concept, the LLC offers the benefits that have made the "S" corporation so popular: it is taxed like a partnership and offers the centralized management and limited liability features of the corporation (the only loss members risk is the loss of their original investment).

But the LLC has two drawbacks that small entrepreneurs should consider. First, unlike "S" corporations, LLCs are a very new form of business. There has not been time yet to develop a substantial body of law and tax rules and regulations lawyers can look to in giving advice about LLCs. Even if your lawyer thinks he or she dots every "i" and crosses every "t," the possibility exists that a court reviewing a case involving an LLC may think a particular "i" was not dotted, and the entrepreneur's tax break or limited liability protection may go down the drain.

"S" corporations, on the other hand, have existed for decades. Lawyers and accountants have a vast body of case law and tax rules and regulations they can look to for guidance. In fact, "S" corporation law is so clear and settled that the average person can set up a solid, working "S" corporation without professional assistance. That simply is not the case with LLCs. The uncertainty surrounding them today is enormous, although that may not be true ten years from now, but it is the case today. Any individual who tries to set up an LLC without professional advice would be foolhardy at best. Most lawyers, in fact, profess to know little if anything about LLCs and urge their clients to use the "S" corporation, a business format about which they can provide meaningful advice.

In short, the LLC promises the benefits of "S" incorporation and avoids some limitations on "S" corporations (none of which are significant to most small companies), but it simply is too new an entity for most people to rely on. The LLC may well become the medium of choice 10 or 20 years from now, but it is a highly risky vehicle today.

The "S" Corporation

Unlike a regular corporation, which is treated as a separate person for tax purposes, an "S" corporation avoids separate taxation for most purposes. Essentially, the "S" corporation more closely resembles the partnership for tax purposes because its income, deductions, losses and credits flow through to the corporation shareholders, who account for those items on their returns. The tax form filled out by an "S" corporation is, in fact, a reporting form that breaks down the various types of income, deductions, losses and business credits that will become part of the shareholders' income tax filing.

There are exceptions to the rules stated above. First, an "S" corporation may be liable for certain capital gains, usually where a regular corporation converts to an "S" corporation in order to avoid double taxation. Second, certain types of "passive income" may be subject to double taxation if the "S" corporation was previously a regular corporation. Both exceptions are discussed in the chapters on "S" corporation taxation.

Despite its favorable tax position, the "S" corporation suffers no concomitant loss of nontax benefits available to regular corporations. Its shareholders are immune from personal liability for the business debts. Shares are transferable to anyone willing to buy into the "S" corporation (although there are limits on the number of shareholders the corporation can have). Corporate existence remains perpetual, and an individual can maintain the same degree of anonymity available in regular incorporation.

What then are the drawbacks to "S" incorporation? There are very few. First, unlike a regular corporation, an "S" corporation may not get the benefit of a business deduction for fringe benefit payments made on behalf of its shareholder-employees. Given the cost of certain fringe benefits, particularly health benefits, this is a meaningful concern. However, there are techniques available that make it possible for the small business to enjoy "S" corporation status and obtain the advantages and deductions inherent in fringe benefit programs (see Chapter 9).

STATE TAX CONSEQUENCES

Whether to use an LLC or an "S" corporation may depend on the state tax consequences. Some states do not follow the federal tax treatment of either "S" corporations or the partnership treatment of LLCs. Some states tax an LLC as a corporation regardless of its federal tax status. Other states tax an "S" corporation's income wholly or partially.

Converting from an existing corporation to an LLC treated as a partnership for federal taxes could result in a tax liability. The conversion will be treated as a taxable liquidation with gain being taxed at both the corporate and shareholder levels. The "S" corporation rules may provide the only available relief because the conversion usually is not considered to be a taxable event.

IF YOU HAVE AN EXISTING CORPORATION

Even if you have already established a business that operates as a "C" corporation, you can obtain the benefits of "S" incorporation. The procedure for switching to "S" corporation status is quite simple and is explained in subsequent chapters. Once the switch is made, almost all "S" corporation benefits become available to your business. Furthermore, those few areas for which you do not get the benefit of single taxation are treated no worse than they would have been had you not made the switch.

The First Step:
Creating Your Corporation

THE NEED TO INCORPORATE

In order to have a valid "S" corporation, you must first form a valid corporation under state law. Although many people believe it is difficult and expensive to form a corporation, nothing could be further from the truth. It is possible to form a corporation in Delaware for $74, and your corporation can operate anywhere in the United States. Why Delaware? Because the Delaware corporation laws take particular notice of requirements for "S" corporation status and expressly permit your business to do everything legally necessary to qualify for and maintain your company's status as an "S" corporation.

In addition to being one of the most favorable, if not the most favorable, taxing jurisdictions, Delaware provides a speedy and inexpensive incorporation process. You do not have to use either an attorney or an accountant to incorporate your business. The Company Corporation, founded to assist in low-cost incorporation, is headquartered at 1013 Centre Road, Wilmington, DE 19805, 1-800-499-6315, and can incorporate your business for as little as $119.

BENEFITS OF DELAWARE INCORPORATION

In addition to the fact that Delaware's corporation laws are specifically tailored to meet the precise needs of "S" corporations, there are at least 24 other good reasons for incorporation in Delaware:

1. *There is no minimum capital requirement.* A corporation can be organized with zero capital, if desired. Many states require that a corporation have at least $1,000 in capital.
2. *One person can hold the offices of president, treasurer and secretary and be all the directors.* Many states require at least three officers and/or directors. Therefore, there is no need to bring other persons into a Delaware corporation if the owner does not desire it.
3. *No formal operating agreements.* Delaware has a specific body of corporation law that permits a corporation to function through its shareholders, thereby avoiding many of the formalities of corporate operations.
4. *An established body of law relevant to corporations has been tested in the Delaware courts over the years.* In the event of legal matters that involve Delaware courts, there is a high degree of predictability of the outcome of any legal proceedings based on past history and experience. This can be meaningful to investors in a corporation. The Court of Chancery in Delaware is the only separate business court system in the United States and has a long record of pro-management decisions.
5. *There is no corporation income tax for any corporation formed in Delaware, but doing no business in the state.*
6. *Delaware's franchise tax on corporations compares favorably with any other state's.*
7. *Shares of stock owned by a person outside the state are not subject to any Delaware taxes.*
8. *A person can operate as the owner of a Delaware corporation anonymously, if desired.*
9. *A person can form a corporation by mail and never visit the state, even to conduct annual meetings.* Meetings can be held anywhere, at the option of the directors.
10. The Delaware Corporation Department welcomes new corporations and is organized to process them the same day their incorporation paperwork is received.
11. *Delaware is the state friendliest to corporations.* The state depends on its corporation department as a prime source of revenue. Because corporation revenue is exceeded by income taxes, the state depends on attracting a high volume of corporations. It has, historically, kept its laws and fees relevant to corporations favorable.

12. *Delaware charges no inheritance tax on shares of stock held by nonresidents.* These shares are taxed only in the states of residence of corporation owners.
13. *Directors may fix a sales price on any stock that the corporation issues and wishes to sell.*
14. *Shareholders, directors and committee members may act by unanimous written consent in lieu of formal meetings.*
15. *Directors may determine what part of consideration received for stock is capital.*
16. *Corporations can pay dividends out of profits as well as surplus.*
17. *Corporations can hold stocks, bonds or securities of other corporations and real and personal property, within or without the state, without limitation as to amount.*
18. *Corporations may purchase shares of their own stock and hold, sell or transfer them.*
19. *Corporations may conduct different kinds of business in combination.* If the corporate documents filed with Delaware have the broadest type "purpose clause," as outlined in this book, business activity of any kind may be conducted. More than one type of business can be conducted by the same corporation without any changes in the documents filed with the state.
20. *Corporations have perpetual existence (unless specified in their certificates of incorporation).*
21. *Directors have power to make or alter bylaws.*
22. *Shareholder liability is limited to stock held in the corporation (with the exception of taxes and assuming the business is conducted in a legal manner).*
23. *Only one person acting as the incorporator is required. Many states require three.*
24. *Directors' personal liability is either entirely eliminated or strictly limited under the Delaware Code.*

FORMING THE CORPORATION WITHOUT ENGAGING A REGISTERED AGENT

Any person can form a Delaware corporation. The owner need never visit the state. Annual meetings may be held anywhere.

Below is the least costly way to accomplish the incorporation. (This approach, while the least costly, does not include the benefits of the services a registered agent can provide.)

The following steps are involved:

- *Establish a street mailing address in Delaware.* This can be a private home or office that is open and staffed during business hours. (Without engaging a registered agent to provide assistance, this is usually the most difficult problem to solve.)
- *Complete a certificate of incorporation for a Delaware close corporation using the format provided on the sample certificate that follows.* The language in this certificate has been prepared by the Secretary of State, Corporation Department, Dover, Delaware. Be sure to fill in the name and address of one incorporator who resides in any state. (Two blank certificates have been included for your convenience.)

    Send two signed copies of this certificate to the Secretary of State, Corporation Department, Townsend Building, Dover, DE 19901. Include a check in the amount of $50, which is the total cost of the incorporation. (This fee breaks down as follows: $25 for receiving and indexing; $15 for the minimum state filing fee; and $10 for data entry.)

    If the corporate name you pick is not available, you will be notified. Otherwise, you will receive notice of the date that your corporation has been filed.
- When you receive one certified copy of the certificate of incorporation plus a receipted bill from the state, file this copy with the recorder of deeds office in the county where the registered street address of the corporation is located.

    There are three counties in Delaware. The addresses for the recorder of deeds offices in the three counties are as follows:

    Kent County—County Courthouse, Dover, DE 19901
    Sussex County—Box 505, Georgetown, DE 19947
    New Castle County—800 French St., Wilmington, DE 19801
    Enclose a check for $24*

    Conventional certificates prepared and typed on legal-size paper run four to ten pages, costing the filers $42 to $96. This is the reason that the certificates of incorporation we have supplied are printed on *one page.*

    In some states other than Delaware, a similar incorporation procedure applies. If a reader is interested in forming a non-Delaware corporation, he or she can obtain specific information by writing to the Corporation Department, Secretary of State, in any state. However, no state offers as many benefits of incorporating as Delaware.

------

*Applies to New Castle County only.

Some legal-stationery companies can supply a complete kit of the above forms, at a cost ranging from $60 to $99. A corporate seal and stock certificates cost $25 to $30.

Not only can the Company Corporation file the certificate of incorporation for you, it can check to make sure your company name is available and reserve it for you free of charge. In addition, The Company Corporation can provide you with a "Corporate Kit," including a corporate seal, stock certificates, forms for minutes and forms for Section 1244 of the Internal Revenue Code, for $49.95, plus $8.00 for U.P.S. delivery.

If you prefer to engage a registered agent to act in your behalf, such services can be obtained easily. See "Registered Agents" later in this chapter.

A CLOSE CORPORATION

A close corporation is a corporation whose certificate of incorporation sets out the basic elements contained in a standard Delaware corporation and, in addition, provides the following:

- All the corporation's issued stock shall be held by not more than a specified number of persons, not exceeding 30.
- All the issued stock shall be subject to one or more restrictions on transfer. The most widely used restriction is one that obligates a shareholder to offer to the corporation or other holders of shares of the corporation a prior opportunity to acquire the restricted securities within a reasonable time.

Sometimes other restrictions are included in the certificate of incorporation. These restrictions

- obligate the corporation or any holder of shares of the corporation to purchase the shares that are the subject of an agreement regarding the purchase and sale of the restricted shares;
- require the corporation or shareholders of the corporation to consent to any proposed transfer of the restricted shares or prohibit the transfer of restricted shares to designated persons or classes of persons, if such designation is not unreasonable;
- state that any restriction on the transfer of shares of a corporation for the purpose of maintaining its status as an electing small-business corporation under Subchapter "S" of the Internal Revensue Code is presumed to be for a reasonable purpose; or
- provide that the business of the corporation shall be managed by the shareholders. No directors need be elected so that there are no directors' meetings necessary. This provision has the effect of eliminating the formality of having

directors' meetings. Under this feature, the shareholders of the corporation have the powers and responsibilities that directors would normally have.

A close corporation is not permitted to make a "public" offering of its shares within the meaning of the Securities Act of 1933.

If a person running a corporation wishes to limit shareholders in number and also wishes himself, herself and/or other shareholders to have the first opportunity to buy shares from a selling shareholder, a close corporation is the ideal form of business. This first option to buy shares of stock can be the key to preventing undesirable persons from becoming shareholders in a corporation.

An existing Delaware corporation can also elect to be a close corporation if two-thirds of the shareholders vote in favor of it. An amendment to this effect is filed with the Secretary of State in Dover, Delaware.

A close corporation can change its status to a regular or an "open" corporation by filing a certificate of amendment with the Secretary of State.

On the following pages are a specimen certificate of incorporation and a blank copy that can be completed should a person wish to form a close corporation. Each contains the instructions referred to in the list above.

As with other Delaware corporations, the certificate of incorporation can be filed using any address initially. However, it is preferable to have the certificate filed through a registered agent because a Delaware mailing address is necessary.

REGISTERED AGENTS

Help is available in setting up a new corporation and with all aspects of your existing corporation—through a registered agent. In Delaware, more than 30 companies provide registered agent services to corporations. Some of these companies are listed later in this section. One of the main functions of such companies is to provide street addresses for corporations. All corporations formed in Delaware are required to have mailing addresses in the state and offices must be open and staffed during business hours. Companies that can provide this service (and others) are known as *Registered Agents*.

The annual fee charged by registered agents for providing a Delaware address ranges from $75 to $250. One of the largest registered agents (who owns several registered agent companies) charges $175 per year. If a lawyer's services are used, there are additional fees of $300 to $3,000. Registered agents generally charge an additional fee of $60 to $300 for the initial formation of a corporation.

CERTIFICATE OF INCORPORATION
OF
ABC Corporation
A CLOSE CORPORATION

FIRST: The name of this corporation is ABC Corporation.

SECOND: Its registered office in the State of Delaware is to be located at 1013 Centre Road, Wilmington DE 19805, County of New Castle. The registered agent in charge thereof is The Company Corporation, address same as above.

THIRD: The nature of the business and, the objects and purposes proposed to be transacted, promoted and carried on, are to engage in any lawful act or activity for which corporations may be organized under the General Corporation Law of Delaware.

FOURTH: The amount of the total authorized shares of stock of this corporation is 1500 shares of NO par value.

FIFTH: The name and mailing address of the incorporator is
(Leave blank if using The Company Corporation as agent, otherwise use your name and address)

SIXTH: All of the corporation's issued stock, exclusive of treasury shares, shall be held of record by not more than thirty (30) persons.

SEVENTH: All of the issued stock of all classes shall be subject to one or more of the restrictions on transfer permitted by Section 202 of the General Corporation Law.

EIGHTH: The corporation shall make no offering of any of its stock of any class which would constitute a "public offering" within the meaning of the United States Securities Act of 1933, as it may be amended from time to time.

NINTH: Directors of the corporation shall not be liable to either the corporation or its stockholders for monetary damages for a breach of fiduciary duties unless the breach involves: (1) a director's duty of loyalty to the corporation or its stockholders; (2) acts or omissions not in good faith or which involve intentional misconduct or a knowing violation of law; (3) liability for unlawful payments of dividends or unlawful stock purchases or redemption by the corporation; or (4) a transaction from which the director derived an improper personal benefit.

I, THE UNDERSIGNED, for the purpose of forming a corporation under the laws of the State of Delaware, do make, file and record this Certificate and do certify that the facts herein are true; and I have accordingly hereunto set my hand.

DATED: _____   _____

(Signature of person or officer of corporation named in Fifth Article.)
(Leave blank if using The Company Corporation.)

CERTIFICATE OF INCORPORATION
OF
ABC Corporation

FIRST: The name of this corporation is ABC Corporation.

SECOND: Its registered office in the state of Delaware is to be located at 1013 Centre Road, Wilmington DE 19805, New Castle County. The registered agent in charge thereof is The Company Corporation, address "same as above".

THIRD: The nature of the business and, the objects and purposes proposed to be transacted, promoted and carried on, are to do any or all the things herein mentioned as fully and to the same extent as natural persons might or could do, and in any part of the world, viz: The purpose of the corporation is to engage in any lawful act or activity for which corporations may be organized under the General Corporation Law of Delaware.

FOURTH: The amount of the total authorized capital stock of this corporation is divided into 1500 shares of stock at NO par value.

FIFTH: The name and mailing address of the incorporator is as follows: (Leave blank if using The Company Corporation as agent, otherwise use your name and address)

SIXTH: The Directors shall have power to make and to alter or amend the By-Laws; to fix the amount to be reserved as working capital, and to authorize and cause to be executed, mortgages and liens without limit as to the amount, upon the property and franchise of the Corporation.

With the consent in writing, and pursuant to a vote of the holders of a majority of the capital stock issued and outstanding, the Directors shall have the authority to dispose, in any manner, of the whole property of this corporation.

The By-Laws shall determine whether and to what extent the accounts and books of this corporation, or any of them shall be open to the inspection of the stockholders; and no stockholder shall have any right of inspecting any account, or book or document of this Corporation, except as conferred by the law or the By-Laws, or by resolution of the stockholders.

The stockholders and directors shall have power to hold their meetings and keep the books, documents, and papers of the Corporation outside of the State of Delaware, at such places as may be from time to time designated by the By-Laws or by resolution of the stockholders or directors, except as otherwise required by the laws of Delaware.

It is the intention that the objects, purposes and powers specified in the Third paragraph hereof shall, except where otherwise specified in said paragraph, be nowise limited or restricted by reference to or inference from the terms of any other clause or paragraph in this certificate of incorporation, that the objects, purposes and powers specified in the Third paragraph and in each of the clauses or paragraphs of this charter shall be regarded as independent objects, purposes and powers.

SEVENTH: Directors of the corporation shall not be liable to either the corporation or its stockholders for monetary damages for a breach of fiduciary duties unless the breach involves: (1) a director's duty of loyalty to the corporation or its stockholders; (2) acts or omissions not in good faith or which involve intentional misconduct or a knowing violation of law; (3) liability for unlawful payments of dividends or unlawful stock purchase or redemption by the corporation; or (4) a transaction from which the director derived an improper personal benefit.

I, THE UNDERSIGNED, for the purpose of forming a Corporation under the laws of the State of Delaware, do make, file and record this Certificate and do certify that the facts herein are true; and I have accordingly hereunto set my hand.

DATED:

_____

(Signature of person or officer of corporation named in Fifth Article.)
(Leave blank if using The Company Corporation.)

CERTIFICATE OF INCORPORATION
OF

A CLOSE CORPORATION

FIRST: The name of this corporation is   .

SECOND: Its registered office in the State of Delaware is to be located at 1013 Centre Road, Wilmington DE 19805, County of New Castle. The registered agent in charge thereof is The Company Corporation, address same as above.

THIRD: The nature of the business and, the objects and purposes proposed to be transacted, promoted and carried on, are to engage in any lawful act or activity for which corporations may be organized under the General Corporation Law of Delaware.

FOURTH: The amount of the total authorized shares of stock of this corporation is   shares of   par value.

FIFTH: The name and mailing address of the incorporator is

SIXTH: All of the corporation's issued stock, exclusive of treasury shares, shall be held of record by not more than thirty (30) persons.

SEVENTH: All of the issued stock of all classes shall be subject to one or more of the restrictions on transfer permitted by Section 202 of the General Corporation Law.

EIGHTH: The corporation shall make no offering of any of its stock of any class which would constitute a "public offering" within the meaning of the United States Securities Act of 1933, as it may be amended from time to time.

NINTH: Directors of the corporation shall not be liable to either the corporation or its stockholders for monetary damages for a breach of fiduciary duties unless the breach involves: (1) a director's duty of loyalty to the corporation or its stockholders; (2) acts or omissions not in good faith or which involve intentional misconduct or a knowing violation of law; (3) liability for unlawful payments of dividends or unlawful stock purchases or redemption by the corporation; or (4) a transaction from which the director derived an improper personal benefit.

I, THE UNDERSIGNED, for the purpose of forming a corporation under the laws of the State of Delaware, do make, file and record this Certificate and do certify that the facts herein are true; and I have accordingly hereunto set my hand.

DATED: _____

CERTIFICATE OF INCORPORATION
OF

FIRST: The name of this corporation is

SECOND: Its registered office in the state of Delaware is to be located at 1013 Centre Road, Wilmington DE 19805, New Castle County. The registered agent in charge thereof is The Company Corporation, address "same as above".

THIRD: The nature of the business and, the objects and purposes proposed to be transacted, promoted and carried on, are to do any or all the things herein mentioned as fully and to the same extent as natural persons might or could do, and in any part of the world, viz: The purpose of the corporation is to engage in any lawful act or activity for which corporations may be organized under the General Corporation Law of Delaware.

FOURTH: The amount of the total authorized capital stock of this corporation is divided into   shares of stock at   par value.

FIFTH: The name and mailing address of the incorporator is as follows:

SIXTH: The Directors shall have power to make and to alter or amend the By-Laws; to fix the amount to be reserved as working capital, and to authorize and cause to be executed, mortgages and liens without limit as to the amount, upon the property and franchise of the Corporation.

With the consent in writing, and pursuant to a vote of the holders of a majority of the capital stock issued and outstanding, the Directors shall have the authority to dispose, in any manner, of the whole property of this corporation.

The By-Laws shall determine whether and to what extent the accounts and books of this corporation, or any of them shall be open to the inspection of the stockholders; and no stockholder shall have any right of inspecting any account, or book or document of this Corporation, except as conferred by the law or the By-Laws, or by resolution of the stockholders.

The stockholders and directors shall have power to hold their meetings and keep the books, documents, and papers of the Corporation outside of the State of Delaware, at such places as may be from time to time designated by the By-Laws or by resolution of the stockholders or directors, except as otherwise required by the laws of Delaware.

It is the intention that the objects, purposes and powers specified in the Third paragraph hereof shall, except where otherwise specified in said paragraph, be nowise limited or restricted by reference to or inference from the terms of any other clause or paragraph in this certificate of incorporation, that the objects, purposes and powers specified in the Third paragraph and in each of the clauses or paragraphs of this charter shall be regarded as independent objects, purposes and powers.

SEVENTH: Directors of the corporation shall not be liable to either the corporation or its stockholders for monetary damages for a breach of fiduciary duties unless the breach involves: (1) a director's duty of loyalty to the corporation or its stockholders; (2) acts or omissions not in good faith or which involve intentional misconduct or a knowing violation of law; (3) liability for unlawful payments of dividends or unlawful stock purchase or redemption by the corporation; or (4) a transaction from which the director derived an improper personal benefit.

I, THE UNDERSIGNED, for the purpose of forming a Corporation under the laws of the State of Delaware, do make, file and record this Certificate and do certify that the facts herein are true; and I have accordingly hereunto set my hand.

DATED: _____

The Company Corporation

One company, The Company Corporation, charges only $45* during the first year for its registered agent service. This modest fee is less than that charged by others. This fee increases to $125 for subsequent years.

The Company Corporation charges no legal fees, because customers of The Company Corporation *complete the forms themselves.* No counseling service is provided or needed if the forms are completed by the person forming the corporation.

Service is provided in a highly confidential and speedy manner. Upon receipt of forms, a corporation is usually filed with the Secretary of State the *same* day.

Potential savings when you use The Company Corporation for the initial formation of your corporation can add up to $3,000 and up to $250 annually thereafter.

The Company Corporation works differently from other registered agents. It operates on a volume basis and advertises for its customers directly. Its fees are substantially less than its competitors'. All "middle-man" fees are eliminated.

The Company Corporation will provide services to customers referred by lawyers, but does not require this. All it requires is that a certificate of incorporation and a signed confidential information form be completed by the customer and mailed or faxed to The Company Corporation. The certificate is then forwarded to the appropriate places. The Company Corporation handles all the rest.

The Company Corporation *provides no legal advice or counseling.* Only administerial functions are provided. No review or advice on the form itself can be given. However, if the form is complete (instructions are provided) *none is necessary.* If for any reason the certificate of incorporation is not accepted by the Secretary of State in Dover, Delaware, it is returned without comment by The Company Corporation, but with any of the Secretary of State's comments.

In addition to providing a permanent street address in Delaware, The Company Corporation, unlike any other registered agent, provides the following services to its customers:

Initial Services

- Acts as registered agent and provides a service of process address in Delaware. (The Company Corporation provides a mailing address for the purpose of receiving and forwarding all legal documents, not general mail delivery. General mail forwarding can be arranged for an additional fee.)
- Furnishes the incorporator. (A certificate of incorporation can be completed, but unsigned, if desired.)
- Forwards the certificate of incorporation to the Corporation Department in Dover, Delaware, for filing.

---

*Prices and fees are subject to change without notice.

- Files a copy of the certificate of incorporation with the recorder of deeds office.
- Prepares checks for payment of initial recording fees to the state of Delaware.
- Reserves the corporate name and files documents within 24 hours of receipt of a customer's request.
- Orders printed stock certificates, the corporate seal and forms for minutes and bylaws, if the option is desired by the client.
- Supplies the appropriate forms for qualifying the Delaware corporation in any other state in the United States.
- Processes the application for a federal identification number.
- Processes the application for "S"-status filings with the IRS.

Continuing Services

- Acts as registered agent and provides a mailing address in Delaware.
- Forwards the corporation's annual report form to the Secretary of State, Dover, Delaware. (Once each year, the Secretary of State sends to the Delaware mailing address of every corporation chartered in the state an annual report form. The Company Corporation forwards this to its customers. It is completed by each customer and sent back to The Company Corporation, which forwards it to the Secretary of State, Dover, Delaware, for filing. Or you can use The Company Corporation's convenient Tax-on-Time® service, and it will handle everything for you.
- Assists in locating facilities for annual meetings if the client wishes to hold them in Delaware.
- Receives legal documents served on the corporation in Delaware, including lawsuits, and forwards these to the business address of the corporation.
- Makes available to its customers books and manuals, trademark searches, domain name registrations, Web presence programs, mail forwarding, shelf corporations, and express service.
- Provides ongoing customer assistance to the corporation.
- Makes available the Small Business Toolkit™, a program of products and services to help the smart, bottom-line-oriented entrepreneur in every stage of the small business cycle. The program includes health and dental insurance, merchant credit card service, long distance service, 24-hour legal assistance, stationery and office supplies, payroll processing, office equipment leasing, plus many other best-price goods and services. For more information about The Company Corporation's continuing services, contact them at 1013 Centre Road, Wilmington, DE 19805; 1-800-499-6315; fax: 1-302-636-5454; Web site: www.incorporate.com.

In addition, The Company Corporation will furnish upon request the Delaware fee schedule for filing forms with the state. Forms include, but are not limited to, those that increase the number of shares of a corporation's stock, add new classes of stock, amend a certificate of incorporation, dissolve or merge a corporation and establish a limited partnership.

The Company Corporation incorporates people in all 50 states. However, for reasons described in the book *How to Form Your Own Corporation Without a Lawyer for Under $75,* most savvy corporate lawyers, accountants and other experts recommend Delaware as the most attractive state in which to incorporate. In fact, two-thirds of the companies listed in the New York and American stock exchanges were incorporated there. You, too, should review seriously the reasons to incorporate in Delaware.

If you'd like The Company Corporation to set up your corporation and you want fast, one-day service, complete the "Confidential Information Form" included in this chapter. Or, if you prefer or have any questions, call the toll-free number: 1-800-499-6315.

Other Registered Agents

Other companies in Delaware provide services to corporations, including acting as registered agent. A partial list follows. Most of these companies require that clients be referred to them by lawyers. Their fee schedules vary in the amounts shown below:

Initial fee: $60 to $300 for filing corporate documents
Legal fees: $300 to $3,000
Annual fees: $75 to $250

Colonial Charter Company
300 Delaware Avenue, Suite 1130
Wilmington, DE 19801
302-656-9850
302-656-9836 Fax

Corporation Company of Delaware
1105 North Market Street
Wilmington, DE 19899
302-998-0595

Corporation Guarantee & Trust Co.
701 Architects Building
117 South 17th Street
Philadelphia, PA 19103
215-563-6131
215-563-9410 Fax

Delaware Charter Company
1105 North Market Street
Wilmington, DE 19899
302-995-2131

Delaware Charter Guarantee &
   Trust Company
1013 Centre Road
P.O. Box 8963
Wilmington, DE 19899
302-999-9554
302-999-9954 Fax

Delaware Registration Trust Company
913 Market Street, Suite 1001
Wilmington, DE 19801
302-655-7371

The Corporation Trust Company
1209 Orange Street
Wilmington, DE 19899
302-995-2131

United States Corporation Company
229 South State Street
Dover, DE 19901
302-674-1221

CSC
1013 Centre Road
Wilmington, DE 19805
800-927-9800
302-636-5454 Fax

Delaware Registry, Ltd.
3711 Silverside Road, Suite 105
Wilmington, DE 19810
800-321-CORP
302-477-9811 Fax

CHANGING REGISTERED AGENTS

In order for an existing *Delaware* corporation to obtain the advantages offered by The Company Corporation, a simple form is all that is necessary. If a person wishes to change agents, the total cost due that corporation the first year is $99. This is the actual filing cost paid to the state of Delaware and applicable county recording fees.

The Company Corporation will provide its registered agent services at no cost during the first calendar year to existing corporations.

If a reader wishes to take advantage of this low-cost service, write The Company Corporation for a copy of the change of registered agent form in duplicate. When you mail this form and a completed confidential information form with a check for $224 (payable to The Company Corporation), the certification document will be forwarded to the Secretary of State's office in Dover, Delaware, for filing.

TheCompany Corporation

Incorporation Order Form

1. **Corporate Name:** (One of the following corporate endings is required—Inc., Company, Corporation, Incorporated, Corp., Co., Limited Liability Companies may use LLC)

   First Choice: _____

   Alternate : _____

2. **State in which you wish to be incorporated:** _____

   County: _____

3. **Type of Corporation:**
   - ❏ General Corporation   ❏ Limited Liability Company   ❏ Professional
   - ❏ Non Stock/Non-Profit (must provide corporate documents)

4. **Stock:** The corporation will be authorized to issue up to 1,500 shares of no par common stock unless you instruct otherwise

   Shares: _____   Par Value: _____

5. **Corporate Kits:**   ❏ Attache Kit ($99)   ❏ Deluxe Kit ($75)   ❏ Standard Kit ($60)

   Sales tax required for corporate kits and publications shipped to CA, CT, DC, FL, IL, MA, NJ, NY, PA, TX, WA.

Additional Services:	**Publications:**
❏ Express Formation Service ($60)	❏ Business Owners Guide to Accounting ($19.95) 189 pg
❏ Rapid Delivery ($16)	❏ Essential Limited Liability Company Handbook ($19.95) 262 pg
❏ Prepare Tax I.D. Application ($25)	❏ Essential Corporation Handbook ($29.95) 232 pg
❏ Prepare S Corporation Election ($25)	❏ The Successful Business Plan ($24.95) 320 pg

   Please check the Corporate Package you wish to order; see next page for description and prices.
   - ❏ Delaware Basic Package   ❏ Delaware Complete Package
   - ❏ Non-Delaware Basic Package   ❏ Non-Delaware Complete Package

6. **Names of Directors:** (Only one director is required in most states. LLC's require two member names)

   Name: _____   Name: _____

   Address: _____   Address: _____

7. **Shipping Address for Articles and Kit:** (No P.O. Boxes)

   _____

   Phone: ( ) _____ Fax: ( ) _____ Email: _____

8. **Registered Agent:** _____

   Remember to add $45 if TCC is the registered agent or $50 if TCC is not the registered agent. (Registered Agent included in packages) Provide address if TCC is not Registered Agent

9. **Method of Payment:**
   - ❏ Check/Money Order enclosed ❏ Western Union ❏ MasterCard ❏ Visa
   - ❏ Discover ❏ Amex

   Card #: _____ Exp. Date: _____ Total Amount: $ _____

   Name on Card: _____ Authorized Signature: _____

THE COMPANY CORPORATION

1013 CENTRE ROAD   (800) 499-6315   WWW.INCORPORATE.COM/TNP

WILMINGTON, DE 19805 U.S.A.   FAX: (302) 636-5454   INFO@CORPORATE.COM

TNP200

Incorporation/LLC Prices by State

State	Corporation With Service Charge	Corporation State Fee Only	LLC With Service Charge	LLC State Fee Only	State	Corporation With Service Charge	Corporation State Fee Only	LLC With Service Charge	LLC State Fee Only
Alabama	$184	$85	$184	$85	Missouri	157	58	204	105
Alaska	349	250	349	250	Montana	189	90	169	70
Arizona	344	245	344	245	Nebraska†	309	210	374	275
Arkansas	149	50	149	50	Nevada	294	195	294	195
California††	514	415	184*	85	New Hampshire	214	115	184	85
Colorado	149	50	149	50	New Jersey	229	130	209	110
Connecticut	399	300	184	85	New Mexico	199	100	149	50
Delaware	119	74	139	70	New York	269	170	309**	210
District of Columbia	219	120	199	100	North Carolina	224	125	224	125
Florida	169	70	384	285	North Dakota	234	135	234	135
Georgia	299	200	314	215	Ohio	194	95	194	95
Hawaii	249	150	279	180	Oklahoma	149	50	199	100
Idaho	199	100	199	100	Oregon	149	50	139	40
Illinois	219	120	499	400	Pennsylvania†	349	250	199	100
Indiana	219	120	219	120	Rhode Island	249	150	249	150
Iowa	149	50	149	50	South Carolina	309	210	209	110
Kansas	194	95	249	150	South Dakota	189	90	189	90
Kentucky	169	70	139	40	Tennessee	219	120	399	300
Louisiana	219	120	219	120	Texas	409	310	309	210
Maine	254	155	349	250	Utah	174	75	199	100
Maryland	169	70	179	80	Vermont	174	75	174	75
Massachusetts	299	200	599	500	Virginia	180	81	205	106
Michigan	189	90	189	90	Washington	294	195	294	195
Minnesota	234	135	234	135	West Virginia	169	70	199	100
Mississippi	149	50	149	50	Wisconsin	214	115	299	130
					Wyoming	199	100	199	100

The Company Corporation

800-499-6315

An additional $45.00 will be added to all fees for the first year's registered agent service. Subsequently, the charge is $125.00 per year for all states.

If The Company Corporation is not the registered agent, an additional $50.00 will be added to all prices. All prices include The Company Corporation's service fee.

Our Tax-On-Time® service guarantees prompt filing of your annual report, and payment of fees and taxes (available to Delaware corporations only). Call us.

*When formed as a partnership, managed by company members of the franchise, tax is due in three months.

**Does not include publishing fees.

†Includes publishing fees.

‡California minimum franchise tax fee for corporations that plan on $1,000,000 or less in annual revenues.

All fees subject to change without notice.

Choose From Four Corporation Packages*

Basic Delaware Corporation/LLC Package

$289.00 (includes state filing fees)
$55.00 Savings!

- Prepare and file the Certificate of Incorporation for your corporation (for corporations with up to 1,500 shares of no par value stock).
- Provide registered agent representation for the first calendar year.
- Personalized Standard Corporate Kit including: seal, stock certificates and other important documents to simplify record keeping.
- Essential Corporation Handbook
- Express Service

Complete Delaware Corporation/LLC Package

$389.00 (includes state filing fees)
$70.00 Savings!

Includes everything in the *Basic Delaware Corporation Package,* plus:

- Application for federal tax identification number
- Application for Sub Chapter "S"
- E.A.R.N. membership
- Deluxe Corporate Kit

Basic Non-Delaware Corporation/LLC Package

$235.00 (includes state filing fees)
$59.00 Savings!

- Prepare and file the Certificate of Incorporation for your corporation (includes preliminary name check, in most states).
- Provide registered agent service for the first year.
- Personalized Standard Corporate Kit including: seal, stock certificates and other important documents to simplify record keeping.
- Essential Corporation Handbook
- Express Service

Complete Non-Delaware Corporation/LLC Package

$335.00 (plus state filing fees)
$74.00 Savings!

Includes everything in the *Basic Non-Delaware Corporation Package,* plus:

- Application for federal tax identification number
- Application for Sub Chapter "S"
- E.A.R.N. membership
- Deluxe Corporate Kit

*Please add $5.00 to package price if TCC is not appointed registered agent.

PROTECT YOUR CORPORATION'S VALUABLE LEGAL STATUS *with an* EASY-TO-USE CORPORATE KIT

THE COMPLETE PERSONALIZED KIT INCLUDES:

1. Your personalized Corporate Binder with slipcase — protects your corporate records. Your corporate name will be printed on a gold inset on the spine of this handsome binder.

2. Your personalized corporate seal can be kept in a pouch inside your binder. Use your corporate seal for completion of legal documents such as leases and purchase agreements.

Your corporate name and year of incorporation will be permanently etched into the dies which create a raised impression on any paper. *(separately, seal is $25 for up to 45 characters.)*

3. For your permanent records: minutes & by-laws forms printed on three-hole paper for easy record-keeping. Complete forms included for any corporation.

4. 20 personalized stock certificates lithographed with your corporate name on each certificate. Printing also includes number of shares authorized by corporation. *(Additional stock certificates can be purchased. Minimum purchase is 20 @ $30.00 total, extras @ 35¢ each.)*

5. Celluloid tab index separators make it easy to turn to any section in your binder.

6. Stock/transfer ledger — to keep an accurate and complete record of your corporate stock, including stock transfers.

4

Qualifying Your Business

THE BASIC REQUIREMENTS

Corporations that wish to enjoy both traditional corporate advantages and the added benefit of single taxation must elect to become "S" corporations. The election itself is available to any "small business corporation" that satisfies a handful of simple eligibility requirements, none of which poses any burden for the average businessperson operating a business.

The following requirements must be satisfied:

- There must be a domestic U.S. corporation.
- The corporation must have no more than 75 shareholders.
- Each shareholder must be a natural person or an estate (certain trusts and certain tax-exempt organizations may be shareholders). There are limits on estates as shareholders as outlined later in this chapter.
- The corporation may have only one class of stock, although there are limited exceptions to this requirement.
- The corporation must be a small business corporation.

With respect to the small business corporation requirement, it should be noted at the outset that the definition does not limit either the volume or the scope of business that can be conducted. For the most part, it refers to the maximum number of shareholders a corporation can have (75) and the fact that it must be a corporation formed under the laws of a state of the United States.

Need for a Corporation

In order to qualify as an "S" corporation, the business seeking qualification must be a corporation. If your existing or proposed business operates or will operate as a sole proprietorship or partnership, it must first be converted to a corporation.

75 or Fewer Shareholders

The "S" corporation law's requirement that single taxation provisions apply to small-business corporations refers, for the most part, to the number of shareholders the corporation may have. It does not set any limits on the dollar volume of business the corporation may do or, for the most part, on the type of business in which the corporation can engage.

The law limits to 75 the number of shareholders a corporation may have. In calculating whether a corporation may have more than 75 shareholders, the following guidelines should be observed:

- Husbands and wives and their estates are treated as one person, even if they hold stock in their own names. So, for example, if Mr. Smith owns ten shares of an "S" corporation in his name only and Mrs. Smith owns 12 shares in her name only, they will be viewed as one shareholder for "S" corporation purposes.
- Jointly held stock—for example, shares owned by John Smith and Mary Jones as joint tenants or tenants in common—is viewed as being owned by one shareholder.
- Shares held in trust by a trustee or custodian for a beneficiary are viewed as being owned by the beneficiary, not the trustee or custodian. So, for example, if a parent holds shares as trustee or custodian for each of the parent's three children, there are three shareholders for "S" corporation purposes, not one.

In the event shares of an "S" corporation become owned by 76 or more shareholders, the business will lose its "S" corporation status—that is, it will be treated as a regular "C" corporation and will be subject to double taxation. Therefore, if an "S" corporation will have more than one shareholder, all shareholders should sign a shareholders' agreement restricting the right of each person to sell his or her shares if the sale would jeopardize the business's "S" corporation status. A form for just this purpose is provided at the end of this chapter.

If you expect that your corporation will have more than 75 shareholders, "S" incorporation is not the right vehicle for your business. In that case, you may want to consider either the limited partnership or the limited liability company mode of doing business (see Chapter 2). They, too, offer the twin benefits of favorable tax treatment and limited personal liability, although neither is as easy and inexpensive to form as an "S" corporation.

Qualified Shareholders

Estates and certain trusts and also any individual who is either a citizen or resident of the United States may be a shareholder in an "S" corporation. Shareholders who do not fit into any one of those categories are not qualified to be "S" corporation shareholders, and if they obtain shares, the business will lose its "S" corporation status.

Citizens and U.S. residents. Because an individual is a natural person, both partnerships and corporations are disqualified from owning shares in an "S" corporation. Furthermore, the individual must be either a citizen or resident of the United States. An alien who is visiting this country does not qualify as an "S" corporation shareholder. Two cautions should be observed with respect to nonresident aliens:

- If shares are jointly held—by spouses, for example—and one owner is a nonresident alien, the corporation will be viewed as having a disqualified shareholder. "S" corporation status, therefore, will be denied to the business.
- Only residence in the United States qualifies an alien for shareholder status in an "S" corporation. Residence in a territory or a possession is not sufficient.

Estates. With respect to estates, it should be noted that a corporation will not lose its "S" corporation status if a qualified shareholder dies and his or her shares pass to the decedent's estate. Nor will such an event preclude an existing corporation from switching from regular "C" status to "S" status.

Two cautions must be observed with respect to estates. First, the shares cannot remain in the estate indefinitely. Assuming the decedent's estate is processed in the time it ordinarily takes to process estates in the local jurisdiction, there should be no problem. Second, care should be taken to avoid having the shares in the decedent's estate go to a beneficiary not qualified to be an "S" corporation shareholder.

A second type of estate, the estate of a bankrupt, may also be a shareholder in an "S" corporation. If an individual shareholder files for bankruptcy, the shareholder's assets, including his or her shares in the corporation, are placed in the bankrupt's estate. That estate is qualified to be a shareholder in an "S" corporation. As is the case with decedents' estates, care should be taken to avoid placing the shares with an individual or entity not qualified to be an "S" corporation shareholder.

Trusts. The matter is far more complex when it comes to trusts. Although certain trusts may qualify to become shareholders in an "S" corporation, the applicable rules are complicated and highly detailed. In the event that a shareholder in an "S" corporation intends to establish a trust that includes the corporation shares, qualified legal counsel should be obtained. The matter of trusts is not insignificant. Many people today use trusts to hold their assets as a means of asset protection. One fairly common technique involves the use of foreign-based asset protection trusts. The use of such a trust, however, would disqualify a corporation from obtaining "S" status.

The term *eligible shareholders* includes five types of trusts:

1. Grantor trusts
2. Voting trusts
3. Continuing grantor and testamentary trusts
4. Electing small business trusts (ESBTs)
5. Qualified subchapter "S" trusts (QSSTs)

In a *grantor trust,* the grantor is regarded as a shareholder. Grantor trust status must apply to all the income of the trust (both capital gains and ordinary income). The "deemed owner" of the trust, for income tax purposes, may be the individual who created the trust or a beneficiary with certain powers to vest the assets of the trust in himself.

Each beneficiary is treated as a shareholder in a *voting trust.* It is created primarily to exercise voting power of stock transferred to it.

Both *continuing grantor trusts* and *testamentary trusts* may be "S" corporation shareholders. If a trust qualifies as a grantor trust at the death of the deemed owner, the trust will continue as an eligible "S" corporation shareholder for a two-year period following the owner's death. A trust that receives stock pursuant to a will is an eligible "S" corporation shareholder for the two-year period beginning on the day the stock is transferred to the trust.

The beneficiaries of the *electing small business trusts* are not taxable on the "S" corporation's income. Rather, the ESBT is the shareholder and pays tax on its share of the distributable income of the "S" corporation. If the trust has other assets, the regular rules of trust taxation will apply to those assets.

ESBTs facilitate financial planning by permitting "S" corporation owners to spread income among a class of people. The trustee of an ESBT can have the right to spray or sprinkle "S" corporation income among all beneficiaries without violating the "S" corporation rules permitting only one class of stock.

For a trust to qualify for ESBT treatment, it must meet the following requirements:

- All of the trust's beneficiaries must be qualified to own "S" corporation stock.
- Although nonresident aliens do not qualify to hold "S" corporation stock directly, they can be the beneficiaries of an ESBT.
- No interest in the trust may be acquired by purchase, but only by gift or bequest.
- A specific election to be treated as an electing trust must have been filed by the trustee. Such an election will be irrevocable without the consent of the IRS.

Each potential current beneficiary of the ESBT is treated as a shareholder. However, if there is no potential current beneficiary of the trust, the trust itself will be treated as the shareholder during such period.

A *qualified subchapter "S" trust,* may also be a shareholder of an "S" corporation if the individual beneficiary of the trust, or his legal representative, elects to be treated as the owner of the portion of the trust that consists of the "S" corporation stock. This election may be revoked only with the consent of the IRS.

QSSTs may only have one beneficiary during the beneficiary's lifetime. All income of the QSST must be either distributed or required to be distributed to the beneficiary, who must be either a citizen or a resident of the United States.

A conversion from a QSST to an ESBT can be made on the election of both the trustee and the current income beneficiary for each "S" corporation held by the trust, if the trust has not converted from an ESBT to a QSST within the three-year period ending on the effective date of the new ESBT election.

A trust that is eligible for a QSST election will usually be eligible for an ESBT election. An ESBT has three principal advantages over a QSST: (1) the election is easier to make, (2) the ESBT is a more flexible trust for nontax reasons, and (3) the ESBT has certain transfer tax advantages.

A testator can require that a trustee make the ESBT election. A testator cannot direct the beneficiary of a QSST to make the QSST election but may penalize a beneficiary for failing to make a requested election. A successor income beneficiary of a QSST may refuse to consent to the election, which is not a problem with an ESBT.

An ESBT provides greater flexibility for distributions. Current distributions of income, which are required for a QSST, may be inappropriate if a beneficiary is not capable of handling the funds. A testator or donor may wish to create a single trust benefiting multiple beneficiaries that distributes income based on a beneficiary's needs.

The ESBT's ability to accumulate income and spray income and principal has several tax advantages. The income beneficiary does not receive income that unnecessarily builds up his estate. An ESBT provides more flexibility in maximizing the use of a generation-skipping tax (GST) exemption.

The primary disadvantage of an ESBT is that the income is taxed at the highest income tax bracket. The existence of an ESBT may eliminate "S" corporation treatment under such state laws as Pennsylvania.

Because a corporation can lose its "S" corporation status if a shareholder transfers shares to an unqualified recipient, all shareholders should enter into an agreement that would prevent such a happening. The sample shareholders' agreement that appears at the end of this chapter was designed with this concern in mind.

If your corporation cannot qualify for "S" corporation status because it has an ineligble shareholder or a shareholder wishes to put his or her shares into a trust, you might want to consider the limited partnership or limited liability company as an alternative to "S" incorporation.

One Class of Stock

An "S" corporation may have only one class of stock issued and outstanding. Essentially, this requirement means that if a corporation is authorized to create more than one class of stock and wishes to qualify as an "S" corporation, it may sell only one class of stock to its shareholders.

To determine whether a corporation has more than one class of stock, one need only ask whether, in the event of a redemption of shares or a liquidation, every shareholder would be entitled to receive (1) the same dividend at the same time as every other shareholder and (2) the same amount for each share he or she holds and at the same time as every other shareholder. If all aspects of each share's economic rights are the same, the shares will be treated as being of the same class.

The mere fact that shares may have different voting rights (e.g., voting and nonvoting common stock) will not cause the IRS to rule that more than one class of stock exists. Voting rights may be differentiated without danger; economic rights—that is, dividend and liquidation rights—may not be differentiated.

However, differences in voting rights are permitted. A corporate obligation that qualifies as "straight debt" is not considered a second class of stock. Buy-sell and redemption agreements restricting transferability of the stock are usually disregarded in determining whether there is a single class of stock. Stock of an "S" corporation does not include stock received for the performance of services that is substantially nonvested, unless the holder has made an election to include the value of the stock in income.

When debt may be treated as a second class of stock. In a regular "C" corporation, shareholders may lend money to the corporation rather than put all of their investment in stock. Their reasons may be:

- To avoid the double tax by taking interest payments rather than dividend payments (interest is a business expense and is not taxed at the corporate level)
- To minimize the risk in their investment because they become creditors of the corporation and, in the event the business fails, they have a better chance to recoup part of their investment
- To balance control if one shareholder puts up more money than another, but both want an equal number of shares

Although the first reason listed above does not apply to the "S" corporation, which is not subject to the double tax process imposed on "C" corporation profits, the two other reasons are equally applicable to "S" corporations.

However, the use of shareholder-provided loans can create a major problem for either a regular "C" corporation or an "S" corporation: the IRS may treat the loan as if it is an equity investment—that is, an investment in shares.

When that happens in the context of a "C" corporation, the interest paid on the loan is treated as a dividend and the double-taxation rule is imposed. If a shareholder loan to an "S" corporation is treated as an investment in equity by the IRS, it will be treated as an investment in a different class of stock. The result here is that the corporation will lose its "S" status and will be subject to double taxation on all of its profits and gains.

In order to permit "S" corporation shareholders to lend money to their corporations with a measure of security, the Internal Revenue Code provides a safe harbor provision that, if followed, will ensure that an intended loan will not be treated as a second class of stock. Essentially, the safe harbor rule provides that if the loan from the shareholder is comparable to a loan that would have been offered by a stranger, it will be treated as a loan and not a second class of shares.

To be protected under the safe harbor rule, the shareholder loan must

- be in writing;
- require the corporation to pay interest at fixed times—for example, monthly, quarterly, annually—and to set a rate of interest that is in keeping with current interest rates and that does not depend on the corporation's profits, the corporation's discretion or similar factors;
- oblige the corporation to repay the entire principal amount of the loan; and
- not allow the loan to be convertible to stock at either the borrower's or lender's option.

As suggested above, the safe harbor rules do not present any real problem for a shareholder who seeks to hedge his or her risk by lending money to an "S" corporation. The loan terms required by the rule are exactly those that any creditor would demand before lending money.

Prudent investors will closely follow these safe harbor rules. The IRS can be quick to challenge a shareholder loan to an "S" corporation. If it determines the loan is really an investment in a second class of stock, the result can be disastrous. The actual date of the loan becomes the date the second class of stock was created and, therefore, the date on which "S" corporation status ends. That might mean the corporation would owe back taxes as a "C" corporation starting from the date of the loan.

Small Business Corporation

The congressional intent that the "S" incorporation be limited to small business corporations has never really been defined by law. In fact, a definition of that term is available only by determining what kinds of enterprises cannot take advantage of the "S" corporation option.

The only forms of businesses that may not take advantage of "S" incorporation are

- financial institutions such as banks, insurance companies, building and loan associations or mutual savings and loan associations (unless they do not use the reserve method of accounting for bad debts);

- foreign corporations (an "S" corporation must be incorporated under the laws of any state, possession or territory of the United States);
- corporations that operate in possessions of the United States and use the possessions' tax credits against their U.S. income tax;
- Domestic International Sales Corporations (DISCs) or former DISCs; and
- affiliated corporations. (An "S" corporation may not be a subsidiary of a parent corporation. This follows from the fact that shareholders of an "S" corporation must be natural persons, estates or certain trusts.)

An "S" corporation is also permitted to own a qualified subchapter "S" subsidiary (QSSS). Any domestic corporation that qualifies as an "S" corporation and is 100 percent owned by an "S" corporation parent can elect to be treated as a QSSS.

The QSSS is not to be treated as a separate corporation for tax purposes. Its assets, liabilities, items of income deduction, and credit are treated as though they belong to the parent corporation. The nontax benefit of a QSSS is that an "S" corporation may segregate assets for liability purposes by creating a QSSS.

To qualify as a QSSS, the corporation must be wholly owned by its "S" corporation parent. An "S" election can be made for a number of wholly owned subsidiaries within a chain of corporations.

ADDITIONAL REQUIREMENTS FOR EXISTING CORPORATIONS

"S" incorporation is also available to existing regular "C" corporations. If such a corporation elects to switch to "S" status, it must satisfy the requirements previously discussed in this chapter, as well as two additional requirements.

Prior Elections—The Five-Year Rule

If the regular corporation was previously an "S" corporation and its status was revoked within the past five years, it will not be qualified to become an "S" corporation again. This provision exists to deter shareholders from electing "S" status in only those years during which their enterprise will lose money. In a losing year, any losses the regular "C" corporation incurs are of no benefit to its shareholders. In the past, shareholders would opt to have their corporation taxed as an "S" corporation for a year during which the corporation lost money. The loss, then, would flow to the shareholders, who would use it to offset other income. The next year, if the corporation became profitable, the shareholders would revoke the election, and the corporation would have its profits taxed at the lower corporate rates that existed before the 1986 Tax Reform Act.

Because of this, the Internal Revenue Service will not approve an "S" corporation election if the shareholders of the corporation revoked or lost their "S" corporation election during the past five years. However, any termination of a subchapter

"S" election in a tax year beginning before January 1, 1997, is not taken into account. A possible exception to this rule exists if the corporation's shares (or at least a controlling interest) are held by shareholders different from those who revoked or lost the election to be treated as an "S" corporation.

Planning Note

It should be observed that shareholders can opt to be treated as an "S" corporation during the enterprise's first year (when it is likely to lose money because of start-up costs) and switch to regular "C" status the following year. If this is done, the shareholders will be barred from making an "S" corporation election for another five years.

Passive Investment Income

If a "C" corporation elects to become an "S" corporation and has no accumulated earnings and profits, it can qualify for "S" status regardless of the type or sources of income the corporation has had.

If, on the other hand, the regular "C" corporation has accumulated earnings and profits when it makes its election for "S" incorporation, its election may not be recognized. Under this rule, if an "S" corporation has (1) accumulated earnings and profits from its "C" corporation operations at the end of the "S" corporation tax year and (2) more than 25 percent of its gross income from passive investment income sources (dividends, interest, annuities, rents, royalties and gain from the sale of securities), the election will be lost.

Planning Note

For the passive income rule to apply, the corporation must fall within both sides of the test for three years. In other words, during each of the first three years, starting with the election year, the corporation must have accumulated "C" corporation earnings and profits and must have passive investment income that is more than 25 percent of its gross income.

If that does happen, the "S" corporation election is lost in the fourth year—but it remains valid for each of the first three years. What happens if the election is lost in the fourth year? First, the corporation profits will be taxed as if the corporation is a regular "C" corporation. Second, the ability to elect to become an "S" corporation will be lost for five years.

One note of interest if you intend to form a corporation that will engage in the equipment leasing business: Until recently, it was believed that because these corporations have primarily passive income (i.e., income from the rental of the equipment they lease), they would not be able to qualify for "S" corporation status. A recent letter ruling indicates that the IRS will now look at the substance of an equipment lessor's activities and will not object to such a company qualifying for "S" corporation status.

PROTECTING AGAINST LOSS OF ELIGIBILITY

The greatest threat to a corporation's continued eligibility as an "S" corporation stems from the possibility that an existing, qualified shareholder may sell his or her shares to an unqualified shareholder or to more than one person, thereby bringing the total number of shareholders to more than 75 persons.

This threat can be effectively and safely eliminated by taking two relatively easy steps: adopting a shareholders' agreement under which each shareholder agrees not to make a transfer that would endanger the "S" status of the corporation and placing a notice of that restriction on each share certificate.

The shareholders' agreement should be entered into by the corporation and every shareholder. Use the services of an objective third person, ideally the corporation's lawyer, to determine whether a proposed share transfer would jeopardize the company's "S" corporation standing. The agreement also should contain penalty provisions that give it real teeth.

A notice of the restriction on share transfer should be placed on each share certificate to provide innocent buyers with a warning that the corporation may not be required to issue new shares to them if that would cause the business to lose its "S" corporation status. Without such a warning, an unknowing buyer who pays fair value for the shares may be in a position to force the corporation to issue new shares to him or her, even if that would disqualify it from "S" corporation status.

Although a state court might order such a buyer to sell his or her shares to either the "S" corporation or its shareholders, this process can be costly. First, the lawsuit that must be brought to force the sale will be expensive. Second, the buyer must be paid an amount equal to the money he or she paid for the shares, which may be more than the fair market value of the shares.

Samples of both a shareholders' agreement and a legend for use on share certificates follow.

SHAREHOLDERS' AGREEMENT

This agreement is made on the 12th day of January, 20___, by and between ABC Products, Inc., a Delaware corporation, and John Smith, Jane Roberts, and Peter Brown, who are all shareholders (Shareholders) of ABC Products, Inc.

In consideration of the facts that (a) The Corporation has elected to be taxed as an "S" corporation as permitted by the Internal Revenue Code of the United States, and that each Shareholder has consented to that election; and (b) the Shareholders believe it is in their mutual interests for The Corporation to continue as an "S" corporation as long as the holders of 51 percent of the outstanding shares of stock agree the corporation shall be an "S" corporation, it is hereby mutually agreed that:

1. Unless the approval of all of the Shareholders is obtained, no Shareholder shall sell, donate, or in any way transfer shares of stock in The Corporation without first obtaining (a) the written opinion of the legal counsel to The Corporation that the transfer will not cause The Corporation to lose its status as an "S" corporation and (b) the transferee's written consent that he or she will be bound by all the terms of this Agreement.

2. No Shareholder shall refuse to provide any consent or other document that may be required by the Internal Revenue Code, any regulations promulgated under the Internal Revenue Code or the Internal Revenue Service that may be as a condition for maintaining The Corporation election to be taxed as an "S" corporation.

3. Any actual or attempted transfer of shares of stock in violation of Paragraph One above will be null, void, and without legal effect.

4. In the event any Shareholder violates or refuses to perform in accordance with the provisions of Paragraphs One and/or Two above, the other Shareholders shall not be limited to seeking money damages, and, in addition to monetary damages, may enforce this Agreement by requesting any form of legal or equitable relief or remedy that requires specific performance from the Shareholder in accordance with this Agreement.

5. In the event that The Corporation loses its "S" corporation status and such loss is attributable in whole or in any part to the failure of one or more Shareholders to act in accordance with the provisions of Paragraphs 1 and/or 2 above, then each Shareholder who failed to comply with the provisions of Paragraphs 1 and/or 2 above shall be jointly and severally liable for all losses incurred by The Corporation and the other Shareholders.

6. Each Shareholder, upon the signing of this agreement, shall return to ABC Products, Inc., all ABC Products, Inc.'s, share certificates he or she may now own and shall receive in substitution therefor a share certificate for the same number of shares. The new certificate shall contain a printed legend stating that the shares represented by the certificate are subject to the restrictions on transfer set out in this Agreement.

7. In the event that the Internal Revenue Code provisions governing "S" corporation status are amended or changed in any way, this Agreement will be modified by the parties to comply with such changes or amendments if advised by legal counsel to The Corporation that such modification or modifications are necessary in order for the Shareholders to continue to receive the benefits of "S" incorporation status.

8. This agreement shall end upon the happening of any one of the following events:
   a. The written agreement of the holders of 51 percent of the outstanding shares of the corporation or
   b. The repeal of the Internal Revenue Code provisions allowing for the election of "S" corporation status and the failure of the Internal Revenue Code, or any future law replacing the Internal Revenue Code, to provide a substitute for the single taxation approach to corporate profits and dividends currently provided by the existing "S" corporation provisions of the Internal Revenue Code.

9. This Agreement will be binding upon and exists for the benefit of the parties to this Agreement, and, subject to the restrictions set out in this Agreement, upon their heirs, legatees, distributees, assigns, personal representatives, and successors.

10. This Agreement has been entered into and will be governed by the laws of Delaware.

IN WITNESS WHEREOF, the parties have executed this Agreement on the day, month, and year first mentioned above.

ABC Products, Inc.

By _____

John Smith
President, ABC Products, Inc.

ATTEST:

By: _____

Peter Brown
Secretary, ABC Products, Inc.

WITNESS: SHAREHOLDERS:

_____   _____

_____   _____

_____   _____

SHAREHOLDERS' AGREEMENT

This agreement is made on the　　　　day of　　　　, 20　　, by and between
　　　　, a　　　　　　corporation, and
　　　　, who are all shareholders (Shareholders) of
In consideration of the facts that (a) The Corporation has elected to be taxed as an "S" corporation as permitted by the Internal Revenue Code of the United States, and that each Shareholder has consented to that election; and (b) the Shareholders believe it is in their mutual interests for The Corporation to continue as an "S" corporation as long as the holders of　　　　percent of the outstanding shares of stock agree The Corporation shall be an "S" corporation, it is hereby mutually agreed that:

1. Unless the approval of all of the Shareholders is obtained, no Shareholder shall sell, donate, or in any way transfer shares of stock in The Corporation without first obtaining (a) the written opinion of the legal counsel to The Corporation that the transfer will not cause The Corporation to lose its status as an "S" corporation and (b) the transferee's written consent that he or she will be bound by all the terms of this Agreement.

2. No Shareholder shall refuse to provide any consent or other document that may be required by the Internal Revenue Code, any regulations promulgated under the Internal Revenue Code or the Internal Revenue Service that may be as a condition for maintaining The Corporation election to be taxed as an "S" corporation.

3. Any actual or attempted transfer of shares of stock in violation of Paragraph 1 above will be null, void, and without legal effect.

4. In the event any Shareholder violates or refuses to perform in accordance with the provisions of Paragraphs 1 and/or 2 above, the other Shareholders shall not be limited to seeking money damages, and, in addition to monetary damages, may enforce this Agreement by requesting any form of legal or equitable relief or remedy that requires specific performance from the Shareholder in accordance with this Agreement.

5. In the event that The Corporation loses its "S" corporation status and such loss is attributable in whole or in any part to the failure of one or more Shareholders to act in accordance with the provisions of Paragraphs 1 and/or 2 above, then each Shareholder who failed to comply with the provisions of Paragraphs 1 and/or 2 above shall be jointly and severally liable for all losses incurred by The Corporation and the other Shareholders.

6. Each Shareholder, upon the signing of this agreement, shall return to _____ all _____ share certificates he or she may now own and shall receive in substitution therefor a share certificate for the same number of shares. The new certificate shall contain a printed legend stating that the shares represented by the certificate are subject to the restrictions on transfer set out in this Agreement.

7. In the event that the Internal Revenue Code provisions governing "S" corporation status are amended or changed in any way, this Agreement will be modified by the parties to comply with such changes or amendments if advised by legal counsel to The Corporation that such modification or modifications are necessary in order for the Shareholders to continue to receive the benefits of "S" incorporation status.

8. This agreement shall end upon the happening of any one of the following events:
   a. The written agreement of the holders of _____ percent of the outstanding shares of the corporation or
   b. The repeal of the Internal Revenue Code provisions allowing for the election of "S" corporation status and the failure of the Internal Revenue Code, or any future law replacing the Internal Revenue Code, to provide a substitute for the single taxation approach to corporate profits and dividends currently provided by the existing "S" corporation provisions of the Internal Revenue Code.

9. This Agreement will be binding upon and exists for the benefit of the parties to this Agreement, and, subject to the restrictions set out in this Agreement, upon their heirs, legatees, distributees, assigns, personal representatives, and successors.

10. This Agreement has been entered into and will be governed by the laws of

IN WITNESS WHEREOF, the parties have executed this Agreement on the day, month, and year first mentioned above.

By _____

ATTEST:

By: _____

WITNESS: SHAREHOLDERS:

_____   _____

_____   _____

_____   _____

INCORPORATED UNDER THE LAWS OF THE STATE OF DELAWARE

Number:

Shares:

TOTAL AUTHORIZED ISSUE
1,000 SHARES WITHOUT PAR VALUE

This is to Certify that _____ *is the owner of*

_____

fully paid and non-assessable shares of the above Corporation transferrable only on the books of the Corporation by the holder hereof in person or by duly authorized Attorney upon surrender of this Certificate properly endorsed.

Witness, the seal of the Corporation and the signatures of its duly authorized officers.

Dated:

Treasurer

President

_____ 20 ___

THE SALE, GIFT, OR ANY OTHER TRANSFER OF THE SHARES REPRESENTED BY THIS CERTIFICATE ARE SUBJECT TO AN AGREEMENT, DATED _____
A COPY OF THE AGREEMENT IS ON FILE AND AVAILABLE FOR INSPECTION IN THE PRINCIPAL OFFICE OF THE CORPORATION.

5

Timing and Mechanics of Filing

The mechanics of making an "S" corporation election are quite simple. In fact, it is a one-step process that involves filing a very simple form: IRS Form 2553, entitled "Election by a Small Business Corporation." The key to a successful filing, therefore, amounts to no more than filling in the blanks accurately and doing it on time to get the "S" corporation benefits that will save you money. Those two requirements, however, should not be taken lightly. If the electing corporation does not file on time, or if its filings are inaccurate, the benefits of "S" incorporation may be lost.

This chapter describes the mechanics of filing, the types of information needed and the dates by which a filing must be made and supplies a blank Form 2553 (and several other forms)—all designed to make your filing as easy as rolling off a log.

SECURING YOUR EMPLOYER ID NUMBER

If you operate an existing business, it should have an employer identification number (EIN). This number is comparable to an individual's Social Security number and is used by the Internal Revenue Service to identify your business. Your existing corporation's EIN can serve as the EIN for your "S" corporation.

If you are starting a new business, you will have to obtain an EIN—a fairly simple process. Just fill out IRS Form SS-4, a copy of which appears at the end of this chapter. Then you can either mail or fax the form to the appropriate IRS office for your region. It will take about three to four weeks for the IRS to respond. A quicker, more efficient method is to call your local IRS office and do it by phone. Before calling, fill out the form. The agent will ask you to read off the information on the form and will assign your business an EIN over the phone. You must also have access to a fax machine because after assigning the EIN to your corporation, the agent will ask you to fax a copy of your Form SS-4 to the IRS.

THE DOCUMENTS THAT MUST BE FILED

For most filings, only one document is needed: Form 2553. It is available from any IRS office, or file the copy of the current Form 2553 included at the end of this chapter.

Form 2553 asks the applying corporation to supply the following information:

- Corporation's name
- Corporation's employer identification number (EIN). If yours is a new business and does not yet have an EIN, just fill in the words *applied for.* If you have not yet applied for an EIN, see above and use the application for an EIN (IRS Form SS-4) at the end of this chapter. Try to avoid using the phrase *applied for* because it will require you to make a second filing when you get the number. As explained, you can get your corporation's EIN simply by calling the IRS and faxing a copy of the EIN application form to the agency. As a practical matter, there really is no need to turn a one-step process into two steps.
- Corporation's address
- Whether the corporation has already operated as a regular "C" corporation
- Whether the filing is made for the corporation's first year of existence, the earliest of the dates the corporation had shareholders, had assets or began doing business
- Corporation's principal business and product or service. This entry requires you to use the "Codes for Principal Business Activity" contained in IRS Form 1120S. A current listing of the codes is reproduced in Appendix A.
- Number of shares actually held by shareholders at the time the election is filed. (Note: The information sought here relates to the number of shares, not share certificates, held by shareholders. One shareholder, for example, may own ten shares that are represented by one share certificate. In this case, the number to fill in would be ten, not one.)
- Date and state of incorporation
- Corporation's tax year. If you want a tax year other than a calendar year, fill out Parts II, III, and IV of Form 2553. Noncalendar years will be approved only in limited circumstances.

- Consent of each shareholder, along with information stating how many shares each shareholder owns, when the shares were acquired and each person's tax year

The completed Form 2553 must be signed by a corporate officer and mailed to the IRS Service Center where you file your income tax return. A procedure followed by cautious lawyers, and one that you should adopt, uses two safeguards whenever filing a form with the IRS by mail. First, send it by certified mail, return receipt requested. The receipt—which you should keep on permanent file with your incorporation documents—will supply you with proof of timely filing should the question ever arise.

Second, enclose a photocopy of your form with a self-addressed, stamped envelope, and ask to have a time-stamped and date-stamped copy of your Form 2553 returned to you. File this document with the return receipt from your certified mailing. This will demonstrate both timeliness and accuracy should the IRS claim you never filed.

Caution

Filing does not occur until Form 2553 is postmarked by the post office. A filing that is even one day late will cause the corporation to lose the benefit of "S" incorporation for a full year. If time has run down to the last day, you may wish to consider hand delivering your Form 2553 to the IRS rather than taking a chance on a late postmark by the somewhat erratic post office. If you do hand carry your Form 2553, take along a photocopy and have it stamped by the person to whom you submit the original. Unless you take this precaution, you will run into problems if the IRS should misplace your form and later claim it never received the document.

Caution

The stress given to timeliness, certified mail and stamped photocopies should not be ignored. At least two or three times a year, we see IRS litigation involving individuals (and sometimes their attorneys or accountants) who swear in open court that they mailed a form to the IRS on or before its due date. The IRS then claims it never received the form, and if the taxpayer cannot prove the IRS received it, the IRS wins.

TIMING YOUR FILING

The timing of a filing for the "S" corporation election is strictly defined by law. If the election is to be effective for the corporation's existing tax year, Form 2553 must be filed no later than the fifteenth day of the third month of the corporation's taxable year. Note, the rule refers to months and days. Timing, therefore, works as follows:

- A new corporation, with a taxable year that starts on June 6, 1999, counts two months to August 6th, and adds 14 more days (August 6th was two months and one day). It must file on or before August 20, 2000.
- An existing corporation that wishes to switch to "S" corporation status in 2000 can file at any time during 1999 and no later than March 15, 2000.

Planning Note

It is vital that you allow yourself enough time to meet the two-month-and-fifteen-day time frame. However, the IRS can treat a late-filed election as timely made. The "S" corporation must file an election within 12 months of the original due date of an election (but in no event later than the unextended due date of the tax return for the first year the corporation intended to be an "S" corporation). A statement that the filing is made pursuant to Rev. Proc. 97-40 must be at the top of Form 2553. The reasons why the election was not made on time must be attached to the election. The act also gave the IRS the authority to waive defects in "S" corporation elections and to treat an untimely election as timely filed if reasonable cause is found.

Relief for Certain Late ESBT and QSST Elections

A corporation is eligible for inadvertent invalid election relief or inadvertent termination relief if it meets the following requirements:

1. The "S" corporation election was invalid or terminated solely because the beneficiary of a QSST (or the beneficiary's legal representative) failed to file a timely QSST election, or the trustee of a trust that would otherwise qualify as an ESBT failed to file a timely ESBT election.
2. All taxpayers whose tax liability and tax returns would be affected by the QSST or ESBT election (including the trust itself and, in the case of a QSST, the beneficiary of the trust) have reported their income (on all affected returns) consistent with the corporation's "S" corporation election for the year the QSST or ESBT election should have been made, as well as for any subsequent year.

3. The failure to file a timely QSST or ESBT election was inadvertent.
4. Within 24 months of the original due date of the election, the beneficiary of the QSST or the trustee of the ESBT files the election pursuant to this revenue procedure. The current income beneficiary (in the case of a QSST) or the trustee (in the case of an ESBT) of the trust must sign and file the appropriate election with the applicable service center. This election must state at the top, "Filed pursuant to Rev. Proc. 98-55," and include the following material:
   - The names, addresses and taxpayer identification numbers of the current income beneficiary (in the case of a QSST), the trust and the corporation
   - A statement identifying the election as an election under §1361(d)(2) or §1361(e)(3)
   - The date the stock of the corporation was originally transferred to the trust
   - In the case of a QSST, an affidavit from the trustee stating that the trust satisfies the QSST requirements of §1361(d)(3) and that the income distribution requirements have been and will continue to be met
   - In the case of an ESBT, an affidavit from the trustee stating that all potential current beneficiaries meet the shareholder requirements under §1361(b)(1) and that the trust satisfies the requirements of an ESBT under §1361(e)(1) other than the requirement to make an ESBT election
   - An affidavit from the current income beneficiary (in the case of a QSST) or the trustee (in the case of an ESBT) stating that the failure to file the relevant election was inadvertent and that the beneficiary or trustee acted diligently to correct the mistake on discovery
   - Affidavits from all shareholders during the period between the date the "S" corporation election terminated or was to have become effective and the date the completed election was filed (including the trust itself and, in the case of a QSST, the beneficiary of the trust) stating that they have reported their income (on all affected returns) consistent with the "S" corporation election for the year the election should have been made and for any subsequent year
   - A dated declaration signed by the current income beneficiary (in the case of a QSST) or the trustee (in the case of an ESBT) that states: "Under penalties of perjury, I, _____ , declare that, to the best of my knowledge and belief, the facts presented in support of this election are true, correct and complete."

Corporations that satisfy the requirements of this revenue procedure will automatically be granted relief. Thus, the corporation will be treated as an "S" corporation for the period beginning on the date of termination or the date on which the election was to have become effective, whichever applies, and ending on the date the completed ESBT or QSST election is filed, and thereafter, unless the "S" corporation election is otherwise terminated. In addition, during such period, the trust will be treated as a trust and the rules applicable to ESBTs or QSSTs will apply. In the case of a QSST, the beneficiary of the trust will be treated as the owner of that portion of the trust consisting of "S" corporation stock.

FILING AND ELIGIBILITY

For a filing to be effective, not only must it be made in a timely fashion, but the corporation must have conformed to all of the eligibility requirements described in Chapter 4 on both the filing date and every day of the taxable year for which it seeks "S" corporation treatment.

Example

XYZ, Inc., a "C" corporation, elects to be taxed as an "S" corporation. A calendar-year corporation, it files its election on March 1, 1999, in ample time to satisfy the two-month-and-fifteen-day requirement. Knowing it intended to make this election, XYZ, Inc., redeemed all of its preferred stock on January 1, 1999. However, it is not eligible for "S" corporation treatment in 1999 and must wait until 2000 to obtain the benefits of single taxation. This results from the fact that it was ineligible to be an "S" corporation in 1999 because it had two classes of stock in that year, even though it was for only one day. It should have redeemed its preferred stock on December 31, 1998.

SHAREHOLDER CONSENT

All shareholders must consent to the corporation's election to be taxed as an "S" corporation. Equally important, the shareholder consents must be filed within the time limits for a filing. In determining which shareholders should file consents, the following rules apply:

- Every person who owned shares during the taxable year must file a consent—even if the person sold his or her shares before the election was filed.

Example

John Doe owned three shares of XYZ Corporation, which he sold on January 3rd. XYZ Corporation files its election on March 1st. Mr. Doe must file a consent.

- If shares are held for the benefit of a second person, the beneficiary should file a consent. A beneficial owner of stock ordinarily is held by the courts to be the person entitled to the financial benefits (dividends or other distributions) of the shares. A safe course to follow would be to get consents from both the beneficiary and the person who holds the stock for the beneficiary.
- Owners of nonvoting common stock should file consents.
- If stock is held jointly by husbands and wives, or others, each joint owner or tenant in common should file a consent.

Caution

In community property states, even if shares of stock are listed in the name of only one spouse, both husband and wife should file consents.

- If shares have passed to an estate, it is generally safe to cover all bases by obtaining consents from both the executor of the estate as well as the beneficiaries or legatees of the stock.

Extensions are available for the filing of shareholder consents. If, for example, a former shareholder whose consent is required has left the immediate area, the corporation can obtain an extension of time for the filing of that person's consent. A sample form for this purpose is included at the end of the chapter.

Filing Shareholder Consents

This process involves little, if any, paperwork for most corporations. Form 2553 has a section in which shareholder consents can be included.

On occasion, however, one or more shareholders may not be available to sign the Form 2553 consent provision. Assume, for example, your corporation has three or four shareholders and two of them reside in distant communities. It may not be possible for you to mail Form 2553 to different parts of the country and get it back on time to file within the two-month-and-fifteen-day limit. In such cases, the corporation should request an extension of time within which to file the shareholder's consent and, when the other consents are received, promptly file them with the IRS.

Sample copies of forms asking the IRS for an extension and of a separate consent statement are included at the end of this chapter.

SHAREHOLDERS' CONSENT

March 1, 20

Director
Internal Revenue Service Center
100 Main Street
Anytown, USA 10000

Dear Sir:

I, Robert Jones, by means of this letter, state my consent to have the Ace Corporation, a Delaware corporation with offices at 123 High Street, Wilmington, DE 10000, treated as an "S" corporation under Section 1362(a) of the Internal Revenue Code. In accordance with the information requested by Form 2553, I offer the following data:

1. My name is Robert Jones.
2. I own ten shares of stock of the Ace Corporation.
3. I acquired that stock on May 1, 20 .
4. My Social Security number is: 999-99-9999.
5. My tax year ends on December 31.

_____

Robert Jones
Date: March 1, 20

Director
Internal Revenue Service Center

Dear   :

I,   , by means of this letter, state my consent to have the
                          , a   corporation with offices at
                          , treated as an "S" corporation under Section 1362(a) of
the Internal Revenue Code. In accordance with the information requested by Form
2553, I offer the following data:

1. My name is   .
2. I own   shares of stock of the   .
3. I acquired that stock on   .
4. My Social Security number is: .
5. My tax year ends on   .

_____

                          Date:

REQUEST FOR EXTENSION TO FILE
SHAREHOLDERS' CONSENT

March 14, 20

Director

Internal Revenue Service Center

100 Main Street

Anytown, USA 10000

Dear Sir:

By means of this letter, the Ace Corporation (hereinafter, "The Corporation") requests an extension of the time for the filing of shareholder consents with respect to The Corporation's election to be subject to the "S" incorporation provisions of the Internal Revenue Code. In support of this request, the following information is provided:

1. The Corporation was incorporated under the laws of the State of Delaware on January 2, 20 .

2. The Corporation first had assets* on January 2, 20 .

3. All of the shareholders' consents to The Corporation election to be taxed under the "S" incorporation provisions of the Internal Revenue Code have not and could not be filed on Form 2553, which is being filed with this letter, for the following reason:

   John Doe, the holder of 10 shares out of 100 issued and outstanding shares, after agreeing to sign a consent, transferred his shares to Robert Greene on January 10, 20 . Mr. Greene has signed the consent. Mr. Doe, believing his signature would not be needed, has embarked on a two-month vacation.

4. Other than John Doe, all other shareholders have consented to the election, and each of those shareholders has consented in writing on Form 2553.

5. The government's interest will not be jeopardized by treating the election to be chaptered under the "S" incorporation provisions of the Internal Revenue Code as valid.

Ace Corporation

By: _____

Jane Smith

Title: President

*Or "did business" or "had shareholders"

Director

Internal Revenue Service Center

:

By means of this letter, the _____ (hereinafter, "The Corporation") requests an extension of the time for the filing of shareholder consents with respect to The Corporation's election to be subject to the "S" incorporation provisions of the Internal Revenue Code. In support of this request, the following information is provided:

1. The Corporation was incorporated under the laws of _____ on _____, 20 __ .
2. The Corporation first _____ on _____, 20 __ .
3. All of the shareholders' consents to The Corporation election to be taxed under the "S" incorporation provisions of the Internal Revenue Code have not and could not be filed on Form 2553, which is being filed with this letter, for the following reason:

4. Other than _____, all other shareholders have consented to the election, and each of those shareholders has consented in writing on Form 2553.
5. The government's interest will not be jeopardized by treating the election to be chaptered under the "S" incorporation provisions of the Internal Revenue Code as valid.

By: _____

Title:

Form **2553**

(Rev. September 1997)

Department of the Treasury
Internal Revenue Service

Election by a Small Business Corporation

(Under section 1362 of the Internal Revenue Code)

▶ For Paperwork Reduction Act Notice, see page 2 of instructions.

▶ See separate instructions.

OMB No. 1545-0146

Notes:
1. *This election to be an S corporation can be accepted only if all the tests are met under* **Who May Elect** *on page 1 of the instructions; all signatures in Parts I and III are originals (no photocopies); and the exact name and address of the corporation and other required form information are provided.*

2. *Do not file* **Form 1120S,** *U.S. Income Tax Return for an S Corporation, for any tax year before the year the election takes effect.*

3. *If the corporation was in existence before the effective date of this election, see* **Taxes an S Corporation May Owe** *on page 1 of the instructions.*

Part I	**Election Information**	

Please Type or Print

Name of corporation (see instructions)	**A** Employer identification number
Number, street, and room or suite no. (If a P.O. box, see instructions.)	**B** Date incorporated
City or town, state, and ZIP code	**C** State of incorporation

D Election is to be effective for tax year beginning (month, day, year) . . . . ▶ / /

E Name and title of officer or legal representative who the IRS may call for more information

F Telephone number of officer or legal representative ( )

G If the corporation changed its name or address after applying for the EIN shown in **A** above, check this box . . . . ▶ ☐

H If this election takes effect for the first tax year the corporation exists, enter month, day, and year of the **earliest** of the following: (1) date the corporation first had shareholders, (2) date the corporation first had assets, or (3) date the corporation began doing business . . . . ▶ / /.

I Selected tax year: Annual return will be filed for tax year ending (month and day) ▶ . . . .

If the tax year ends on any date other than December 31, except for an automatic 52-53-week tax year ending with reference to the month of December, you **must** complete Part II on the back. If the date you enter is the ending date of an automatic 52-53-week tax year, write "52-53-week year" to the right of the date. See Temporary Regulations section 1.441-2T(e)(3).

J Name and address of each shareholder; shareholder's spouse having a community property interest in the corporation's stock; and each tenant in common, joint tenant, and tenant by the entirety. (A husband and wife (and their estates) are counted as one shareholder in determining the number of shareholders without regard to the manner in which the stock is owned.)	**K** Shareholders' Consent Statement. Under penalties of perjury, we declare that we consent to the election of the above-named corporation to be an S corporation under section 1362(a) and that we have examined this consent statement, including accompanying schedules and statements, and to the best of our knowledge and belief, it is true, correct, and complete. We understand our consent is binding and may not be withdrawn after the corporation has made a valid election. (Shareholders sign and date below.)		**L** Stock owned		**M** Social security number or employer identification number (see instructions)	**N** Shareholder's tax year ends (month and day)
	Signature	Date	Number of shares	Dates acquired		

Under penalties of perjury, I declare that I have examined this election, including accompanying schedules and statements, and to the best of my knowledge and belief, it is true, correct, and complete.

Signature of officer ▶   Title ▶   Date ▶

See Parts II and III on back.   Cat. No. 18629R   Form **2553** (Rev. 9-97)

Part II **Selection of Fiscal Tax Year** (All corporations using this part must complete item O and item P, Q, or R.)

O Check the applicable box to indicate whether the corporation is:
   1. ☐ A new corporation adopting the tax year entered in item I, Part I.
   2. ☐ An existing corporation retaining the tax year entered in item I, Part I.
   3. ☐ An existing corporation changing to the tax year entered in item I, Part I.

P Complete item P if the corporation is using the expeditious approval provisions of Rev. Proc. 87-32, 1987-2 C.B. 396, to request **(1)** a natural business year (as defined in section 4.01(1) of Rev. Proc. 87-32) or **(2)** a year that satisfies the ownership tax year test in section 4.01(2) of Rev. Proc. 87-32. Check the applicable box below to indicate the representation statement the corporation is making as required under section 4 of Rev. Proc. 87-32.

   1. Natural Business Year ► ☐ I represent that the corporation is retaining or changing to a tax year that coincides with its natural business year as defined in section 4.01(1) of Rev. Proc. 87-32 and as verified by its satisfaction of the requirements of section 4.02(1) of Rev. Proc. 87-32. In addition, if the corporation is changing to a natural business year as defined in section 4.01(1), I further represent that such tax year results in less deferral of income to the owners than the corporation's present tax year. I also represent that the corporation is not described in section 3.01(2) of Rev. Proc. 87-32. (See instructions for additional information that must be attached.)

   2. Ownership Tax Year ► ☐ I represent that shareholders holding more than half of the shares of the stock (as of the first day of the tax year to which the request relates) of the corporation have the same tax year or are concurrently changing to the tax year that the corporation adopts, retains, or changes to per item I, Part I. I also represent that the corporation is not described in section 3.01(2) of Rev. Proc. 87-32.

Note: *If you do not use item P and the corporation wants a fiscal tax year, complete either item Q or R below. Item Q is used to request a fiscal tax year based on a business purpose and to make a back-up section 444 election. Item R is used to make a regular section 444 election.*

Q Business Purpose—To request a fiscal tax year based on a business purpose, you must check box Q1 and pay a user fee. See instructions for details. You may also check box Q2 and/or box Q3.

   1. Check here ► ☐ if the fiscal year entered in item I, Part I, is requested under the provisions of section 6.03 of Rev. Proc. 87-32. Attach to Form 2553 a statement showing the business purpose for the requested fiscal year. See instructions for additional information that must be attached.

   2. Check here ► ☐ to show that the corporation intends to make a back-up section 444 election in the event the corporation's business purpose request is not approved by the IRS. (See instructions for more information.)

   3. Check here ► ☐ to show that the corporation agrees to adopt or change to a tax year ending December 31 if necessary for the IRS to accept this election for S corporation status in the event (1) the corporation's business purpose request is not approved and the corporation makes a back-up section 444 election, but is ultimately not qualified to make a section 444 election, or (2) the corporation's business purpose request is not approved and the corporation did not make a back-up section 444 election.

R Section 444 Election—To make a section 444 election, you must check box R1 and you may also check box R2.
   1. Check here ► ☐ to show the corporation will make, if qualified, a section 444 election to have the fiscal tax year shown in item I, Part I. To make the election, you must complete **Form 8716**, Election To Have a Tax Year Other Than a Required Tax Year, and either attach it to Form 2553 or file it separately.

   2. Check here ► ☐ to show that the corporation agrees to adopt or change to a tax year ending December 31 if necessary for the IRS to accept this election for S corporation status in the event the corporation is ultimately not qualified to make a section 444 election.

Part III **Qualified Subchapter S Trust (QSST) Election Under Section 1361(d)(2)***

Income beneficiary's name and address	Social security number
Trust's name and address	Employer identification number

Date on which stock of the corporation was transferred to the trust (month, day, year) . . . . ►   /   /

In order for the trust named above to be a QSST and thus a qualifying shareholder of the S corporation for which this Form 2553 is filed, I hereby make the election under section 1361(d)(2). Under penalties of perjury, I certify that the trust meets the definitional requirements of section 1361(d)(3) and that all other information provided in Part III is true, correct, and complete.

_____   _____
Signature of income beneficiary or signature and title of legal representative or other qualified person making the election   Date

*Use Part III to make the QSST election only if stock of the corporation has been transferred to the trust on or before the date on which the corporation makes its election to be an S corporation. The QSST election must be made and filed separately if stock of the corporation is transferred to the trust after the date on which the corporation makes the S election.

✪

Instructions for Form 2553

(Revised September 1997)

Election by a Small Business Corporation

Section references are to the Internal Revenue Code unless otherwise noted.

Department of the Treasury
Internal Revenue Service

General Instructions

Purpose.— To elect to be an S corporation, a corporation must file Form 2553. The election permits the income of the S corporation to be taxed to the shareholders of the corporation rather than to the corporation itself, except as noted below under **Taxes an S Corporation May Owe.**

Who May Elect.— A corporation may elect to be an S corporation only if it meets all of the following tests:

1. It is a domestic corporation.

2. It has no more than 75 shareholders. A husband and wife (and their estates) are treated as one shareholder for this requirement. All other persons are treated as separate shareholders.

3. Its only shareholders are individuals, estates, certain trusts described in section 1361(c)(2)(A), or, for tax years beginning after 1997, exempt organizations described in section 401(a) or 501(c)(3). Trustees of trusts that want to make the election under section 1361(e)(3) to be an electing small business trust should see Notice 97-12, 1997-3 I.R.B. 11.

Note: *See the instructions for Part III regarding qualified subchapter S trusts.*

4. It has no nonresident alien shareholders.

5. It has only one class of stock (disregarding differences in voting rights). Generally, a corporation is treated as having only one class of stock if all outstanding shares of the corporation's stock confer identical rights to distribution and liquidation proceeds. See Regulations section 1.1361-1(1) for more details.

6. It is not one of the following ineligible corporations:

a. A bank or thrift institution that uses the reserve method of accounting for bad debts under section 585;

b. An insurance company subject to tax under the rules of subchapter L of the Code;

c. A corporation that has elected to be treated as a possessions corporation under section 936; or

d. A domestic international sales corporation (DISC) or former DISC.

7. It has a permitted tax year as required by section 1378 or makes a section 444 election to have a tax year other than a permitted tax year. Section 1378 defines a permitted tax year as a tax year ending December 31, or any other tax year for which the corporation establishes a business purpose to the satisfaction of the IRS. See Part II for details on requesting a fiscal tax year based on a business purpose or on making a section 444 election.

8. Each shareholder consents as explained in the instructions for column K.

See sections 1361, 1362, and 1378 for additional information on the above tests.

An election can be made by a parent S corporation to treat the assets, liabilities, and items of income, deduction, and credit of an eligible wholly-owned subsidiary as those of the parent. For details, see Notice 97-4, 1997-2 I.R.B. 24.

Taxes an S Corporation May Owe.— An S corporation may owe income tax in the following instances:

1. If, at the end of any tax year, the corporation had accumulated earnings and profits, and its passive investment income under section 1362(d)(3) is more than 25% of its gross receipts, the corporation may owe tax on its excess net passive income.

2. A corporation with net recognized built-in gain (as defined in section 1374(d)(2)) may owe tax on its built-in gains.

3. A corporation that claimed investment credit before its first year as an S corporation will be liable for any investment credit recapture tax.

4. A corporation that used the LIFO inventory method for the year immediately preceding its first year as an S corporation may owe an additional tax due to LIFO recapture.

For more details on these taxes, see the Instructions for Form 1120S.

Where To File.— File this election with the Internal Revenue Service Center listed below.

If the corporation's principal business, office, or agency is located in	Use the following Internal Revenue Service Center address
New Jersey, New York (New York City and counties of Nassau, Rockland, Suffolk, and Westchester)	Holtsville, NY 00501
New York (all other counties), Connecticut, Maine, Massachusetts, New Hampshire, Rhode Island, Vermont	Andover, MA 05501
Florida, Georgia, South Carolina	Atlanta, GA 39901
Indiana, Kentucky, Michigan, Ohio, West Virginia	Cincinnati, OH 45999
Kansas, New Mexico, Oklahoma, Texas	Austin, TX 73301
Alaska, Arizona, California (counties of Alpine, Amador, Butte, Calaveras, Colusa, Contra Costa, Del Norte, El Dorado, Glenn, Humboldt, Lake, Lassen, Marin, Mendocino, Modoc, Napa, Nevada, Placer, Plumas, Sacramento, San Joaquin, Shasta, Sierra, Siskiyou, Solano, Sonoma, Sutter, Tehama, Trinity, Yolo, and Yuba), Colorado, Idaho, Montana, Nebraska, Nevada, North Dakota, Oregon, South Dakota, Utah, Washington, Wyoming	Ogden, UT 84201
California (all other counties), Hawaii	Fresno, CA 93888
Illinois, Iowa, Minnesota, Missouri, Wisconsin	Kansas City, MO 64999
Alabama, Arkansas, Louisiana, Mississippi, North Carolina, Tennessee	Memphis, TN 37501
Delaware, District of Columbia, Maryland, Pennsylvania, Virginia	Philadelphia, PA 19255

When To Make the Election.— Complete and file Form 2553 **(a)** at any time before the 16th day of the 3rd month of the tax year, if filed during the tax year the election is to take effect, or **(b)** at any time during the preceding tax year. An election made no later than 2 months and 15 days after the beginning of a tax year that is less than 2½ months long is treated as timely made for that tax year. An election made after the 15th day of the 3rd month but before the end of the tax year is effective for the next year. For example, if a calendar tax year

corporation makes the election in April 1998, it is effective for the corporation's 1999 calendar tax year.

However, an election made after the due date will be accepted as timely filed if the corporation can show that the failure to file on time was due to reasonable cause. To request relief for a late election, the corporation generally must request a private letter ruling and pay a user fee in accordance with Rev. Proc. 97-1, 1997-1 I.R.B. 11 (or its successor). But if the election is filed within 6 months of its due date and the original due date for filing the corporation's initial Form 1120S has not passed, the ruling and user fee requirements do not apply. To request relief in this case, write "FILED PURSUANT TO REV. PROC. 97-40" at the top of page 1 of Form 2553, attach a statement explaining the reason for failing to file the election on time, and file Form 2553 as otherwise instructed. See Rev. Proc. 97-40, 1997-33 I.R.B. 50, for more details.

See Regulations section 1.1362-6(b)(3)(iii) for how to obtain relief for an inadvertent invalid election if the corporation filed a timely election, but one or more shareholders did not file a timely consent.

Acceptance or Nonacceptance of Election.— The service center will notify the corporation if its election is accepted and when it will take effect. The corporation will also be notified if its election is not accepted. The corporation should generally receive a determination on its election within 60 days after it has filed Form 2553. If box Q1 in Part II is checked on page 2, the corporation will receive a ruling letter from the IRS in Washington, DC, that either approves or denies the selected tax year. When box Q1 is checked, it will generally take an additional 90 days for the Form 2553 to be accepted.

Do not file Form 1120S for any tax year before the year the election takes effect. If the corporation is now required to file **Form 1120,** U.S. Corporation Income Tax Return, or any other applicable tax return, continue filing it until the election takes effect.

Care should be exercised to ensure that the IRS receives the election. If the corporation is not notified of acceptance or nonacceptance of its election within 3 months of date of filing (date mailed), or within 6 months if box Q1 is checked, take follow-up action by corresponding with the service center where the corporation filed the election. If the IRS questions whether Form 2553 was filed, an acceptable proof of filing is **(a)** certified or registered mail receipt (timely filed) from the U.S. Postal Service or its equivalent from a designated private delivery service (see Notice 97-26, 1997-17 I.R.B. 6); **(b)** Form 2553 with accepted stamp; **(c)** Form 2553 with stamped IRS received date; or **(d)** IRS letter stating that Form 2553 has been accepted.

End of Election.— Once the election is made, it stays in effect until it is terminated. If the election is terminated in a tax year beginning after 1996, the corporation (or a successor corporation) can make another election on Form 2553 only with IRS consent for any tax year before the 5th tax year after the first tax year in which the termination took effect. See Regulations section 1.1362-5 for more details.

Cat. No. 49978N

Specific Instructions

Part I

Note: *All corporations must complete Part I.*

Name and Address of Corporation.— Enter the true corporate name as stated in the corporate charter or other legal document creating it. If the corporation's mailing address is the same as someone else's, such as a shareholder's, enter "c/o" and this person's name following the name of the corporation. Include the suite, room, or other unit number after the street address. If the Post Office does not deliver to the street address and the corporation has a P.O. box, show the box number instead of the street address. If the corporation changed its name or address after applying for its employer identification number, be sure to check the box in item G of Part I.

Item A. Employer Identification Number (EIN).— If the corporation has applied for an EIN but has not received it, enter "applied for." If the corporation does not have an EIN, it should apply for one on **Form SS-4,** Application for Employer Identification Number. You can order Form SS-4 by calling 1-800-TAX-FORM (1-800-829-3676).

Item D. Effective Date of Election.— Enter the beginning effective date (month, day, year) of the tax year requested for the S corporation. Generally, this will be the beginning date of the tax year for which the ending effective date is required to be shown in item I, Part I. For a new corporation (first year the corporation exists) it will generally be the date required to be shown in item H, Part I. The tax year of a new corporation starts on the date that it has shareholders, acquires assets, or begins doing business, whichever happens first. If the effective date for item D for a newly formed corporation is later than the date in item H, the corporation should file Form 1120 or Form 1120-A for the tax period between these dates.

Column K. Shareholders' Consent Statement.— Each shareholder who owns (or is deemed to own) stock at the time the election is made must consent to the election. If the election is made during the corporation's tax year for which it first takes effect, any person who held stock at any time during the part of that year that occurs before the election is made, must consent to the election, even though the person may have sold or transferred his or her stock before the election is made.

An election made during the first 2½ months of the tax year is effective for the following tax year if any person who held stock in the corporation during the part of the tax year before the election was made, and who did not hold stock at the time the election was made, did not consent to the election.

Each shareholder consents by signing and dating in column K or signing and dating a separate consent statement described below. The following special rules apply in determining who must sign the consent statement.

- If a husband and wife have a community interest in the stock or in the income from it, both must consent.
- Each tenant in common, joint tenant, and tenant by the entirety must consent.
- A minor's consent is made by the minor, legal representative of the minor, or a natural or adoptive parent of the minor if no legal representative has been appointed.
- The consent of an estate is made by the executor or administrator.

- The consent of an electing small business trust is made by the trustee.
- If the stock is owned by a trust (other than an electing small business trust), the deemed owner of the trust must consent. See section 1361(c)(2) for details regarding trusts that are permitted to be shareholders and rules for determining who is the deemed owner.

*Continuation sheet or separate consent statement.—*If you need a continuation sheet or use a separate consent statement, attach it to Form 2553. The separate consent statement must contain the name, address, and EIN of the corporation and the shareholder information requested in columns J through N of Part I. If you want, you may combine all the shareholders' consents in one statement.

Column L.— Enter the number of shares of stock each shareholder owns and the dates the stock was acquired. If the election is made during the corporation's tax year for which it first takes effect, do not list the shares of stock for those shareholders who sold or transferred all of their stock before the election was made. However, these shareholders must still consent to the election for it to be effective for the tax year.

Column M.— Enter the social security number of each shareholder who is an individual. Enter the EIN of each shareholder that is an estate, a qualified trust, or an exempt organization.

Column N.— Enter the month and day that each shareholder's tax year ends. If a shareholder is changing his or her tax year, enter the tax year the shareholder is changing to, and attach an explanation indicating the present tax year and the basis for the change (e.g., automatic revenue procedure or letter ruling request).

Signature.— Form 2553 must be signed by the president, treasurer, assistant treasurer, chief accounting officer, or other corporate officer (such as tax officer) authorized to sign.

Part II

Complete Part II if you selected a tax year ending on any date other than December 31 (other than a 52-53-week tax year ending with reference to the month of December).

Box P1.— Attach a statement showing separately for each month the amount of gross receipts for the most recent 47 months as required by section 4.03(3) of Rev. Proc. 87-32, 1987-2 C.B. 396. A corporation that does not have a 47-month period of gross receipts cannot establish a natural business year under section 4.01(1).

Box Q1.— For examples of an acceptable business purpose for requesting a fiscal tax year, see Rev. Rul. 87-57, 1987-2 C.B. 117.

In addition to a statement showing the business purpose for the requested fiscal year, you must attach the other information necessary to meet the ruling request requirements of Rev. Proc. 97-1 (or its successor). Also attach a statement that shows separately the amount of gross receipts from sales or services (and inventory costs, if applicable) for each of the 36 months preceding the effective date of the election to be an S corporation. If the corporation has been in existence for fewer than 36 months, submit figures for the period of existence.

If you check box Q1, you will be charged a $250 user fee (subject to change). Do not pay the fee when filing Form 2553. The service center will send Form 2553 to the IRS in

Washington, DC, who, in turn, will notify the corporation that the fee is due.

Box Q2.— If the corporation makes a back-up section 444 election for which it is qualified, then the election will take effect in the event the business purpose request is not approved. In some cases, the tax year requested under the back-up section 444 election may be different than the tax year requested under business purpose. See **Form 8716,** Election To Have a Tax Year Other Than a Required Tax Year, for details on making a back-up section 444 election.

Boxes Q2 and R2.— If the corporation is not qualified to make the section 444 election after making the item Q2 back-up section 444 election or requesting a fiscal tax year, it can make the election in item R1, and therefore it later files a calendar year return, it should write "Section 444 Election Not Made" in the top left corner of the first calendar year Form 1120S it files.

Part III

Certain qualified subchapter S trusts (QSSTs) may make the QSST election required by section 1361(d)(2) in Part III. Part III may be used to make the QSST election only if corporate stock has been transferred to the trust on or before the date on which the corporation makes its election to be an S corporation. However, a statement can be used instead of Part III to make the election.

Note: *Use Part III* **only** *if you make the election in Part I (i.e., Form 2553 cannot be filed with only Part III completed).*

The deemed owner of the QSST must also consent to the S corporation election in column K, page 1, of Form 2553. See section 1361(c)(2).

Paperwork Reduction Act Notice.— We ask for the information on this form to carry out the Internal Revenue laws of the United States. You are required to give us the information. We need it to ensure that you are complying with these laws and to allow us to figure and collect the right amount of tax.

You are not required to provide the information requested on a form that is subject to the Paperwork Reduction Act unless the form displays a valid OMB control number. Books or records relating to a form or its instructions must be retained as long as their contents may become material in the administration of any Internal Revenue law. Generally, tax returns and return information are confidential, as required by section 6103.

The time needed to complete and file this form will depend on individual circumstances. The estimated average time is:

Recordkeeping .... 6 hr., 28 min.

**Learning about the
law or the form**.................................. 3 hr., 41 min.

**Preparing, copying,
assembling, and sending
the form to the IRS**........................... 3 hr., 56 min.

If you have comments concerning the accuracy of these time estimates or suggestions for making this form simpler, we would be happy to hear from you. You can write to the Tax Forms Committee, Western Area Distribution Center, Rancho Cordova, CA 95743-0001. **DO NOT** send the form to this address. Instead, see **Where To File** on page 1.

Page 2

Form **SS-4**
(Rev. February 1998)
Department of the Treasury
Internal Revenue Service

Application for Employer Identification Number

(For use by employers, corporations, partnerships, trusts, estates, churches, government agencies, certain individuals, and others. See instructions.)

► Keep a copy for your records.

EIN _____

OMB No. 1545-0003

Please type or print clearly.

1 Name of applicant (legal name) (see instructions)

2 Trade name of business (if different from name on line 1)	**3** Executor, trustee, "care of" name

4a Mailing address (street address) (room, apt., or suite no.)	**5a** Business address (if different from address on lines 4a and 4b)

4b City, state, and ZIP code	**5b** City, state, and ZIP code

6 County and state where principal business is located

7 Name of principal officer, general partner, grantor, owner, or trustor—SSN or ITIN may be required (see instructions) ► _____

8a Type of entity (Check only one box.) (see instructions)

Caution: *If applicant is a limited liability company, see the instructions for line 8a.*

☐ Sole proprietor (SSN) _____
☐ Partnership   ☐ Personal service corp.
☐ REMIC   ☐ National Guard
☐ State/local government ☐ Farmers' cooperative
☐ Church or church-controlled organization
☐ Other nonprofit organization (specify) ► _____
☐ Other (specify) ►

☐ Estate (SSN of decedent) _____
☐ Plan administrator (SSN) _____
☐ Other corporation (specify) ► _____
☐ Trust
☐ Federal government/military
          (enter GEN if applicable) _____

8b If a corporation, name the state or foreign country (if applicable) where incorporated

State	Foreign country

9 Reason for applying (Check only one box.) (see instructions)
☐ Started new business (specify type) ►_____

☐ Hired employees (Check the box and see line 12.)
☐ Created a pension plan (specify type) ►

☐ Banking purpose (specify purpose) ► _____
☐ Changed type of organization (specify new type) ► _____
☐ Purchased going business
☐ Created a trust (specify type) ► _____
☐ Other (specify) ►

10 Date business started or acquired (month, day, year) (see instructions)	**11** Closing month of accounting year (see instructions)

12 First date wages or annuities were paid or will be paid (month, day, year). **Note:** *If applicant is a withholding agent, enter date income will first be paid to nonresident alien. (month, day, year)* . . . . ►

13 Highest number of employees expected in the next 12 months. **Note:** *If the applicant does not expect to have any employees during the period, enter -0-. (see instructions)* . . . . ►	Nonagricultural	Agricultural	Household

14 Principal activity (see instructions) ►

15 Is the principal business activity manufacturing? . . . . ☐ Yes ☐ No
If "Yes," principal product and raw material used ►

16 To whom are most of the products or services sold? Please check one box. ☐ Business (wholesale)
☐ Public (retail)   ☐ Other (specify) ►   ☐ N/A

17a Has the applicant ever applied for an employer identification number for this or any other business? . . . . ☐ Yes ☐ No
Note: *If "Yes," please complete lines 17b and 17c.*

17b If you checked "Yes" on line 17a, give applicant's legal name and trade name shown on prior application, if different from line 1 or 2 above.
Legal name ►   Trade name ►

17c Approximate date when and city and state where the application was filed. Enter previous employer identification number if known.

Approximate date when filed (mo., day, year)	City and state where filed	Previous EIN

Under penalties of perjury, I declare that I have examined this application, and to the best of my knowledge and belief, it is true, correct, and complete.

Business telephone number (include area code)

Fax telephone number (include area code)

Name and title (Please type or print clearly.) ►

Signature ►   Date ►

Note: *Do not write below this line. For official use only.*

Please leave blank ►	Geo.	Ind.	Class	Size	Reason for applying

For Paperwork Reduction Act Notice, see page 4.   Cat. No. 16055N   Form **SS-4** (Rev. 2-98)

General Instructions

Section references are to the Internal Revenue Code unless otherwise noted.

Purpose of Form

Use Form SS-4 to apply for an employer identification number (EIN). An EIN is a nine-digit number (for example, 12-3456789) assigned to sole proprietors, corporations, partnerships, estates, trusts, and other entities for tax filing and reporting purposes. The information you provide on this form will establish your business tax account.

Caution: *An EIN is for use in connection with your business activities only. Do NOT use your EIN in place of your social security number (SSN).*

Who Must File

You must file this form if you have not been assigned an EIN before and:

• You pay wages to one or more employees including household employees.

• You are required to have an EIN to use on any return, statement, or other document, even if you are not an employer.

• You are a withholding agent required to withhold taxes on income, other than wages, paid to a nonresident alien (individual, corporation, partnership, etc.). A withholding agent may be an agent, broker, fiduciary, manager, tenant, or spouse, and is required to file **Form 1042,** Annual Withholding Tax Return for U.S. Source Income of Foreign Persons.

• You file **Schedule C,** Profit or Loss From Business, **Schedule C-EZ,** Net Profit From Business, or **Schedule F,** Profit or Loss From Farming, of **Form 1040,** U.S. Individual Income Tax Return, **and** have a Keogh plan or are required to file excise, employment, or alcohol, tobacco, or firearms returns.

The following must use EINs even if they do not have any employees:

• State and local agencies who serve as tax reporting agents for public assistance recipients, under Rev. Proc. 80-4, 1980-1 C.B. 581, should obtain a separate EIN for this reporting. See **Household employer** on page 3.

• Trusts, except the following:

    1. Certain grantor-owned trusts. (See the **Instructions for Form 1041.**)

    2. Individual Retirement Arrangement (IRA) trusts, unless the trust has to file **Form 990-T,** Exempt Organization Business Income Tax Return. (See the **Instructions for Form 990-T.**)

• Estates

• Partnerships

• REMICs (real estate mortgage investment conduits) (See the **Instructions for Form 1066,** U.S. Real Estate Mortgage Investment Conduit Income Tax Return.)

• Corporations

• Nonprofit organizations (churches, clubs, etc.)

• Farmers' cooperatives

• Plan administrators (A plan administrator is the person or group of persons specified as the administrator by the instrument under which the plan is operated.)

When To Apply for a New EIN

New Business. If you become the new owner of an existing business, **do not** use the EIN of the former owner. IF YOU ALREADY HAVE AN EIN, USE THAT NUMBER. If you do not have an EIN, apply for one on this form. If you become the "owner" of a corporation by acquiring its stock, use the corporation's EIN.

Changes in Organization or Ownership. If you already have an EIN, you may need to get a new one if either the organization or ownership of your business changes. If you incorporate a sole proprietorship or form a partnership, you must get a new EIN. However, **do not** apply for a new EIN if:

• You change only the name of your business,

• You elected on **Form 8832,** Entity Classification Election, to change the way the entity is taxed, or

• A partnership terminates because at least 50% of the total interests in partnership capital and profits were sold or exchanged within a 12-month period. (See Regulations section 301.6109-1(d)(2)(iii).) The EIN for the terminated partnership should continue to be used. This rule applies to terminations occurring after May 8, 1997. If the termination took place after May 8, 1996, and before May 9, 1997, a new EIN must be obtained for the new partnership unless the partnership and its partners are consistent in using the old EIN.

Note: *If you are electing to be an "S corporation," be sure you file* **Form 2553,** *Election by a Small Business Corporation.*

File Only One Form SS-4. File only one Form SS-4, regardless of the number of businesses operated or trade names under which a business operates. However, each corporation in an affiliated group must file a separate application.

EIN Applied for, But Not Received. If you do not have an EIN by the time a return is due, write "Applied for" and the date you applied in the space shown for the number. **Do not** show your social security number (SSN) as an EIN on returns.

If you do not have an EIN by the time a tax deposit is due, send your payment to the Internal Revenue Service Center for your filing area. (See **Where To Apply** below.) Make your check or money order payable to Internal Revenue Service and show your name (as shown on Form SS-4), address, type of tax, period covered, and date you applied for an EIN. Send an explanation with the deposit.

For more information about EINs, see **Pub. 583,** Starting a Business and Keeping Records, and **Pub. 1635,** Understanding your EIN.

How To Apply

You can apply for an EIN either by mail or by telephone. You can get an EIN immediately by calling the Tele-TIN number for the service center for your state, or you can send the completed Form SS-4 directly to the service center to receive your EIN by mail.

Application by Tele-TIN. Under the Tele-TIN program, you can receive your EIN by telephone and use it immediately to file a return or make a payment. To receive an EIN by telephone, complete Form SS-4, then call the Tele-TIN number listed for your state under **Where To Apply.** The person making the call must be authorized to sign the form. (See **Signature** on page 4.)

An IRS representative will use the information from the Form SS-4 to establish your account and assign you an EIN. Write the number you are given on the upper right corner of the form and sign and date it.

Mail or fax (facsimile) the signed SS-4 **within 24 hours** *to the Tele-TIN Unit at the service center address for your state.* The IRS representative will give you the fax number. The fax numbers are also listed in Pub. 1635.

Taxpayer representatives can receive their client's EIN by telephone if they first send a fax of a completed **Form 2848,** Power of Attorney and Declaration of Representative, or **Form 8821,** Tax Information Authorization, to the Tele-TIN unit. The Form 2848 or Form 8821 will be used solely to release the EIN to the representative authorized on the form.

Application by Mail. Complete Form SS-4 at least 4 to 5 weeks before you will need an EIN. Sign and date the application and mail it to the service center address for your state. You will receive your EIN in the mail in approximately 4 weeks.

Where To Apply

The Tele-TIN numbers listed below will involve a long-distance charge to callers outside of the local calling area and can be used only to apply for an EIN. THE NUMBERS MAY CHANGE WITHOUT NOTICE. Call 1-800-829-1040 to verify a number or to ask about the status of an application by mail.

If your principal business, office or agency, or legal residence in the case of an individual, is located in:	Call the Tele-TIN number shown or file with the Internal Revenue Service Center at:
Florida, Georgia, South Carolina	Attn: Entity Control Atlanta, GA 39901 770-455-2360
New Jersey, New York City and counties of Nassau, Rockland, Suffolk, and Westchester	Attn: Entity Control Holtsville, NY 00501 516-447-4955
New York (all other counties), Connecticut, Maine, Massachusetts, New Hampshire, Rhode Island, Vermont	Attn: Entity Control Andover, MA 05501 978-474-9717
Illinois, Iowa, Minnesota, Missouri, Wisconsin	Attn: Entity Control Stop 6800 2306 E. Bannister Rd. Kansas City, MO 64999 816-926-5999
Delaware, District of Columbia, Maryland, Pennsylvania, Virginia	Attn: Entity Control Philadelphia, PA 19255 215-516-6999
Indiana, Kentucky, Michigan, Ohio, West Virginia	Attn: Entity Control Cincinnati, OH 45999 606-292-5467

| Kansas, New Mexico, Oklahoma, Texas | Attn: Entity Control Austin, TX 73301 512-460-7843 |

| Alaska, Arizona, California (counties of Alpine, Amador, Butte, Calaveras, Colusa, Contra Costa, Del Norte, El Dorado, Glenn, Humboldt, Lake, Lassen, Marin, Mendocino, Modoc, Napa, Nevada, Placer, Plumas, Sacramento, San Joaquin, Shasta, Sierra, Siskiyou, Solano, Sonoma, Sutter, Tehama, Trinity, Yolo, and Yuba), Colorado, Idaho, Montana, Nebraska, Nevada, North Dakota, Oregon, South Dakota, Utah, Washington, Wyoming | Attn: Entity Control Mail Stop 6271 P.O. Box 9941 Ogden, UT 84201 801-620-7645 |

| California (all other counties), Hawaii | Attn: Entity Control Fresno, CA 93888 209-452-4010 |

| Alabama, Arkansas, Louisiana, Mississippi, North Carolina, Tennessee | Attn: Entity Control Memphis, TN 37501 901-546-3920 |

| If you have no legal residence, principal place of business, or principal office or agency in any state | Attn: Entity Control Philadelphia, PA 19255 215-516-6999 |

Specific Instructions

The instructions that follow are for those items that are not self-explanatory. Enter N/A (nonapplicable) on the lines that do not apply.

Line 1. Enter the legal name of the entity applying for the EIN exactly as it appears on the social security card, charter, or other applicable legal document.

Individuals. Enter your first name, middle initial, and last name. If you are a sole proprietor, enter your individual name, not your business name. Enter your business name on line 2. Do not use abbreviations or nicknames on line 1.

Trusts. Enter the name of the trust.

Estate of a decedent. Enter the name of the estate.

Partnerships. Enter the legal name of the partnership as it appears in the partnership agreement. **Do not** list the names of the partners on line 1. See the specific instructions for line 7.

Corporations. Enter the corporate name as it appears in the corporation charter or other legal document creating it.

Plan administrators. Enter the name of the plan administrator. A plan administrator who already has an EIN should use that number.

Line 2. Enter the trade name of the business if different from the legal name. The trade name is the "doing business as" name.

Note: *Use the full legal name on line 1 on all tax returns filed for the entity. However, if you enter a trade name on line 2 and choose to use the trade name instead of the legal name, enter the trade name on all returns you file. To prevent processing delays and errors, always use either the legal name only or the trade name only on all tax returns.*

Line 3. Trusts enter the name of the trustee. Estates enter the name of the executor, administrator, or other fiduciary. If the entity applying has a designated person to receive tax information, enter that person's name as the "care of" person. Print or type the first name, middle initial, and last name.

Line 7. Enter the first name, middle initial, last name, and SSN of a principal officer if the business is a corporation; of a general partner if a partnership; of the owner of a single member entity that is disregarded as an entity separate from its owner; or of a grantor, owner, or trustor if a trust. If the person in question is an alien individual with a previously assigned individual taxpayer identification number (ITIN), enter the ITIN in the space provided. You are not required to enter an SSN or ITIN if the reason you are applying for an EIN is to make an entity classification election (see Regulations section 301.7701-1 through 301.7701-3), and you are a nonresident alien with no effectively connected income from sources within the United States.

Line 8a. Check the box that best describes the type of entity applying for the EIN. If you are an alien individual with an ITIN previously assigned to you, enter the ITIN in place of a requested SSN.

Caution: *This is not an election for a tax classification of an entity. See "Limited liability company" below.*

If not specifically mentioned, check the "Other" box, enter the type of entity and the type of return that will be filed (for example, common trust fund, Form 1065). Do not enter N/A. If you are an alien individual applying for an EIN, see the **Line 7** instructions above.

Sole proprietor. Check this box if you file Schedule C, C-EZ, or F (Form 1040) and have a Keogh plan, or are required to file excise, employment, or alcohol, tobacco, or firearms returns, or are a payer of gambling

winnings. Enter your SSN (or ITIN) in the space provided. If you are a nonresident alien with no effectively connected income from sources within the United States, you do not need to enter an SSN or ITIN.

REMIC. Check this box if the entity has elected to be treated as a real estate mortgage investment conduit (REMIC). See the **Instructions for Form 1066** for more information.

Other nonprofit organization. Check this box if the nonprofit organization is other than a church or church-controlled organization and specify the type of nonprofit organization (for example, an educational organization).

If the organization also seeks tax-exempt status, you must file either **Package 1023,** Application for Recognition of Exemption, or **Package 1024,** Application for Recognition of Exemption Under Section 501(a). Get **Pub. 557,** Tax Exempt Status for Your Organization, for more information.

Group exemption number (GEN). If the organization is covered by a group exemption letter, enter the four-digit GEN. (Do not confuse the GEN with the nine-digit EIN.) If you do not know the GEN, contact the parent organization. Get Pub. 557 for more information about group exemption numbers.

Withholding agent. If you are a withholding agent required to file Form 1042, check the "Other" box and enter "Withholding agent."

Personal service corporation. Check this box if the entity is a personal service corporation. An entity is a personal service corporation for a tax year only if:

• The principal activity of the entity during the testing period (prior tax year) for the tax year is the performance of personal services substantially by employee-owners, and

• The employee-owners own at least 10% of the fair market value of the outstanding stock in the entity on the last day of the testing period.

Personal services include performance of services in such fields as health, law, accounting, or consulting. For more information about personal service corporations, see the **Instructions for Form 1120,** U.S. Corporation Income Tax Return, and **Pub. 542,** Corporations.

Limited liability company (LLC). See the definition of limited liability company in the **Instructions for Form 1065.** An LLC with two or more members can be a partnership or an association taxable as a corporation. An LLC with a single owner can be an association taxable as a corporation or an entity disregarded as an entity separate from its owner. See Form 8832 for more details.

• If the entity is classified as a partnership for Federal income tax purposes, check the "partnership" box.

• If the entity is classified as a corporation for Federal income tax purposes, mark the "Other corporation" box and write "limited liability co." in the space provided.

• If the entity is disregarded as an entity separate from its owner, check the "Other" box and write in "disregarded entity" in the space provided.

Plan administrator. If the plan administrator is an individual, enter the plan administrator's SSN in the space provided.

Other corporation. This box is for any corporation other than a personal service corporation. If you check this box, enter the type of corporation (such as insurance company) in the space provided.

Household employer. If you are an individual, check the "Other" box and enter "Household employer" and your SSN. If you are a state or local agency serving as a tax reporting agent for public assistance recipients who become household employers, check the "Other" box and enter "Household employer agent." If you are a trust that qualifies as a household employer, you do not need a separate EIN for reporting tax information relating to household employees; use the EIN of the trust.

QSSS. For a qualified subchapter S subsidiary (QSSS) check the "Other" box and specify "QSSS."

Line 9. Check only **one** box. Do not enter N/A.

Started new business. Check this box if you are starting a new business that requires an EIN. If you check this box, enter the type of business being started. **Do not** apply if you already have an EIN and are only adding another place of business.

Hired employees. Check this box if the existing business is requesting an EIN because it has hired or is hiring employees and is therefore required to file employment tax returns. **Do not** apply if you already have an EIN and are only hiring employees. For information on the applicable employment taxes for family members, see Circular E, Employer's Tax Guide (Publication 15).

Created a pension plan. Check this box if you have created a pension plan and need this number for reporting purposes. Also, enter the type of plan created.

Note: *Check this box if you are applying for a trust EIN when a new pension plan is established.*

Banking purpose. Check this box if you are requesting an EIN for banking purposes only, and enter the banking purpose (for example, a bowling league for depositing dues or an investment club for dividend and interest reporting).

Changed type of organization. Check this box if the business is changing its type of organization, for example, if the business was a sole proprietorship and has been incorporated or has become a partnership. If you check this box, specify in the space provided the type of change made, for example, "from sole proprietorship to partnership."

Purchased going business. Check this box if you purchased an existing business. **Do not** use the former owner's EIN. **Do not** apply for a new EIN if you already have one. Use your own EIN.

Created a trust. Check this box if you created a trust, and enter the type of trust created. For example, indicate if the trust is a nonexempt charitable trust or a split-interest trust.

Note: *Do not check this box if you are applying for a trust EIN when a new pension plan is established. Check "Created a pension plan."*

Exception. Do **not** file this form for certain grantor-type trusts. The trustee does not need an EIN for the trust if the trustee furnishes the name and TIN of the grantor/owner and the address of the trust to all payors. See the Instructions for Form 1041 for more information.

Other (specify). Check this box if you are requesting an EIN for any reason other than those for which there are checkboxes, and enter the reason.

Line 10. If you are starting a new business, enter the starting date of the business. If the business you acquired is already operating, enter the date you acquired the business. Trusts should enter the date the trust was legally created. Estates should enter the date of death of the decedent whose name appears on line 1 or the date when the estate was legally funded.

Line 11. Enter the last month of your accounting year or tax year. An accounting or tax year is usually 12 consecutive months, either a calendar year or a fiscal year (including a period of 52 or 53 weeks). A calendar year is 12 consecutive months ending on December 31. A fiscal year is either 12 consecutive months ending on the last day of any month other than December or a 52-53 week year. For more information on accounting periods, see **Pub. 538,** Accounting Periods and Methods.

Individuals. Your tax year generally will be a calendar year.

Partnerships. Partnerships generally must adopt one of the following tax years:
- The tax year of the majority of its partners,
- The tax year common to all of its principal partners,
- The tax year that results in the least aggregate deferral of income, or
- In certain cases, some other tax year.

See the **Instructions for Form 1065,** U.S. Partnership Return of Income, for more information.

REMIC. REMICs must have a calendar year as their tax year.

Personal service corporations. A personal service corporation generally must adopt a calendar year unless:
- It can establish a business purpose for having a different tax year, or
- It elects under section 444 to have a tax year other than a calendar year.

Trusts. Generally, a trust must adopt a calendar year except for the following:
- Tax-exempt trusts,
- Charitable trusts, and
- Grantor-owned trusts.

Line 12. If the business has or will have employees, enter the date on which the business began or will begin to pay wages. If the business does not plan to have employees, enter N/A.

Withholding agent. Enter the date you began or will begin to pay income to a nonresident alien. This also applies to individuals who are required to file Form 1042 to report alimony paid to a nonresident alien.

Line 13. For a definition of agricultural labor (farmwork), see **Circular A,** Agricultural Employer's Tax Guide (Publication 51).

Line 14. Generally, enter the exact type of business being operated (for example, advertising agency, farm, food or beverage establishment, labor union, real estate agency, steam laundry, rental of coin-operated vending machine, or investment club). Also state if the business will involve the sale or distribution of alcoholic beverages.

Governmental. Enter the type of organization (state, county, school district, municipality, etc.).

Nonprofit organization (other than governmental). Enter whether organized for religious, educational, or humane purposes, and the principal activity (for example, religious organization—hospital, charitable).

Mining and quarrying. Specify the process and the principal product (for example, mining bituminous coal, contract drilling for oil, or quarrying dimension stone).

Contract construction. Specify whether general contracting or special trade contracting. Also, show the type of work normally performed (for example, general contractor for residential buildings or electrical subcontractor).

Food or beverage establishments. Specify the type of establishment and state whether you employ workers who receive tips (for example, lounge—yes).

Trade. Specify the type of sales and the principal line of goods sold (for example, wholesale dairy products, manufacturer's representative for mining machinery, or retail hardware).

Manufacturing. Specify the type of establishment operated (for example, sawmill or vegetable cannery).

Signature. The application must be signed by (a) the individual, if the applicant is an individual, (b) the president, vice president, or other principal officer, if the applicant is a corporation, (c) a responsible and duly authorized member or officer having knowledge of its affairs, if the applicant is a partnership or other unincorporated organization, or (d) the fiduciary, if the applicant is a trust or an estate.

How To Get Forms and Publications

Phone. You can order forms, instructions, and publications by phone. Just call 1-800-TAX-FORM (1-800-829-3676). You should receive your order or notification of its status within 7 to 15 workdays.

Personal computer. With your personal computer and modem, you can get the forms and information you need using:
- IRS's Internet Web Site at **www.irs.ustreas.gov**
- Telnet at **iris.irs.ustreas.gov**
- File Transfer Protocol at **ftp.irs.ustreas.gov**

You can also dial direct (by modem) to the Internal Revenue Information Services (IRS) at 703-321-8020. IRIS is an on-line information service on FedWorld.

For small businesses, return preparers, or others who may frequently need tax forms or publications, a CD-ROM containing over 2,000 tax products (including many prior year forms) can be purchased from the Government Printing Office.

CD-ROM. To order the CD-ROM call the Superintendent of Documents at 202-512-1800 or connect to **www.access.gpo.gov/su_docs**

Privacy Act and Paperwork Reduction Act Notice. We ask for the information on this form to carry out the Internal Revenue laws of the United States. We need it to comply with section 6109 and the regulations thereunder which generally require the inclusion of an employer identification number (EIN) on certain returns, statements, or other documents filed with the Internal Revenue Service. Information on this form may be used to determine which Federal tax returns you are required to file and to provide you with related forms and publications. We disclose this form to the Social Security Administration for their use in determining compliance with applicable laws. We will be unable to issue an EIN to you unless you provide all of the requested information which applies to your entity.

You are not required to provide the information requested on a form that is subject to the Paperwork Reduction Act unless the form displays a valid OMB control number. Books or records relating to a form or its instructions must be retained as long as their contents may become material in the administration of any Internal Revenue law. Generally, tax returns and return information are confidential, as required by section 6103.

The time needed to complete and file this form will vary depending on individual circumstances. The estimated average time is:

Recordkeeping . . . . 7 min.

Learning about the law or the form . . . . 19 min.

Preparing the form . . . . 45 min.

Copying, assembling, and sending the form to the IRS . . 20 min.

If you have comments concerning the accuracy of these time estimates or suggestions for making this form simpler, we would be happy to hear from you. You can write to the Tax Forms Committee, Western Area Distribution Center, Rancho Cordova, CA 95743-0001. **Do not** send this form to this address. Instead, see **Where To Apply** on page 2.

6

Four Situations in Which "S" Corporations May Be Taxed

The chief attraction of the "S" corporation is the fact that it is a pass-through entity. In other words, its income, losses, deductions and credits are passed along—untaxed—to its shareholders, who include each of those items on their personal tax returns. Every rule, however, has its exceptions, and there are four limited situations in which the "S" corporation itself may be liable for taxes.

Before reviewing those special circumstances, however, we should hasten to give you the good news: If you are starting a new business, none of the four exceptions will affect your "S" corporation. Similarly, if your corporation always operated as an "S" corporation, none of the exceptions will affect your business. The four occasions on which an "S" corporation pays a tax all involve businesses that started out as regular "C" corporations.

The four possible occasions when an "S" corporation may pay a tax involve:

1. Capital gains
2. Excess passive investment income
3. The sale or disposition of property on which an investment tax credit was taken when the enterprise was not an "S" corporation
4. Sale or another disposition of property in a liquidation if (1) there is a gain, (2) the gain arose before the corporation converted from "C" to "S" status, and (3) the

sale or other disposition occurs within ten years of the date the corporation converted from "C" to "S" status

Each of these situations is reviewed in this chapter.

CAPITAL GAINS

A capital gain results when a "capital asset" is sold for more money than it cost to purchase and improve the asset. A capital asset usually is an asset used to produce income. So, for example, an office building that produces rental income is a capital asset. The rent it produces is income; if the building is sold at a profit, that profit is a capital gain.

Although many people believe the Tax Reform Act of 1986 did away with capital gains treatment, that is only partially true. Before the 1986 act, the significance of labeling an asset a "capital asset" stemmed from the fact that for many years, capital gains received highly favored tax treatment. This benefit was eliminated by the Tax Reform Act of 1986, which provides that capital gains are to be taxed as if they constitute ordinary income. Nevertheless, the Tax Reform Act left unchanged the format for determining that segment of a taxpayer's income that is capital gain. Most observers believe this was done so that if economic conditions warrant it, a new tax law can reinstitute favorable tax treatment for capital gains without causing disruption and reporting problems for taxpayers. Certain "S" corporations that made their "S" election before 1987 (or during 1987 or 1988 and qualify for transitional relief from the built-in gains tax) are potentially subject to an income tax on net gain (net long-term capital gain over net short-term loss).

Given the benefits formerly available through capital gains treatment (up to a 60 percent exclusion of gain for the taxpayer), Congress sought to ensure that taxpayers would not form "S" corporations solely to take advantage of a one-time capital gain situation. With this concern in mind, Congress determined that an "S" corporation must pay a tax on capital gains if four criteria are satisfied:

1. The net capital gain involved is more than $25,000.
2. The net capital gain is more than half of the corporation's taxable income for the year.
3. The corporation has more than $25,000 of taxable income.
4. The corporation (a) was not an "S" corporation for each of the three years before the tax year in question or (b) has been in business for less than four years and it has not been an "S" corporation throughout that period.

Each of the four criteria must be present if the "S" corporation is to pay a tax on capital gains. The tax is imposed on the amount of net capital gain in excess of $25,000; the tax rate applied is the lower of 28 percent or the rate that would have been used had the corporation not been an "S" corporation.

Based on the four criteria listed above, however, it is clear that an "S" corporation will not be subject to a capital gains tax if it has always been an "S" corporation (regardless of how short its period of existence) or if it was once a "C" corporation, but transferred to "S" status at least three taxable years before the tax year in which the capital gain arose.

This means that if you are about to embark on a new business, you need not fear that your "S" corporation will pay a capital gains tax.

If you have an existing corporation and wish to pick up the various advantages of "S" incorporation, you can do so knowing that if you wait at least three years before selling a capital asset at a gain, the corporation will not pay a capital gains tax. If you opt not to wait three years, your corporation may not pay a capital gains tax if the gain is less than $25,000. Even if the corporation must pay the capital gains tax, the situation will be no different, for capital gains tax purposes, than if you had not made the change. Furthermore, you can still use the other benefits of "S" corporation status to minimize the federal government's overall tax bite.

EXCESS PASSIVE INVESTMENT GAINS

An "S" corporation will be required to pay a tax on excess passive investment income totaling more than 25 percent of gross receipts earned in a year during which it also has regular corporation earnings and profits. The tax, in this situation, clearly affects only those "S" corporations that started life as "C" corporations. A business that has been only an "S" corporation (e.g., a new enterprise), need not concern itself with the tax on excess passive investment income.

Only a limited number of ways exist for an "S" corporation to obtain "C" corporation profits and earnings. The shareholders of a "C" corporation may have elected to seek "S" status when the "C" corporation had earnings and profits, or a merger may have occurred between a "C" corporation and an "S" corporation. Should either situation arise, the "S" corporation tax can be avoided if, before the end of the tax year, the corporation distributes its accumulated earnings and profits to its shareholders. Although the shareholders must report the distribution as a dividend, the corporation will not be required to pay a tax if the distribution is made before the end of the tax year.

Passive investment income, for purposes of the "S" corporation tax, includes earnings from royalties, rents, dividends, interest, annuities, and sales or exchanges of stock or other securities.

LIQUIDATIONS

One tax benefit available to shareholders in regular corporations before the enactment of the Tax Reform Act of 1986 involved distributions of appreciated property by the corporation. So, for example, under the prior law, if a corporation sold appreciated property as part of a complete liquidation, it would not be taxed on the gain it made. Instead, that gain would be taxed in the shareholders' hands if the total distribution they received was greater than the investment they made in their stock. The Tax Reform Act repealed this provision.

Today, if a regular corporation disposes of an appreciated asset, it must pay a tax on its gain, and the shareholders will pay a second tax if the distribution they receive from the corporation represents a gain to them.

Assume a corporation wishes to get around the 1986 changes and converts to "S" status to do so. Its efforts will go for naught. The 1986 provisions require the "S" corporation to pay a tax on any appreciation of its property that occurred before the conversion to "S" status—but only if the sale or distribution that is part of the liquidation comes within ten years of the date the election to be treated as an "S" corporation became effective.

Again, this problem is one that exists only for corporations that convert from "C" status to "S" status. Furthermore, the tax that can be assessed against the "S" corporation is limited to the appreciation that took place before the conversion; appreciation that occurs after the conversion to "S" status is gain that flows through to the shareholders of the "S" corporation.

7

Maximizing Your Benefits on Corporate Losses

Although "S" corporation losses flow through to shareholders, those losses can be deducted by shareholders on their returns only if the losses do not exceed the total of shareholders' bases in their stock and any debt owed to them by the corporation. *Basis* is a tax term that generally refers to the cost of an item.

If an "S" corporation's losses exceed a shareholder's basis in stock and debt, the shareholder cannot deduct his or her pro rata share of the loss, but must carry it over until such time as he or she has sufficient basis to cover the loss.

To make maximum use of "S" corporation losses, therefore, a shareholder must know how basis is determined, how it can be increased or decreased and how the carryover rules work.

One other area of interest in this respect involves the unwelcome but always real possibility that the corporation may fail. If that happens and the shareholder's stock becomes worthless, he or she will be required to take a capital loss on the worthless stock. For many investors, however, an alternative permits the loss on the original investment to be treated as an ordinary loss. This tool—Section 1244 stock—is available to most small corporations.

Assume Mr. Jones transferred title to a small office building to his newly formed "S" corporation. When the transfer took place, the carryover basis of the building, in Mr. Jones's hands, was $50,000. Now assume that Mr. Jones received 10,000 shares of the "S" corporation stock valued at $4 a share and $15,000 in cash for the building. His basis in his stock would be $40,000. ($50,000 in carryover basis minus the $15,000 cash payment plus $5,000 of recognized gain equals $40,000. The $5,000 of recognized gain is determined by adding together the value of the stock and the cash, $55,000, and subtracting the original basis, $50,000.)

If the stock was issued for property and the transfer was a taxable event, the basis of the stock would be the property's fair market value at the time of transfer.

Two other commonplace transfers of stock in small corporations arise when the owner of the stock dies or makes a gift of the shares. If the stock is inherited because of the original owner's death, the person who receives the stock uses as his or her basis the fair market value of the stock at the time of the decedent's death. If, on the other hand, the stock is given as a gift, the recipient takes the stock with a basis equal to the donor's basis at the time the gift was made.

DETERMINING BASIS IN DEBT

If a shareholder loans money to an "S" corporation, his or her basis in the loan is the amount of money actually loaned. Occasionally, a shareholder will supply either services or property in return for an IOU (a note) from the "S" corporation. In that case, the shareholder's basis in the note equals the amount of the note the shareholder includes when reporting his or her income for tax purposes.

Caution

First, a shareholder should not confuse money he or she lends to the "S" corporation with loans or other debts the corporation may incur with respect to other persons, but that the shareholder may guarantee. A shareholder has basis only in money he or she lends to the corporation, not money lent to the corporation by other persons.

Second, a shareholder does not obtain a basis in debt merely because he or she guarantees a corporate loan. If, however, the corporation does not meet its obligations under a loan and the shareholder must make good on his or her guarantee, the shareholder will have increased his or her basis in corporate debt by the amount actually paid out on the guarantee.

HOW BASIS CHANGES

After it is initially determined, a shareholder's basis changes every year during which the "S" corporation operates at a profit or loss. For example, assume an "S" corporation has a profit of $3,000 in 1999. The "S" corporation has one shareholder, Ms. Smith, who had a basis of $10,000 in her stock when the year began. Her basis at the end of the year would be $13,000. Similarly, if the corporation had lost $3,000, her basis would have been reduced to $7,000 at the end of the year.

When determining annual adjustments in basis, each "S" corporation shareholder increases or decreases the basis by the amount of his or her pro rata share of profits or losses.

Caution

If an "S" corporation makes a nontaxable distribution to its shareholders, their bases are reduced by the amount of the distribution each receives. Such distributions can occur when the "S" corporation has assets it no longer needs or if it has accumulated earnings and profits (from its regular "C" corporation days) and wishes to distribute the accumulations to its shareholders.

Assume an "S" corporation's sole shareholder believes the corporation will incur losses in the current year and that those losses will exceed the shareholder's basis in stock or debt. The shareholder wants to use those losses in the current year rather than carry them forward. Therefore, the shareholder should consider buying more stock in the corporation or lending it additional sums. Either would increase the shareholder's basis and, if the amount invested is projected with care, should permit the shareholder to deduct all anticipated "S" corporation loss.

If a shareholder has basis in both stock and debt, a formula will determine which of the two bases is increased when the corporation operates at a profit or loss. The general rule is that both accounts are determined separately unless operating losses exceed the shareholder's basis in his or her stock. In that case, the shareholder may deduct the loss only if the shareholder has sufficient basis in debt owed to him or her by the corporation to cover the loss. If the corporation operates at a profit the next year, the increase in basis would be applied to the debt basis first, and the excess, if any, to create basis in stock.

> ### Example
>
> Assume Mr. Jones is the sole shareholder of an "S" corporation. He has a basis of $40,000 in his stock, and he has loaned the corporation $20,000. In 1999, the corporation operates at a loss of $48,000. Mr. Jones can deduct the entire loss, but in doing so, he reduces his basis in stock to zero and reduces his basis in debt to $12,000. If the same corporation operates at a profit of $12,000 in 2000, Mr. Jones's basis in debt would be increased to its original amount, $20,000, and his basis in stock would go from zero to $4,000.

This example should make clear the following rules for determining how basis can be increased or decreased:

- A shareholder's basis in stock or debt can be reduced to zero, but cannot be reduced to a negative amount. If losses exceed the basis in debt and stock, they must be carried forward.
- Decreases in basis caused by operating losses are applied first to the basis in stock and then to the basis in debt.
- If operating losses have been used to decrease the basis in debt and there is a profit in a succeeding year, the debt basis must be increased until it is completely replaced; then remaining profits can increase the basis of stock.

CARRYING LOSSES FORWARD

As explained above, a shareholder can deduct losses only if the losses do not exceed the total amount of the shareholder's bases in stock and debt. If losses exceed the combined bases, the shareholder may carry them forward indefinitely and until such time as the shareholder has increased his or her basis through additional investments in stock or loans to the corporation or operating profits supply sufficient basis to cover the losses.

MAKING THE MOST OF A LOSING SITUATION

Although most entrepreneurs embark on new ventures convinced they will succeed, the more realistic businessperson anticipates the possibility of failure and takes measures that would make failure as painless as possible. One technique used by such businesspeople involves Section 1244 stock, which enables shareholders to make maximum use of their losses should a business fail and their stock become worthless.

Under existing tax rules, losses suffered by a shareholder when his or her stock becomes worthless are capital losses and can be used only in a restricted manner. If the losses are long-term losses (where the asset is held for more than six months), they can be applied to offset capital gains. Excess capital losses can be used to offset ordinary income, but only to a maximum of $3,000. This means that if a taxpayer has $2,000 of capital gains and $10,000 of long-term capital losses, $5,000 of the capital losses cannot be used in the current tax year, but must be carried forward ($2,000 of the losses will offset the $2,000 gain, and another $3,000 can be used to offset ordinary income; that leaves a balance of $5,000 of the total $10,000 loss that is unused in the current tax year).

Section 1244 stock addresses just this situation. Created by Congress to assist small businesses, Section 1244 of the Internal Revenue Code provides a special rule for losses incurred when stock of small corporations is sold or transferred at a loss or becomes worthless. The loss suffered by the shareholder is treated as an ordinary loss and can offset up to $50,000 of income ($100,000, if the taxpayer files a joint return).

Example

Assume that Mr. Taxpayer has ordinary income of $50,000 and that during the current tax year, he sold an asset for a long-term capital gain of $2,000. Mr. Taxpayer operates a small business as a sideline, and he holds Section 1244 stock in this business. Mr. Taxpayer's basis in his Section 1244 stock is $12,000. If the sideline business does not work out and Mr. Taxpayer dissolves the business, which has no assets (i.e., his stock is worthless), Mr. Taxpayer's total income of $52,000 ($50,000 of ordinary income plus $2,000 of capital gain) would be reduced to $40,000 because he can deduct all of the $12,000 loss he suffered when his stock became worthless.

To use Section 1244 stock, a corporation must satisfy five standards, none of which conflicts with "S" corporation requirements:

1. The corporation was created in the United States.
2. The corporation is not a holding company.
3. The total amount paid by shareholders for their stock is not more than $1 million.
4. The stock was issued for cash or property and was not issued for services or in exchange for other shares of stock.
5. During the five tax years that preceded the year in which the stock became worthless, the corporation derived more than half of its income from non-passive sources. (Passive sources include royalties, rents, dividends, interest, annuities and sales or exchanges of stock or other securities.)

Although no one should start a new venture expecting to fail, prudent investors will try to anticipate that possibility. Section 1244 stock, which is much the same as other forms of common stock, provides a cost-free benefit: In the event the business fails, the losses suffered by the taxpayer will become somewhat less painful when they show up as full deductions on the taxpayer's tax return.

8

Compensation and the "S" Corporation

Most individuals who start a new business expect that enterprise to supply them with regular income. Usually, their expectations include a weekly or monthly salary, combined with fringe benefits and, perhaps, some form of retirement plan. If the business is started as an "S" corporation and if it is run profitably, it can satisfy two of those needs without difficulty—salary and retirement plans—but the "S" corporation does not have the capacity to provide the wide range of fringe benefits available when regular "C" incorporation is adopted. As we shall see, however, this weakness is a small price to pay for the other benefits provided by "S" incorporation. Furthermore, alternatives offer the businessperson who forms an "S" corporation the capability of enjoying the same range of fringe benefits he or she would enjoy with a "C" corporation.

COMPENSATION

We have stressed throughout this book the fact that an "S" corporation is a flow-through enterprise that is not taxed on its earnings. More so than in any other area, the flow-through concept takes on added import when compensation is considered.

Although not apparent to most nonlawyers, one major benefit of "S" incorporation is that it permits shareholder-employees to pay themselves compensation that reaches the uppermost limits of "reasonableness" without inviting an audit by the IRS. This element of comfort is not so readily available in regular "C" incorporation. An understanding of this difference in outlook requires a reexamination of just how "C" and "S" corporations are taxed.

A "C" corporation's profits are taxed twice: once as corporate profits then a second time when those profits are distributed to shareholders as dividends. The shareholder-employees of a "C" corporation, therefore, will seek to pay themselves as high a salary as possible to reduce the amount of tax their corporation will have to pay on its earnings. (Salaries are costs deducted from the "C" corporation's gross income to determine taxable income.)

The IRS is aware of this technique and monitors the efforts of "C" corporation shareholders to avoid the double tax on corporate profits by paying themselves high salaries. As a result, the IRS regularly challenges executive salaries, claiming they are really dividends. If the IRS is successful, as it often is, the unreasonable segment of the salary is not allowed as a corporate deduction and the corporation must pay an added tax for the year in question.

This problem, however, does not arise in the "S" corporation. This is because the goal the "C" corporation shareholder-employee pursues—single taxation—is already present in the "S" corporation. Let's assume an "S" corporation pays its sole shareholder-employee an unreasonably high salary. If the IRS does not pick it up, the corporation will take a deduction for that salary, but the shareholder must declare it when reporting his or her earnings and will be taxed on the compensation. However, if the IRS challenges the unreasonable portion of the salary and wins the point, the payment will be termed a *distribution* and will not be taxed to the shareholder. But the "S" corporation will be denied a deduction for the overpayment—that is, the distribution. It will end the year having net profits that are increased by the amount of the unreasonable segment of the compensation. That additional profit, in turn, will flow through to the shareholder and will be taxed as income in his or her hands.

Whichever of the two approaches is taken, however, the result remains the same: the shareholder has the same amount of taxable income. The IRS, therefore, is less likely to be concerned about unreasonable salaries in "S" corporation situations than it would be in "C" corporation operations.

Exceptions

In two situations, the payment of unreasonable compensation may cause serious problems for shareholder-employees. One involves "S" corporations that have more than one shareholder-employee; the other involves shareholders who have little or no bases in their stock.

Multiple shareholders. Assume that an "S" corporation has two shareholders, John and Mary, who are unrelated. Both own 50 percent of the "S" corporation shares. Although they agree that both will share profits equally, John, who put up most of the money to get the business off the ground, does not work for the corporation, nor does he draw a salary. Mary works for the corporation full time and is compensated for her services.

Let's now assume that the IRS determines that Mary's salary is unreasonable to the extent of $10,000. The result would be that the payment to Mary would be considered a distribution. She would not have to include the $10,000 when reporting her taxable income.

The story does not end here, however. Because the $10,000 payment to Mary is a distribution, the corporation cannot claim it as a deduction for salary. That means the corporation will have an additional $10,000 of income that will flow through to its shareholders. John and Mary will each have to report an extra $5,000 of income. In John's case, he will pay tax on money he never received; Mary, on the other hand, will receive $10,000 and pay tax on $5,000.

Nor do the consequences end here. John's basis in his stock will be increased by $5,000—his share of the distribution that was treated as a corporate profit. Mary, however, will see her basis reduced by $5,000 (the amount she is credited with receiving as a distribution).

The situation described above, particularly its impact on John, is not improbable. Also, an even more serious danger exists in this scenario. The IRS has proposed rules under which salary it determines to be unreasonably high would be viewed as creating a second form of stock. Under these guidelines, the corporation would lose its "S" status because it has more than one class of stock and the two classes have different economic rights. Although these proposed rules have been withdrawn for reconsideration, they clearly indicate the direction the IRS is taking. Prudent "S" corporation shareholders, therefore, would be well advised to heed the suggestions set out in "Determining Reasonable Compensation" below.

Shareholders without basis. In the example above, we assumed the shareholders each had sufficient basis in his or her stock and debt to cover the amount of unreasonable compensation that was treated as a distribution. For instance, Mary's $10,000 of unreasonable compensation was treated as a tax-free distribution. We assumed Mary had a basis of at least $10,000 in her stock and debt. If Mary did not have that basis, the distribution would have been treated as taxable income. Mary, therefore, would have been taxed twice—first on the $10,000 distribution; then when her half of the $10,000 of added corporate income flowed through to her.

Determining reasonable compensation. Although no one fixed guideline establishes precisely what constitutes reasonable compensation, accepted references exist for this purpose. Perhaps the most objective test looks to salaries paid to individuals performing comparable services for comparable businesses. Even this test is subject to other considerations. So, for example, a new development may have required the executive in question to have offered services far greater in effort or scope than would ordinarily be expected. In such cases, a bonus may very well be in order. Straight salary (or bonuses) can be tied to performance standards (e.g., gross sales), an approach that may lead to justifiably high or, if performance is poor, low salaries.

Other factors that may be considered when determining whether compensation is reasonable include the following:

- Extensive experience: An employee who has years of experience or special knowledge in a given field generally justifies higher compensation than a less experienced person.
- Business performance: If the business enjoys a meaningful increase in sales volume or net profits, higher compensation can be justified.
- Unusual services: The ability of a shareholder-employee to obtain goods or services in a time of shortage or to successfully introduce operational efficiencies would justify either a raise or bonus in most arm's-length employment relationships and should be a valid criterion if the employee is also an owner.

WHY IT PAYS TO MINIMIZE COMPENSATION

All things being equal, it does not matter to a shareholder-employee if his or her income from the "S" corporation takes the form of a salary or a distribution. Either way, the shareholder will have the benefit "C" corporation shareholders strive for—single tax on corporate income. This being the case, it is probably wiser for the "S" corporation shareholder-employee to set his or her salary at the lowest end of reasonableness. This observation flows from the following two considerations.

Withholding taxes. Even though an "S" corporation does not pay taxes, it is an entity in the eyes of the law. As an employer, it must withhold a portion of its employees' wages for income tax, Social Security tax and unemployment insurance tax. Should the "S" corporation seek to avoid withholding for these taxes by not paying its owner-employees salaries, it would do so by making distributions to those employees. Distributions, because they are not wages, would not be subject to withholding taxes.

Both the Internal Revenue Service and the Social Security Administration are alert to the possibility just described. Both will be quick to challenge that distributions are disguised wages subject to withholding. Both have been successful in making this argument. Older shareholders, otherwise entitled to Social Security benefits, have another concern: if they work for their "S" corporation without salary, the Social Security Administration will take the position that distributions they receive are, in fact, wages and that those wages should be applied to reduce the amount of Social Security benefits the shareholder-employees are entitled to receive. (This problem, it should be noted, exists for both "C" and "S" corporations.)

One way to minimize the impact of the withholding problem is to reduce wages to the lowest reasonable amount that can be justified for the services in question.

Impact on basis.   In Chapter 7, we noted that "S" corporation losses flow through to the corporation's shareholders and may be used as deductions against their other income. We also noted a limitation on that rule: a loss can be used as a deduction only if the shareholder has sufficient basis in his or her stock and debt to cover the amount of the loss. If a shareholder-employee draws all of his or her income from the "S" corporation in the form of wages, the shareholder's basis in his or her stock remains unchanged. If, on the other hand, the shareholder draws only a portion of his or her income as wages, the part the shareholder does not draw will become corporate profit at the end of the year. If the money is removed as a distribution of profits, the amount taken in this form will be added to the shareholder's basis in his or her stock.

Example No. 1

John Taxpayer, the sole shareholder of an "S" corporation, has a basis of $15,000 in the corporate stock. He estimates that if he does not draw any salary in 1999, the corporation will have $40,000 of profits. John determines that a reasonable compensation for his services would be $20,000, and he pays himself that amount over the course of 1999. At the end of the year, his projections prove correct, and the corporation has $20,000 left in its coffers. John takes the $20,000 as a distribution.

Result

John's basis in his stock is now $35,000.

Example No. 2

Assume all of the facts set out in Example No. 1. As John plans for 2000, he determines that the business will require additional personnel, but that the fruits of their labor will not be seen until 2001. He hires the new people. As a result, the corporation runs at a $30,000 loss in 2000.

Result

John can apply the entire $30,000 loss against his income from other sources next year. Had he taken this year's income from the corporation entirely as wages, his basis in his stock would have remained at $15,000, and he would have been able to apply only $15,000 of next year's losses against his other income.

DOVETAILING COMPENSATION AND TAX YEARS

A business may operate on either the cash or accrual method of accounting. If it operates on the cash basis, it deducts its expenses for tax purposes when the payments are actually made. Similarly, a cash basis taxpayer reports income when it is actually received.

A taxpayer who uses the accrual method of accounting, on the other hand, can deduct expenses when the amount of an expense is positively known and the person who is to receive the payment becomes legally entitled to demand payment. The business using the accrual method of accounting can work out a form of tax deferral at the end of a tax year. By deferring payment to those individuals or businesses whose claim for payment has matured, they can take a current-year deduction for an expense that is not paid until the following year.

Example

An "S" corporation orders $5,000 of supplies from Mr. Vendor. The supplies are delivered and accepted in late November this year. Mr. Vendor submits his bill when the goods are delivered. The "S" corporation, however, does not pay the bill until January 3rd of next year.

Result

If the "S" corporation operates on the accrual method of accounting, it can deduct the $5,000 expense this year. If Mr. Vendor is a cash basis taxpayer, he will not report the $5,000 payment until he files his next year's taxes.

Given the fact that most individuals use the cash method of accounting, it would seem possible for most "S" corporations to use the accrual method in order to take a current-year deduction for wages owed to shareholder-employees. The cash method shareholder-employee, in theory, would not report the income until the following tax year.

That, however, is not the case. The Internal Revenue Code specifically anticipates this possibility and permits an "S" corporation to deduct the salary it pays to a shareholder-employee only in the year the employee actually receives the salary. Therefore, the deferral option described above cannot be used even if the "S" corporation operates on the accrual method of accounting and the shareholder-employee uses the cash method.

Furthermore, this approach is taken when wage payments are made to employees who are related to a shareholder. An "S" corporation, therefore, can deduct wage payments made to the following recipients only in the year each receives the payments:

- The husband, wife, brother, sister, parent, grandparent or grandchild of a shareholder, regardless of how small an interest the shareholder has in the "S" corporation.
- A partnership in which the people who own 50 percent of the right to profits (or who have invested more than 50 percent of the capital) also own more than 50 percent of the shares of the "S" corporation.
- An "S" corporation or a "C" corporation in which the people who own more than 50 percent of the shares of stock also own more than 50 percent of the shares of stock of the "S" corporation making the payment.

It must be stressed, however, that the rules described above apply only to "S" corporation payments to shareholder-employees. Payments made to employees who are not shareholders of the corporation (or who do not fit within one of the three related groups described above) may be deferred so that the corporation takes the deductions in the year the payments become due, even though the employees will not report the payments as income until the following tax year.

Although the focus here has been on the benefits of the accrual method of accounting, there are also benefits to be obtained if a business uses the cash method of accounting. So, for example, a business that bills heavily at the end of the year but does not receive payment until the beginning of the next year may prefer to use the cash method of accounting. The corporation will be able to include the expenses it incurs producing its products in its current tax year and need not report the payments it receives until the next tax year.

In this respect, "S" corporations enjoy an advantage over "C" corporations. All "S" corporations are permitted to use the cash method of accounting. Only those "C" corporations with average gross receipts of $5 million or less that used the cash method when the Tax Reform Act of 1986 was enacted may use the cash method.

DANGERS IN INCOME SPLITTING

At this time, there are five basic tax rates for individuals: 15 percent, 28 percent, 31 percent, 36 percent and 39.6 percent. Given the difference of 24.6 percent between the highest and lowest rates, many taxpayers who form small businesses will be sorely tempted to underpay themselves and maximize the salaries they pay to family members—usually children or parents—who are often in lower tax brackets. In the case of parents, the situation ordinarily involves retired persons who receive Social Security income. Although they may bring a high degree of expertise to the business, they do not want to receive salaries that would jeopardize their Social Security benefits.

Example

Assume Mr. and Mrs. Smith operate an "S" corporation. They anticipate the company will generate about $180,000 in profits at the end of the year. However, if nothing is done to cushion the blow, the profits will be heavily taxed. For instance, the profits between $89,150 and $140,000 will be taxed at the rate of 31 percent. The profits exceeding $140,000 will be taxed at 36 percent. Therefore, the total tax bill will be $45,330.

In order to reduce their tax bill, the Smiths hire each of their four teenage children to work at the office, answering the telephone, doing janitorial work, operating the photocopying machine and typing. Each child is paid $20,000 a year and saves that money for his or her college education. The Smiths then hire their parents, each of whom they pay $5,500 to act as full-time sales representatives. The parents refuse to take higher salaries for three reasons: first they do not need the money; second, motivated by parental love, they refuse to take money they view as belonging to their children and grandchildren; and third, they do not want to reduce their Social Security retirement income. The Smiths pay themselves $44,500 each.

Result

The "S" corporation will have no profits for the year and will supply no flow-through income to the Smiths. The Smiths, with $89,000 of income, will not have any portion of their income taxed at more than 28 percent. Therefore, their tax bill will be $15,124.

> Each child will be in the 15 percent tax bracket and will pay $3,000 in taxes. The likelihood is that the Smiths' parents have enough deductions to avoid paying any tax on each couple's combined earnings of $11,000. So, instead of paying $45,330, the entire Smith family will pay only $27,124 in income taxes—a savings of $18,206. The savings came about because the Smiths removed $91,000 from the 31 percent and 36 percent tax brackets and put that money into 15 percent and zero percent brackets.

The machinations of the Smith family, however, point out how overly aggressive people can get in trouble with the Internal Revenue Service. Because of the possibilities raised in the example, the Internal Revenue Code allows the IRS to reallocate income in situations where a family member draws an unreasonably high or low salary for his or her efforts.

The family member in question does not have to be a shareholder in the "S" corporation, but may be a spouse, parent, grandparent, child or grandchild of a shareholder. A parent, for example, may be willing to work full time to assist a child and may prefer not to draw a salary either as an act of parental generosity or to avoid reducing Social Security benefits.

What factors does the IRS look at when determining whether a person has received an unreasonably low salary? It is safe to assume the agency looks at the same factors it relies on when determining whether an individual has received an unreasonably high salary (see "Determining Reasonable Compensation," earlier in this chapter).

The fact that the IRS can reallocate "S" corporation income should not dissuade entrepreneurs from using the services of family members who are in lower or higher tax brackets. Entrepreneurs must simply act within reason. In the previous discussion, for example, the Smiths made two mistakes. First, they underpaid their parents as full-time employees. Their parents should have been employed as part-time sales representatives and the $5,500 payment probably would have passed muster if challenged by the IRS. Second, they paid their children almost as much for janitorial and ministerial services (a total of $80,000) as they paid themselves for running the business ($89,000). The Smiths, therefore, virtually invited the IRS to reallocate income. Had they paid their children more realistic amounts, perhaps as much as $10,000 a year per child, for services honestly rendered, they might not have had a problem if questioned by the IRS. If they had taken this approach, Mr. and Mrs. Smith would have had combined earnings of $129,000 and would have paid $27,518 in taxes. Each child would have paid at most $1,500 in taxes, and the Smiths' parents probably would have paid nothing. The entire Smith family would have paid $33,518 in taxes—a savings of $11,812. Although this savings is less than the savings in the example set out above, it would not have been reallocated and completely lost.

THE DANGER INVOLVED IN INTEREST-FREE LOANS

It is not unusual for a financially comfortable family member to lend money to another family member at no interest or at a low or modest interest rate. The loan may be made to enable the relative to start a business or to help an existing business. If a loan to an "S" corporation is set below market rate in such a situation, the Internal Revenue Code authorizes the IRS to reallocate "S" corporation income so that the lender is attributed with the amount of interest the loan would have received had it been made in an arm's length transaction. This rule—which undercuts the most basic and honorable family feelings—can put a loved one between a rock and a hard place if he or she cannot afford to make a gift of the sum involved, but does not want to charge a child's corporation interest.

One way out of this morass might be for the family member to make a loan at an interest rate keyed to the rate on short-term Treasury bills. Upon receipt of the interest, the lender could make a gift to the entrepreneur (not to the "S" corporation) of the interest the lender received (perhaps net of any income tax he or she paid on the interest). This gift would be tax-free income to the entrepreneur. Note that if this approach is taken, the "S" corporation will have a deduction for the interest paid— a deduction that flows through to the benefit of the entrepreneur.

9

Fringe Benefits and Retirement Plans

FRINGE BENEFITS

In 1982, when it thoroughly revamped the laws governing "S" corporations, Congress sought to provide the "S" corporation with as many partnership tax attributes as possible. Most of the changes worked to assist entrepreneurs who sought the benefits of limited liability associated with incorporation and the single tax on earnings available in a sole proprietorship or partnership. Not everything worked to the favor of the "S" corporation, however.

Prior to the 1982 changes, an "S" corporation could provide the same fringe benefits—medical, accident, disability and life insurance plans, etc.—that a "C" corporation could provide and could do so on the same terms. Premiums paid by the corporation were deductible as business expenses; benefits received by the employee were excluded from taxable income.

Partnerships, on the other hand, did not receive the same treatment. If a partnership provided a fringe benefit to a partner, the cost of the benefit, whether in the form of a premium or a direct payment to the partner, was not eligible for treatment as a business deduction. The partner who received the benefit, furthermore, had to declare it as income.

When it put "S" corporations on a par with partnerships in 1982, Congress applied the rule on partnerships and fringe benefits to "S" corporations. This means that the "S" corporation cannot deduct as a business expense the cost of fringe benefits provided to most shareholder-employees. As is the case with partnerships, the shareholder-employee who receives a benefit must include that benefit when he or she reports taxable income.

Applying the Rules

Consider the following factors when applying the rules just stated:

1. Fringe benefits may be provided for nonshareholder-employees. The cost of those benefits is deductible from the "S" corporation income, and an employee is not required to report any benefits he or she may receive when calculating taxable income.
2. The rules apply to all shareholder-employees who own more than 2 percent of the "S" corporation's stock or, if the corporation has both voting and nonvoting stock, more than 2 percent of the corporation's total combined voting stock. If either of these ownership requirements is satisfied for just one day of the corporation's tax year, the rules apply.

Example

On January 1, 1998, John Taxpayer owned 2.25 percent of an "S" corporation's stock. At 9:00 that morning, he sold his shares to the other shareholders and agreed to continue to work for the corporation. On January 2, 1998, the other shareholder-employees voted to provide Mr. Taxpayer with the same fringe benefit package available to their other employees (e.g., medical, life and disability insurance coverage).

Result

The "S" corporation cannot deduct the cost of the premiums paid on the policies covering Mr. Taxpayer. He, in turn, cannot exclude the benefits when he reports his taxable income. If Mr. Taxpayer remains with the corporation in 1999, the deduction will be available to the business, and he need not include the benefits in his taxable income.

3. The rules applicable to "S" corporations and fringe benefits encompass within their scope both the shareholder-employee who satisfies the more-than-2-percent test and members of that shareholder's family who are employed by the "S" corporation (i.e., husbands, wives, brothers and sisters [including half-brothers and half-sisters], parents, grandparents, children and grandchildren). Furthermore, the rules also cover any relative who owns no stock, but is related to a shareholder who passes the more-than-2-percent test, even if the shareholder is not an employee of the "S" corporation.

4. The partnership rules would seem to apply to any fringe benefit offered by an "S" corporation to its shareholder-employees. Section 1372 of the Internal Revenue Code states simply and directly: "For purposes of applying the provisions . . . which relate to employee fringe benefits—the "S" corporation shall be treated as a partnership . . . ." This would seem to include such traditional benefits as

   • premiums paid by the "S" corporation for medical and disability plans and payments received under the coverage of the plans;
   • premiums paid for $50,000 group life insurance policies;
   • meals and lodging furnished by the "S" corporation to shareholder-employee for the corporation's convenience; and
   • the $5,000 death benefit exclusion available to the estate of an employee whose employer provides this benefit.

5. Forty-five percent of the amount included in income generally may be deducted by the shareholder/employee for the years 1998 and 1999, 50 percent in 2000 and 2001, 60 percent in 2002, 80 percent in 2003 through 2005, 90 percent in 2006, and 100 percent in 2007 and thereafter.

Three Approaches to the Problem

If the endeavor for which an "S" corporation is to be formed will require the full-time efforts of its shareholder-employees, some consideration must be given to their need for the forms of insurance protection provided by most employers. Three possible approaches to this problem follow:

1. Adjust compensation levels so that a shareholder-employee can purchase a comparable package of benefits tailored to his or her specific needs. The drawback here is that the shareholder-employee must include the compensation received for this purpose when determining taxable income and will not receive a deduction for the amount expended to purchase insurance coverage.

2. Assume the business to be formed can be divided into separate parts. Nothing prevents the entrepreneur from forming two corporations—a "C"

corporation and an "S" corporation. The "C" corporation may provide a service or product for the "S" corporation and, given its limited market, should break even or make a slight profit. It, however, can provide all of its employees (including shareholder-employees) with fringe benefits and deduct those expenses as business expenses. The recipients will not be required to include the benefits when determining taxable income.

This approach is available in a host of situations. So, for example, a retail business may be served by a buying corporation that meets all of its product needs. The fact that the same individual or individuals own the stock of both corporations should not defeat the goal of providing deductible fringe benefits through one of the corporations.

3. Use qualified retirement plans that may fund life insurance plans for shareholder-employees, and take a deduction. An employee, if this is done, may not have to report the benefits when determining taxable income.

RETIREMENT PLANS

In 1982, when the Tax Equity and Fiscal Responsibility Act was passed, Congress put "S" corporations, "C" corporations and partnerships on a level playing field with respect to qualified retirement plans. In large measure, few significant differences exist in the treatment accorded the three types of business forms.

A qualified retirement plan provides the following benefits: The corporation is permitted to take a deduction for the full amount of its contribution to the plan, and the shareholder-employee does not include as income either the contribution made on his or her behalf by the corporation or the earnings on the contribution until the time he or she receives a distribution from the qualified plan.

There are limits on the amount an employer may contribute on behalf of the employee. Those limits are very similar to the requirements concerning compensation. Only a reasonable salary will be treated as compensation when paid to a shareholder-employee. Similarly, the contribution made on behalf of a shareholder-employee must be reasonable when considered along with other compensation paid to the shareholder-employee.

The use of a qualified plan may answer one of the problems posed in the previous section—supplying certain fringe benefits to the shareholder-employees of an "S" corporation. If the corporation has an HR-10 plan, it may deduct that portion of contributions it uses to purchase life insurance for shareholder-employees.

Finally, bear in mind that if an "S" corporation intends to set up a qualified retirement plan, its owners should consider getting professional advice before doing so. This advice, available without charge from most financial institutions, is necessary because the average small business, whether it opts for either "S" or "C" status, is likely to have a "top-heavy" plan. Such plans are subject to highly technical and complicated tax rules.

A top-heavy plan exists if 60 percent of the plan's benefits or contributions are for the benefit of key employees. A key employee is someone who satisfies one of the following standards. He or she

- is an officer of the corporation,
- is one of the ten employees who owns the greatest interest in the corporation,
- is a 5 percent owner of the "s" corporation stock, or
- receives more than $150,000 in compensation from the "S" corporation and owns at least 1 percent of the corporation stock.

In determining the percentages of stock ownership listed above, the employee is deemed the owner of shares held by a spouse, children, parents, grandparents, and grandchildren.

10

Transferring Shares Back to the Corporation

A shareholder may transfer his or her shares back to the corporation for a variety of reasons and under a host of circumstances. Among the more commonplace reasons are the following:

- The selling shareholder, wishing to obtain a tax-free distribution from the "S" corporation, offers to sell a portion of his or her shareholdings back to the business.
- The shareholder's basis in his or her stock has been reduced, and the shareholder intends to take a long-term capital loss by selling a portion of the shares in a year when he or she will realize long-term gains on other holdings.
- Given his or her reduced participation in the business, a majority shareholder is willing to sell a portion of the shares back to the corporation to equalize his or her holdings with those of a minority shareholder.
- An existing shareholder, whether because of differences with other shareholders or the desire to retire from active business, wishes to sell all of his or her shareholdings back to the corporation.

Depending on the circumstances, the transfer of shares back to the corporation may be treated as either a distribution, or a sale or an exchange. The consequences for the transferring shareholder, however, may be meaningfully different if the transfer is held to be a distribution rather than a sale or an exchange, or vice versa.

If the transfer of stock is treated as a distribution, the shareholder may receive a tax-free payment of money from the corporation. If a transfer is found to be a sale or an exchange, the shareholder will end up with either a capital gain or loss, depending on the basis he or she had in the stock before the transfer.

WHEN IS A TRANSFER A SALE OR AN EXCHANGE?

A transfer of shares by a shareholder to the "S" corporation is treated as a sale or an exchange if, upon completion of the transfer, there will be a meaningful change at the corporate or shareholder level. A sale or an exchange, therefore, can be found where

- the shareholder transfers all of his or her stock;
- the transfer is viewed as a redemption that is not equivalent to a dividend;
- there is a substantially disproportionate redemption of stock;
- the redemption takes place as part of a partial liquidation of the "S" corporation; or
- the shareholder's stock in the "S" corporation exceeds 35 percent of his or her estate and the shares are sold back to the corporation to provide the estate with money to pay death taxes.

Sale of All Shares

Obviously, if a shareholder sells all of his or her shareholdings back to the corporation, there has been a meaningful change at both the shareholder and corporate levels. Such a transfer will constitute a sale or an exchange only if the selling shareholder completely severs his or her relationship with the "S" corporation. To satisfy this requirement, the selling shareholder may not continue on as an officer, an employee or a director of the "S" corporation. The selling shareholder may, however, offer his or her services to the corporation as an independent contractor.

The selling shareholder will not be viewed as having completely terminated his or her interest if the shareholder's spouse (other than a legally separated spouse), children, grandchildren, or parents will continue to own stock in the corporation. In that case, the sale to the corporation will be viewed as a distribution. The same result is obtained if the selling shareholder retains an option to purchase shares in the "S" corporation.

The fact that the corporation may owe the selling shareholder money based on an earlier loan should not cause the IRS to complain that the sale or exchange is a distribution. The debt in question, however, should carry the same terms as a loan to the corporation would bear if it were made by a stranger; that is, interest rates should be comparable to market rates. There must be a fixed obligation to pay interest and return the principal. If the debt is subordinated to other debts, this fact should be reflected in a higher interest rate.

Transfer Is Not a Dividend

If the selling shareholder can show that a transfer of fewer than all of his or her shares is not a dividend, the transfer will be viewed as a sale or an exchange. Essentially, this test is satisfied if the shareholder can show that as a result of the transfer, there has been a meaningful reduction in the shareholder's pro rata interest in the "S" corporation. This test, therefore, applies only to situations where the corporation has more than one shareholder.

In determining whether there has been a meaningful reduction in the shareholder's proportionate interest, the IRS appears to focus on voting power. As a result of this approach, for example, if a shareholder who owns 75 percent of the corporation stock sells 24 percent back to the corporation, the IRS will view the transfer as a distribution rather than a sale. The logic here is that the transferring shareholder will end up with 51 percent of the stock and will retain voting control.

If, instead, that shareholder sells 25 percent of the outstanding stock so that he or she retains exactly half of the voting stock, the transfer would be viewed as a sale or an exchange because the selling shareholder would no longer have voting control. (He or she would have only the right to veto proposed action because a 50-50 split results in less than the majority needed for most matters determined by shareholder vote.)

According to the IRS, most other partial share redemptions, even those involving a minority shareholder, may qualify as sales or exchanges. Of course, if pro rata transfers by all shareholders occur, there will not be a meaningful change, and the individual transfers will be treated as distributions.

Disproportionate Reductions

A transfer of shares back to the "S" corporation will be treated as a sale or an exchange if the selling shareholder can show three things:

1. The selling shareholder will own less than 50 percent of the total voting power of the corporation after the transfer.
2. After the transfer, the selling shareholder will not own more than 79 percent of the percentage of voting stock the shareholder had before the transfer.
3. If the "S" corporation has nonvoting common stock, the selling shareholder will not be left with more than 79 percent of the total amount of stock he or she held before the transfer. In this test, the percentages are based on the fair market value of the shares.

CONSEQUENCES OF SALE OR EXCHANGE VERSUS DISTRIBUTION

Assuming that an "S" corporation has always been such—or that if it was once a regular "C" corporation, it has distributed any earnings or profits it had from its "C" operations—the consequences to the corporation itself are no different regardless of whether the transfer of shares back to the corporation is treated as a sale or a distribution. The transferring shareholder, however, may not realize his or her goals if the intention is to treat the transfer as a distribution and it is found to be a sale or an exchange.

If a transfer is treated as a sale or an exchange, the following consequences will result:

- If the shareholder receives more for the stock than his or her basis in the shares, the shareholder has a capital gain; if the shareholder receives less than his or her basis, the shareholder has a capital loss. If the shareholder sells fewer than all of his or her shares and remains with an ownership interest of more than 50 percent of the corporation's value, the capital loss will not be allowed by the IRS.
- If the selling shareholder transfers all shares back to the corporation, he or she loses the benefit of all unused carryover losses—that is, losses the shareholder was unable to use in previous years because he or she had an insufficient basis in the stock. Should there be unused losses, the selling shareholder might be better served if he or she sold fewer than all shares and held the remainder until such time that his or her basis permits the shareholder to use the losses.
- If the "S" corporation holds property on which it took an investment tax credit, the selling shareholder may be liable for the recapture of the credit.

If the shareholder is viewed as receiving a distribution when returning his or her shares to the corporation, the following result:

- The amount received from the corporation is tax free to the extent of the shareholder's basis in his or her shares.
- If the distribution exceeds the shareholder's basis in his or her shares, the excess is treated as a capital gain—the shareholder may not apply the excess against any basis he or she may have in corporate debt.
- To the extent the distribution is tax free, the shareholder's basis in his or her stock is reduced.

Based on the factors described above, the primary difference between a distribution and a sale or an exchange occurs when a shareholder transfers fewer than all of his or her shares to the corporation. In such a case, the shareholder receives an immediate benefit (tax-free receipt of money) if the transfer is viewed as a distribution; the cost, however, is a reduced basis in stock. This means the shareholder may not be able to use operating losses of the "S" corporation in subsequent years. Should the shareholder be viewed as having sold or exchanged the shares, he or she may have a capital gain or loss on the shares transferred; the shareholder's basis in the remaining shares will be unchanged, and the shareholder will be in a position to use subsequent losses, if they occur, to the extent of that basis.

Example No. 1

An "S" corporation has two shareholders, John and Mary. John owns 70 shares and has a $7,000 basis in the shares. Mary owns 30 shares. The "S" corporation acquires 30 of John's shares for $6,000. Because the transfer does not fit within any of the sale or exchange categories, it is treated as a distribution.

Result

John has a $6,000 tax-free distribution; his basis in his remaining stock is $1,000 ($7,000 less $6,000). Before the transfer, each of John's 70 shares had a basis of $100; after the transfer, each of John's remaining 40 shares has a basis of $25 ($1,000 divided by 40).

Example No. 2

Assume the same facts as in Example No. 1, except that John transfers 40 shares and receives $6,500. John's transfer is treated as a sale or an exchange because he has given up voting control (John and Mary now own 30 shares apiece).

Result

John has a capital gain of $2,500 ($6,500 less the $4,000 John had as a basis in the 40 shares)). John's basis in his remaining 30 shares remains unchanged ($100 per share, for a total of $3,000).

CLOSING THE BOOKS IF ALL SHARES ARE SOLD

If the selling shareholder transfers all of his or her stock to the corporation, the transaction will be treated as a sale or an exchange. In that situation, the selling shareholder and the remaining shareholders may close the corporation's books as of the sale date or may continue to keep them open. If the books are kept open for the remainder of the tax year, the selling shareholder will report his or her income, losses, deductions and credits from the corporation on a pro rata basis.

If all of the shareholders agree, the corporation is permitted to close its books as of the date the shareholder transfers his or her shares to the "S" corporation. In this event, the corporation will have two short tax years, and the selling shareholder will report only his or her share of flow-through items for that portion of the year during which the shareholder owned stock.

Example No. 1

An "S" corporation has two shareholders, each of whom owns 30 shares of stock in which he has a basis of $10 per share. On July 1st, one shareholder, John Taxpayer, sells all of his shares to the corporation for $500. As of that date, the corporation has $300 of net income; due to losses incurred over the next six months, the corporation has a net loss for the year of $1,200.

When Mr. Taxpayer transfers his stock on July 1st, both shareholders agree the corporation books will be closed.

Result

Mr. Taxpayer reports on only events that occur through July 1st. Therefore, his $150 of income (his half of the $300 net income) raises his basis in his stock to $450. Because he received $500 on shares that have a new basis of $450, his capital gain is $50, which he reports in addition to the $150 of income.

Example No. 2

Assume the same facts as in Example No. 1, except that the shareholders do not agree to close the books on July 1st.

Result

Mr. Taxpayer now reports a loss of $600 (his half of the $1,200 loss). The loss, in turn, reduces his basis in his stock to zero. The $500 he receives for his shares will all be capital gain, but will be negated by the $600 loss. John's bottom line will be a $100 loss.

The examples above are designed for illustrative purposes only. Because there is no way to predict what will happen after a shareholder leaves the corporation, it is impossible to determine which approach will work best in a given situation. If, however, the "S" corporation is running in the red when the shareholder sells his or her shares back to the business, a prudent approach might be to close the books as of the date of the sale. That way, the shareholder gets the benefit of those losses. This approach makes even more sense if the corporation business is seasonal and its high season will follow the sale.

SALES TO A THIRD PERSON

Until this point, we have focused on transfers of shares from a shareholder to the corporation. An "S" corporation shareholder, however, may choose to sell his or her shares to an individual, either another shareholder or a person previously unassociated with the corporation.

If the sale is to an individual, the result for the selling shareholder is exactly what it would have been had there been a sale or an exchange with the corporation. The amount received by the shareholder will be capital gain or loss; and the books of the corporation can be closed (if all shareholders consent) or kept open for the purpose of accounting for the seller's share of income, losses, deductions, and credits during the portion of the year he or she owned shares.

The shareholder who purchases the stock is entitled to participate in the decision to close the books because the shareholder will have to report his or her pro rata share of income and loss that flows through to the shareholder during the period he or she owns the shares.

ELECTION TO CLOSE CORPORATE BOOKS WHEN A SHAREHOLDER SELLS ALL SHARES

The form that appears here must be used if a shareholder sells all of his or her shares and ends his or her relationship with the "S" corporation and if the shareholders agree to create two short tax years. A sample form is completed for illustration.

When completed, the form must be attached to the corporation income tax form (Form 1120S). Every shareholder who owned the "S" corporation stock at any time during the course of the tax year, even if only for one day, must consent to the closing of the corporation books upon the transfer of all of a shareholder's stock.

Note also that the form may be used when a shareholder sells his or her shares either to the "S" corporation or to an individual.

ELECTION TO CLOSE CORPORATE BOOKS

Acme Corporation
100 Main Street
Anywhere, USA 00000

Employer Identification Number:

This Election is hereby made as Attachment to Form 1120S for Acme Corporation's Tax Year which ends December 31, 1999.

Acme Corporation hereby elects to have the provisions of Internal Revenue Code Section 1377(a)(1) enforced as if Acme Corporation's taxable year consisted of two taxable years, the first of which shall end on July 1, 1999.

The reason for this election is that John Taxpayer, a shareholder of Acme Corporation, sold all of his shares in the Corporation, and terminated his interest in the Corporation, on July 1, 1999.

Pursuant to this election, Acme Corporation's tax year, which runs from January 1 through December 31, i.e., a calendar year, will consist of the following two parts: (1) January 1, 1999, through June 30, 1999, and (2) July 1, 1999, through December 31, 1999.

Dated: July 5, 1999   Acme Corporation

By: _____

Philip Brown
President

Shareholder's Consent

The undersigned, who include every person who was a shareholder of Acme Corporation at any time during calendar year 1999, all consent to the election described above.

Name of Shareholder   Signature of Shareholder

_____   _____

_____   _____

_____   _____

SAMPLE

ELECTION TO CLOSE CORPORATE BOOKS

Employer Identification Number:

    This Election is hereby made as Attachment to Form 1120S for Tax Year which ends   , 20   .
                               hereby elects to have the provisions of Internal Revenue Code Section 1377(a)(1) enforced as if   taxable year consisted of two taxable years, the first of which shall end on   , 20   .
    The reason for this election is that   , a shareholder of   , sold all of his shares in the Corporation, and terminated his interest in the Corporation, on   , 20   .
    Pursuant to this election,   tax year, which runs from January 1 through December 31, i.e., a calendar year, will consist of the following two parts: (1)   , 20   , through   , 20   , and (2)   , 20   , through   , 20   .
    Dated: , 20   .

By: _____

Shareholder's Consent

The undersigned, who include every person who was a shareholder of

_____ at any time during calendar year 20___ , all consent to the

election described above.

Name of Shareholder   Signature of Shareholder

_____   _____

_____   _____

_____   _____

11

Revoking or Terminating the "S" Corporation Election

One of the key attributes of a corporation is that it has perpetual life unless its shareholders decide to end its existence or it is run in a manner that causes the state to step in and terminate its existence. Just as "C" corporations enjoy the right to perpetual existence, so do "S" corporations.

The shareholders of any corporation—"S" or "C"—have the right to determine the tax status the corporation will occupy. Having made that decision, the shareholders are not locked in; a corporation's shareholders may switch the business from "C" status to "S" status, or vice versa. If the decision is made to switch from "S" to "C" status, it is termed a *revocation* of "S" status.

"S" corporation status will also end if the corporation fails to satisfy the Internal Revenue Code requirements for a valid election to be taxed as an "S" corporation. The involuntary ending of the "S" corporation election is referred to as a *termination* of the election.

REVOCATION

Shareholders who own more than 50 percent of all outstanding shares—both voting and nonvoting stock—can revoke the "S" corporation election at any time by filing a notice with the District Director of Internal Revenue.

Example No. 1

John owns 50 shares of voting stock in an "S" corporation; Mary owns 51 shares of stock in the corporation. Mary controls the decision to revoke the "S" election because she owns more than one-half of the outstanding stock.

Example No. 2

Assume the same facts as in Example No. 1. Assume also that Mary does not hold an office with the corporation and that John is its only officer. Under these circumstances, Mary votes to revoke the election, and John votes not to.

Result

John may be able to block Mary's decision because the Internal Revenue Code requires the notice of revocation to be signed by an authorized corporate officer and filed with the District Director. Mary might have to bring a lawsuit to compel John to follow the dictates of the majority.

When Revocation Becomes Effective

If shareholders decide to revoke the election to be treated as an "S" corporation, there are three possible dates upon which the revocation will become effective:

1. The year before the tax year during which the notice of revocation is filed. If the notice is filed on or before the 15th day of the third month of the corporation tax year, the corporation "S" status ends with the close of the previous tax year.

Example No. 1

A calendar-year "S" corporation files its notice of revocation on March 15, 1999.

Result

The corporation's last year as an "S" corporation will be 1998; it will be taxed as a "C" corporation in 1999.

2. The tax year during which the notice of revocation is filed. If the notice of revocation is filed at any time after the 15th day of the third month of the corporation tax year, the election will remain in place for the balance of the tax year.

Example No. 2

A calendar-year "S" corporation files its notice of revocation on March 16, 1999.

Result

When the "S" corporation files its return for 1999, it must do so as an "S" corporation. It will not be a "C" corporation for tax purposes until the tax year starting January 1, 2000.

3. A date chosen by the shareholders. The shareholders can choose any effective date for their revocation as long as the date chosen falls on or after the date of the revocation.

Example No. 3

A calendar-year "S" corporation files its notice of revocation on March 15, 1999. The notice specifies that the effective date will be July 1, 1999.

Result

Unlike the result in Example No. 1, the "S" election will end on July 1, 1999, not with the end of 1998.

If the third option is chosen, the corporation will have two short tax years—one for "S" corporation treatment, a second for "C" corporation treatment. This means that the corporation books will be closed as of the day the first short year ends and will be reopened on the day the second year starts. In this example, the corporation would have a short "S" corporation tax year that runs from January 1, 1999, through June 30, 1999, and a short "C" corporation tax year that starts July 1, 1999, and ends December 31, 1999.

TERMINATION

To qualify as an "S" corporation, the corporation must be a small-business corporation (see Chapter 4). To remain qualified for "S" status, the corporation must continue to be a small-business corporation. If the "S" corporation fails to continue to satisfy any one of the requirements needed to qualify it as a small-business corporation, its "S" status ends the day before the terminating or disqualifying event occurs. Disqualifying events (treated more fully in Chapter 4) include the following:

- Share ownership by more than 75 persons. For example, if a husband and wife, who count as one shareholder, divorce and each keeps one-half of the stock they jointly owned, the corporation will have two shareholders instead of one. If the corporation already had 75 shareholders when the divorce took place, it would go over the limit, and its election would terminate.
- Transfer of shares to an entity or a person who is not eligible to be an "S" corporation shareholder. Ineligible shareholders include any corporation or partnership, certain trusts and nonresident aliens.
- Issuance of a second class of stock. An "S" corporation is permitted to have only one class of stock. The exception to this rule allows an "S" corporation to create a second class of common stock that differs from the first class only with respect to voting rights.
- Acquisition of a subsidiary in which the "S" corporation owns more than 80 percent of the outstanding stock.
- Engagement in ineligible business activities. For example, the corporation would lose its "S" status if it becomes a banking or another type of financial institution, a DISC or an insurance company.
- Use of an improper tax year. Although not a violation of the requirements concerning a small-business corporation, an "S" corporation may lose its status if it does not use a proper tax year. In most instances, "S" corporations are required to use a calendar year because they are obliged to use their owner's tax year.
- Excessive passive income. Although not a factor that goes to the question of whether a business is a small-business corporation, an "S" corporation that

has excessive passive income will have its "S" status terminated. This cause of termination can affect only "S" corporations that started out as "C" corporations. The test for excessive passive income applies to an "S" corporation that has (1) accumulated earnings and profits from its "C" corporation operations and those earnings and profits remain in the "S" corporation for three consecutive "S" corporation tax years and (2) passive income for three consecutive tax years that exceeds 25 percent of the "S" corporation's gross receipts for each of those years.

- Passive income includes royalties of all kinds—rents from real or personal property, interest from virtually any source, dividends, annuities and gain on the sale of securities.

Termination Procedure

If a terminating event occurs, that fact must be reported to the IRS in a statement that includes the date the event occurred and the nature of the terminating event. If the event involved an ineligible purchaser of shares, the purchaser must be identified, and the number of shares purchased must be stated.

If the termination was inadvertent or accidental, it is possible to get the IRS to reinstate the corporation "S" status. Waivers may be granted for any of the seven disqualifying events described in the pervious section, other than the use of an improper tax year. Although there are no guidelines as to what will convince the IRS that a disqualifying event was caused by inadvertence, it is clear the agency will not accede to a request if the event was caused by an intentional act.

Example

Assume that an "S" corporation, acting on the advice of its certified public accountant, believed it did not have accumulated earnings and profits from its previous history as a "C" corporation. Based on this error, it violated the passive investment income rules.

Result

The IRS will probably go along with a request to waive the termination.

Effective Date of Termination

A corporation's "S" status ends on the day before a terminating event occurs; that is, it is a "C" corporation on the day of the terminating event. As a result, the corporation will have two tax years for the year during which the terminating event took place: a short tax year for its "S" corporation period of operations, followed by a second short tax year for its "C" operations.

IMPACT OF REVOCATION OR TERMINATION

If a corporation's election to be taxed as an "S" corporation is revoked or terminated, the business becomes a "C" corporation. As a general rule, it cannot elect to return to "S" status until the fifth year after the year in which the revocation or termination occurred. So, for example, if a calendar-year "S" corporation revoked its "S" election on May 15, 1999, it cannot become an "S" corporation again until January 1, 2004.

Although the IRS can waive the five-year rule, it rarely—if ever—does so where there was a revocation or an intentional termination unless there has been a change of more than 50 percent of the corporation stock ownership.

REVOCATION OF "S" CORPORATION ELECTION

Each of the two forms that follow can be used to revoke an "S" election. The first form should be used when the shareholders do not wish to have an effective date different from the date supplied by the Internal Revenue Code. The second form should be used when the shareholders wish to set an effective date on or after the date of the filing of the form. A completed sample form of each is supplied.

When completing the form, the preparer should be careful to include the combined total of both voting and nonvoting shares outstanding on the date of filing.

REVOCATION NOTICE

```
Acme Corporation
100 Main Street
Anywhere, USA 00000
                         March 15, 20
```

District Director of Internal Revenue
```
Upper Taxbite Street
Greedy City, DC 00000
```

Dear Sir:

`Acme Corporation` hereby revokes its election to be taxed as an "S" corporation under the provisions of Section 1362 of the Internal Revenue Code. `Acme Corporation` has a total of one thousand shares of stock issued and outstanding as of this date. This revocation shall be effective as of `July 1, 20` .

```
                         Sincerely,
                         Acme Corporation


                     By: _____:
                         John Taxpayer,
                         President
```

Shareholder's Consent

The undersigned, owners of more than 50 percent of the outstanding stock of Acme Corporation as of the date of this notice, have consented to the revocation of Acme Corporation's election to be treated as an "S" corporation under Section 1362 of the Internal Revenue Code.

Name	Signature	Number of Shares Owned
_____	_____	_____
_____	_____	_____
_____	_____	_____

REVOCATION NOTICE

20

District Director of Internal Revenue

Dear Sir:

hereby revokes its election to be taxed as an "S" corporation under the provisions of Section 1362 of the Internal Revenue Code.

has a total of   shares of stock issued and outstanding as of this date.

This revocation shall be effective as of   20   .

Sincerely,

By: _____ :

Shareholder's Consent

The undersigned, owners of more than 50 percent of the outstanding stock of
_____ as of the date of this notice, have consented to the
revocation of _____ election to be treated as an "S" corporation under
Section 1362 of the Internal Revenue Code.

Name	Signature	Number of Shares Owned
_____	_____	_____
_____	_____	_____
_____	_____	_____

12

Preparing Your "S" Corporation's Annual Tax Return

For many small entrepreneurs, the most difficult and intimidating aspect of business involves filing their corporations' annual tax returns. In the case of the "S" corporation, however, this concern is not really justified. Form 1120S, the annual tax return form for "S" corporations, is fairly straightforward.

In this chapter, we will prepare Form 1120S for an imaginary "S" corporation—International Widgets, Inc. (IWI)—that has three shareholders: Joe and Jane Taxpayer and their son, Deduction Taxpayer. Each line of the form will be reviewed, even if it does not apply to IWI. The appendix to this chapter sets out IWI's completed Form 1120S and Schedule K-1, "Shareholders' Shares of Income, Credits, Deductions, etc.," on which each shareholder reports his or her flow-through items from the corporation. After reading each line-by-line discussion, you should find it helpful to consult the form to see how each number plugs in.

Here is one hint that will help you minimize the time needed to complete your corporation's 1120S: organize your materials before starting on the form. Prepare a topical breakdown of the items listed below. Then all you'll have to do is plug the numbers into your form and do some simple arithmetic.

FORM 1120S: U.S. INCOME TAX RETURN FOR AN "S" CORPORATION

The Heading

Date of return. This is the top line of the form. Most "S" corporations are calendar-year entities. IWI uses a calendar year, so its tax year begins on January 1st and ends on December 31st.

The mailing box. If this is your corporation's first return, type in its employer identification number (EIN), name, street address (including a room or suite number, if appropriate), city, state and zip code, as shown on our sample form. If the corporation filed last year, you should have the label provided by the IRS. Simply paste it in this spot.

Box A. Fill in the exact date on which your corporation made its "S" election. If this is not the corporation's first filing as an "S" corporation, you can get this date from last year's form. *Caution:* This line calls for the date of the "S" election, not the date of incorporation (see box D, below).

Box B. Fill in your corporation's business code. If this is the first year of your corporation's existence, consult the listing of codes that appears at the end of Chapter 5. (IWI obtained its code from the "Miscellaneous Manufacturing" category.) Otherwise, last year's form will have this information (even if you filed as a "C" corporation).

Box C. Fill in your corporation's EIN.

Box D. Fill in the date on which your business was incorporated. In box B, you filled in the date the corporation elected to be an "S" corporation. Box D asks for the date the corporation came into existence. Last year's return will have this information.

Box E. Box E asks you to supply the total assets of your "S" corporation. Simply total the values of all assets as those values are shown in the corporation's books and records. *Caution:* If your corporation has no assets at the end of the year, you must fill in the total of its assets at the beginning of the year.

Line F. Unless one of the next four boxes applies, do not check any of the boxes on this line. The box "Initial return" indicates that this is the first time the corporation has ever filed a tax return. If your corporation went out of business last year, check the box for "Final return." *Caution:* If this is a final return, make sure this fact is also reported on line D-1 of Schedule K-1 (which appears as part of our sample).

If your corporation has changed its address, check the third box; if this is an amended version of a form previously filed, check the fourth box.

Line G. Fill in the total number of shareholders. IWI has three shareholders.

Income (Lines 1 through 6)

These six lines refer only to income derived from your corporation's business activities. In IWI's case, it includes income related to the sale of widgets. Other non-business activity income, such as income from investments in securities or bank interest, is reported on Schedule K.

Line 1a. Fill in the gross amount received by your corporation on the sale of its goods or services. IWI had receipts of $510,081 on the sale of its widgets.

Line 1b. If customers returned your product and you refunded their payments, or if customers were given discounts or allowances after they paid for their goods, fill in those numbers here. IWI had to give three customers refunds totaling $4,430, and eight customers who received dented widgets were given allowances totaling $2,500. The total of $6,930 is entered on line 1b.

Line 1c. Subtract line 1b from line 1a, and fill in the result ($503,151 for IWI) on line 1c.

Line 2. This number is taken from line 8 of Schedule A (page 2 of the form). IWI incurred $315,051 as the cost of goods sold and enters this amount on line 2.

Line 3. Subtract line 2 from line 1c, and fill in the result on line 3. IWI subtracts $315,051 from $503,151 and enters the result of $188,100 on line 3.

Line 4. If your corporation had an ordinary gain or loss from the sale of an asset it used in its business, fill in that amount on this line. *Caution:* This line refers to assets used in your business, not to investment assets owned by the corporation. *Example:* Assume IWI sold $5,000 worth of securities it held for investment purposes and a buffing machine it used to polish widgets. Any gain or loss on the sale of the securities would be reported on Schedule K; any gain or loss on the buffing machine would be reported on Form 1120S, line 4.

Line 5. The reference to "Other income" on this line is to other trade or business income and does not include investment income. Examples of other trade or business income include, but are not limited to, interest paid by customers on overdue accounts, insurance income based on a loss (if that income itself is taxable) and payment on a bill you wrote off and deducted as a bad debt on a previous return.

Line 6. Add lines 3 through 5, and enter the total on line 6. Since IWI has no entries on lines 4 and 5, it simply picks up its total from line 3 ($188,100) and enters it on line 6.

Deductions (Lines 7 through 27)

As was the case with income, the deductions detailed on lines 7 through 21 are trade or business deductions, not investment expenses. Other nonbusiness activity expenses, such as brokerage fees incurred when purchasing securities, are reported on Schedules K and K-1.

Line 7. Include the total compensation of your corporation's president, vice presidents, secretary and treasurer. If a person who owns more than 2 percent of the "S" corporation's shares receives a fringe benefit, that payment must be included as part of the total on line 7. That person must also receive a W-2 that includes the fringe benefit as part of his or her total wages. If a person who owns 2 percent or less of the corporation's stock receives a fringe benefit, do not include the benefit on this line (it will be reported on line 18 as part of the deduction for fringe benefits paid to other employees). IWI paid its officers $56,100 in compensation and enters that amount on line 7.

Line 8. The total salaries and wages paid to all nonofficer employees are reported on this line. If you included salaries and wages as part of the cost of goods sold (line 2, above), do not include them here. In the event that the corporation qualifies for a credit against wages, such as the jobs credit, deduct the credit from total wages, and report the net amount here. IWI paid $47,520 in wages during 1998 and was entitled to a $1,980 credit. It reports a net deduction of $45,540 on line 8. The $1,980 is also reported on line 13 of Schedule K and must be supported by Form 5884.

Line 9. All amounts spent by your corporation on repairs and maintenance are reported as deductions on this line. Include only repairs and maintenance expenses incurred to keep equipment in working order or to fix malfunctioning equipment. Do not include expenses incurred to increase an asset's useful life or value. IWI spent $180 to replace a broken gasket in a widget-forming machine and $84 on semiannual tune-ups of its gasoline-powered widget synchronizer. The total of $264 is reported on this line.

Line 10. In the event that your company delivered goods to a customer who has not paid and you have written off your claim as worthless, you may deduct that debt owed your company as a worthless debt. *Caution No. 1:* Do not include personal debts owed to you as an individual; you may include only bad debts that are owed to your "S" corporation. *Caution No. 2:* If your "S" corporation uses the cash method of accounting, you can deduct a bad debt only if you previously included that debt as income. IWI uses the accrual method of accounting and wrote off $528 during 1998.

Line 11. If your "S" corporation leases office, warehouse or manufacturing space, deduct the rent payments it made over the course of the year on this line. IWI pays $253 per month for its combined office and manufacturing quarters and shows total annual rental of $3,036 as a deduction on line 11.

Line 12. Total and report on this line certain taxes paid by your "S" corporation. If your corporation operates under a license from a governmental authority, you may include the license fee on line 12. *Caution:* If you must have a license to perform services used by your "S" corporation, do not deduct the fee for that license on this form; you must deduct that expense on your personal return. IWI paid licensing fees and local taxes totaling $4,950 and enters that amount on line 12.

Line 13. You may deduct all interest expenses for money borrowed for the corporation's business activities on this line. IWI has an existing credit line with a local bank. The corporation drew against that line to purchase the raw materials it converts to widgets. The interest payments on its credit line borrowing totaled $4,686 during 1998, and that amount is reported on this line. *Caution:* If your corporation borrowed money for investment purposes, the interest paid on such loans is reported on line 11a of Schedule K.

Line 14. Your corporation may deduct depreciation of assets it uses in its business. The information needed to complete lines 14a and 14b is taken from Form 4562. *Caution:* If your corporation has incurred a Section 179 expense (see Form 4562), do not include that expense here; instead, report it on Schedule K-1 because it is passed directly through to shareholders. IWI claims a depreciation deduction of $5,016, which it reports on line 14c.

Line 15. The depletion deduction applies only to companies that can take a deduction for timber depletion.

Line 16. If your corporation incurred any advertising or promotional expenses (radio, television or newspaper ads; handouts; stuffers; or giveaways, such as pens, calendars or diaries), include those expenses on this line. IWI spent $2,650 on a quarter-page display ad in the *Widgeteers Guidebook,* a magazine for hobbyists, and $221 for pocket diaries it mailed to widget wholesalers and retailers. The total of $2,871 is reported and deducted on line 16.

Line 17. Any expense incurred for pension and profit-sharing plans can be deducted on this line.

Line 18. Include fringe benefits paid or incurred on behalf of employees owning 2 percent or less of the corporation's stock.

Line 19. Any business expense incurred by your corporation that does not fit within the categories listed at lines 7 through 18 should be included on line 19. Typically, line 19 expenses include such items as commissions paid to fees paid to independent contractors; business insurance premiums, such as bank fees on checking accounts; fire, theft and liability coverage; legal fees and expenses; meals (within the current percentage limits set by the IRS); office stationery; and ordinary and necessary travel and entertainment expenses. The expenses included on this line must be explained by a separate schedule attached to your return. The schedule should be typewritten on an 8½-by-11 sheet of white paper. The heading of the schedule should include the name of your "S" corporation and its EIN. Beneath the heading, simply list in column form the other expenses and, alongside each entry, the amount spent on that item. IWI spent $18,500 on fees to its independent contractor sales representatives; $3,500 on legal fees to defend a lawsuit brought by a supplier after IWI refused shipment of water-damaged widget skins; $2,500 for premiums on its fire, theft and liability insurance policies; $1,100 for accounting services; and $239 for office stationery. The total of $25,839 is shown on line 19. *Caution:* Do not include any expenses incurred with respect to investment assets, such as a safe-deposit box fee if the box is used solely to store investment securities.

Line 20. Add the amounts shown on lines 7 through 19, and enter the total here. *Caution:* Include only the entry you make on line 14c, not any amounts you entered on lines 14a and 14b. IWI enters its total of $148,830 on line 20.

Line 21. Subtract line 20 from line 6, and enter the result on line 21. If line 20 is greater than line 6, your corporation has a loss, and that number should be entered in parentheses—for example, ($7,000). IWI, which reported total income of $188,100 on line 6 and total deductions of $148,830 on line 20, reports income of $39,270 on line 21.

Lines 22 through 27. These lines do not apply to the overwhelming majority of "S" corporations. If your corporation has always been an "S" corporation, these lines definitely do not apply to it. If your corporation converted to "S" status from "C" status, it is possible that these lines will apply to it. Review Chapter 6 to determine whether they do. If so, seek out a tax professional to prepare your corporation's return.

Signature Boxes

Whether you are doing it yourself or you have engaged an accountant to prepare your "S" corporation's return, you or another officer of the corporation must sign the return, date it and supply the corporate title of the person who signs. *Caution:* Do not sign in your capacity as a director or shareholder; the person who signs must do so in his or her title as an officer of the corporation.

FORM 1120S: SCHEDULE A— COST OF GOODS SOLD

In this schedule, you are asked to supply information relating to the cost of goods sold by your "S" corporation. The approach taken is straightforward: You start with the inventory your company had at the beginning of the year, then add all costs the corporation accumulated to increase its inventory during the year and subtract the value of the corporation's inventory at the end of the year. That final figure equals the cost of the goods sold by your corporation. *Caution No. 1:* If you operate a corporation that performs services, draw a line through this schedule, and print the words *Not Applicable. Caution No. 2:* Do not include as part of the cost of goods your corporation sells any equipment purchased by the corporation to produce those goods.

Line 1. Enter the value of your inventory at the beginning of the year. If your corporation is a distributor, wholesaler or retailer, you can use the cost of purchasing goods (including shipping costs). IWI, a manufacturer, carried its inventory on its books at a value of $41,580 and enters that total on line 1.

Line 2. Over the course of the tax year, IWI spent $371,943 on raw materials and other supplies used to produce widgets. It enters that number on line 2.

Line 3. Although IWI incurred substantial labor costs producing widgets, it enters a zero on this line. The labor costs were included on lines 7 and 8 of the deductions block (see above), and all repair and maintenance costs appear on line 9 of this section. Most smaller companies do not track certain production costs very well. For that reason, IWI simply put all of its nonexecutive payroll on line 8 and all of its repair and maintenance costs on line 9. *Example:* IWI's president spends part of his work day supervising production, part of his day selling to customers and part of his day fulfilling administrative tasks. Rather than keep a log of how much time he spends at each, he simply includes his total compensation on line 7 of the deductions block.

Line 4. The costs referred to on this line—those detailed in Section 263A, "Uniform Capitalization Rules"—apply to a limited number of corporations. If these rules apply to your business, you would be better advised to have a professional prepare your corporation's return. The types of companies covered by Section 263A include those that produce films, recordings, books and videos, as well as corporations that buy goods for resale and have gross receipts of more than $10 million. IWI does not fall into any of those categories; therefore, this line does not apply.

Line 5. List any other costs relating to your inventory that have not been included on line 2. If, for example, your corporation rents off-site warehouse space and that rental is not included on line 11 of the deductions block (see above), include it here. Similarly, if the corporation engages an independent contractor to provide security services at its warehouse, that cost could be included on this line.

Line 6. This line is self-explanatory. Add the totals shown on lines 1 through 5, and enter that amount here. IWI has entered the totals of lines 1 ($41,580) and 2 ($371,943), or $413,523.

Line 7. Enter the value of your inventory at the end of the tax year. IWI had inventory it valued at $98,472 at the end of the year and enters this figure on line 7.

Line 8. IWI subtracts line 7 ($98,472) from line 6 ($413,523) and enters $315,051 both here and on line 2 of the income block on page 1 of the return.

Line 9. Item (a) asks for the method your corporation used to value its inventory at the end of the year; simply check the appropriate box. Item (b) should be checked if inventory is valued below cost when the merchandise is unsalable at normal prices or unusable in the normal way because goods are "subnormal" due to damage, imperfections, shop wear, etc., within the meaning of Regulations section 1.471-2(c). These goods may be valued at a current bona fide selling price minus direct cost of dispostion (but not less than scrap value) if such a price can be established. Items (c) and (d) should be answered only if your corporation uses the LIFO (last in, first out) inventory method. Item (e) asks whether Section 263A applies. If it does, consider engaging a professional to prepare the corporation's return (see line 4 of this unit). Item (f) asks whether your corporation changed the way it determined the value of its inventory between the beginning of the year and the end of the year. *Note:* If the corporation changed the way it determined the value of its inventory when it estimated the value at the beginning of the year, and if it kept to the same method for the remainder of the year, the answer to this question will be no because the question asks whether the corporation's methods remained the same for the current tax year.

FORM 1120S: SCHEDULE B–
OTHER INFORMATION

Line 1. This line is self-explanatory. All you need do is check off the method of accounting used by your corporation. IWI uses the accrual method and checks that box.

Line 2. The first part of this line, item (a), asks for the same number you supplied in box B of the heading (see page 1 of the form). The second part of the line, item (b), asks for a description of your product or service. In most instances, the descriptions supplied with the codes will be adequate; in IWI's case, they are not. IWI has described its service as "widget manufacturing."

Lines 3 through 8. The questions on these lines are self-explanatory. *Caution:* If you answer yes on any of these lines, you would be better advised to engage a professional to prepare—or, at least, review—the corporation's return.

Line 9. If your corporation has a gain of the type described in this question, the return should be prepared by a professional.

Form 1120S: Designation Box

The person the corporation designates as the individual who will answer inquiries from the IRS should be identified in this portion of the return. IWI has selected its president (the person who signed the form; see signature block on page 1), and his name is printed here, as is his address (note he has used his home address, not the corporation's address) and his Social Security number (not the corporation's EIN).

SCHEDULE K: SHAREHOLDERS' SHARES OF INCOME, CREDITS, DEDUCTIONS, ETC.

Schedule K shows the Internal Revenue Service that portion of your "S" corporation's income, deductions and credits that flow through to and are reportable by the corporation's shareholders. Most small "S" corporations find that they do not have entries for most of the line items listed in this schedule. IWI, our sample corporation, probably will show more items on this schedule than will many small "S" corporations.

Income (Lines 1 through 6)

Line 1. IWI's $39,270 total entered on this line was taken from page 1, line 21.

Lines 2 and 3. These lines should be filled out only if your "S" corporation had rental income in addition to the income it had from its primary manufacturing, retailing or service business. IWI did not have such income, and it leaves these lines blank.

Line 4. If your corporation had what the IRS terms *portfolio* income, report that income on lines 4a and 4b. Portfolio income is another way of saying *investment* income (i.e., income from stocks, bonds, money market funds, certificates of deposit and other income-producing investments). IWI invested some of its income in short-term CDs and in the stock of companies listed on the New York and American stock exchanges. It reports $1,320 of interest income on its CDs on line 4a and $5,280 of dividend income on line 4b. Because IWI did not have royalty income, short-term or long-term capital gains or losses, or other portfolio income, it leaves lines c through f blank. *Caution:* If your corporation invested in tax-exempt bonds, do not enter the interest on those bonds on line 4a; tax-exempt interest is entered on line 17, below.

Line 5. This line should be filled out only if your corporation sold or otherwise disposed of real property or personal property it had depreciated (Section 1231 property) and had a gain or loss on the sale or disposition. *Example:* If IWI had owned a widget-forming machine for ten years and had depreciated the machine over that period of time, and in 1998 decided to sell the machine and acquire a newer, faster model, the older machine would have been Section 1231 property. IWI, however, did not sell such property and leaves this line blank. *Caution:* If your "S" corporation sold Section 1231 property, consider engaging professional assistance for this part of the corporation's return.

Line 6. This line should be filled out only if your "S" corporation had income (or loss) that has not been reported on lines 1 through 5.

Deductions (Lines 7 through 10)

The next four lines set out some of the deductions against the income reported on lines 1 through 6. Other deductions against income are reported on lines 11a, 15e and 16a.

Line 7. If your "S" corporation made any charitable donations, report them on this line. IWI made charitable contributions totaling $7,920 and reports that fact on line 7.

Line 8. Line 8 refers to the Section 179 deduction. This deduction relates to property your corporation acquired for use in its business and put into service during the tax year. Up to $17,500 can be taken as a Section 179 deduction. IWI did not make any purchases that qualify for the Section 179 deduction. If it had, it would have filled out Form 4562 (a relatively straightforward form) and would have taken the value reported on that form and entered it on line 8 of this form.

Line 9. Your corporation should include any and all deductions it may have in connection with its portfolio income, *except* for investment interest expenses. Any investment income expenses are reported on line 11a. Because it had no deductions based on its portfolio income other than investment interest expenses, IWI leaves this line blank.

Line 10. Report on this line any deductions in connection with items that were reported on line 6 (other income). Because IWI did not have other income on line 6, it leaves line 10 blank.

Investment Interest (Line 11)

Line 11a. If your "S" corporation incurred interest expense on money it borrowed to produce investment income, list that expense on line 11a. IWI had $990 of investment interest expense and enters that amount on line 11a.

Line 11b. This line asks the preparer of the return to add the amounts shown on lines 4a through 4c and enter the total here. IWI entered $1,320 on line 4a and $5,280 on line 4b. Those entries add up to $6,600, and IWI enters that number on line 11b(1).

Credits (Lines 12 and 13)

Most "S" corporations have no entries for the various specialized credits listed on lines 12a through 12e; however, many businesses do take advantage of the jobs credit. If your corporation does so, too, attach a completed copy of Form 5884 to the return, and enter the employment credit shown on that form on line 13. IWI qualified for a jobs credit in the amount of $1,980 and enters that number on line 13.

Adjustments, Preferences, and Foreign Taxes (Lines 14 and 15)

Line 14. If your corporation has a depreciation deduction on property placed in service after 1986 or has income or deductions in connection with oil, gas or geo-thermal properties, complete lines 14a through 14e. *Caution:* If any part of line 14 applies to your corporation, engage a professional to prepare the corporation's tax return.

Line 15. If your corporation paid taxes to a foreign government, it may qual-ify for a deduction under the Internal Revenue Code. *Caution:* If your corporation pays foreign taxes, engage a professional to prepare the return.

Other (Lines 16 through 23)

Lines 16a and 16b. If your corporation has expenditures to which a Sec-tion 59(e) election applies, complete this line. Section 59(e) covers circulation expen-ditures for publishers; research and experimental expenditures; mining exploration and development costs; and intangible drilling and development costs. *Caution:* If your corporation can use the Section 59(e) election, it would be better advised to engage a professional to prepare its return.

Lines 17 and 18. If your corporation has tax-exempt *interest* income such as income from tax-exempt state or municipal bonds, report that income on line 17. IWI had $1,650 of tax-exempt income and reports that amount on line 17. Report tax-exempt income other than interest income on line 18. *Caution:* If your corpora-tion shows income on lines 17 or 18, that income will not be taxable in the share-holders' hands, but will increase the bases of their stock in the corporation.

Line 19. This line asks your corporation to report nondeductible expenses. For an "S" corporation, these expenses might include any "fringe benefits" provided by the corporation for its employee-shareholders and any reduction of salaries that flowed from the jobs credit (see line 13, above). IWI spent $3,416 on life and health insurance premiums for its officer-shareholders and had a $1,980 reduction of sala-ries that flowed from its jobs credit. Those two items total $5,396, and IWI enters this number on line 19.

Line 20. Report on this line any cash or property distributions made to shareholders—other than dividends. Noncash distributions should be estimated at fair market value. IWI made a total of $21,450 in distributions to its shareholders and enters this amount on line 20. *Caution:* Each shareholder must reduce his or her basis in the corporation's stock by the amount of the distribution he or she received.

Line 21. Note that this line asks only for a schedule; no dollar amount must be entered. A schedule will be required if your corporation

1. is a regulated investment company;
2. has income from oil or gas well properties;
3. has qualified exploratory costs;
4. can use the Section 179 expense deduction;
5. can recapture mining exploration expenses;
6. has shareholders who must file under Section 6111 (registration of tax shelters);
7. is involved in farming or fishing activities;
8. is involved in the sale of timeshares;
9. has disposed of property, with tax deferred under the installment method;
10. has shareholders who must capitalize interest under Section 263A;
11. has expenses that qualify for either the rehabilitation or reforestation credits; or
12. seeks to recapture the investment credit.

Caution

If any of these specialized circumstances applies, engage a professional to prepare your corporation's return.

Line 22. If your corporation has paid a dividend to its shareholders, enter that amount on this line.

Line 23. This line involves three straightforward arithmetic steps. First, add lines 1 through 6 of Schedule K. (IWI adds lines 1, 4a and 4b and arrives at a total of $45,870.) Next, add the totals on lines 7 through 11a, plus 15e and 16a. (IWI has entries on only two of those lines—7 [$7,920] and 11a [$990]—for a total of $8,910.) Third, subtract the deductions numbers ($8,910, in IWI's case) from the income number ($45,870), and enter the total ($36,960) on line 23.

SCHEDULE K-1: SHAREHOLDER'S SHARE OF INCOME, CREDITS, DEDUCTIONS, ETC.

Schedule K-1 must be supplied to every "S" corporation shareholder. This form reports to the shareholder his or her proportionate share of the "S" corporation's income, credits and deductions. The numbers reported on this form are derived from the numbers reported on Schedule K. The shareholder takes the numbers reported on his or her Schedule K-1 and plugs them into the appropriate lines of his or her Form 1040. (The right-hand column on Schedule K-1 gives explicit instructions, showing the taxpayer where to enter on Form 1040 each of the Schedule K-1 line items.)

For the purposes of our example, we will assume that Deduction Taxpayer owns 30 percent of the shares of IWI and that this Schedule K-1 is being prepared for him. As a general rule, the corporation will report 30 percent of each of the various Schedule K items as an income, a deduction or a credit item on Deduction Taxpayer's Schedule K-1.

The Heading

Identification numbers. Immediately above the address boxes is a line that asks for the shareholder's and the corporation's identifying numbers. The shareholder will generally supply his or her Social Security number. The shareholder's identification number must be the same number the shareholder uses on his or her Form 1040. The corporation should supply its EIN, which also appears at the top of Form 1120S.

Addresses. Both the corporation and the shareholder receiving the Schedule K-1 must supply their addresses. In the event that you operate your "S" corporation out of your home, you must show your home address for both yourself and the corporation.

Line A. Unless the shareholder held his or her interest for less than a full year, all you need do is fill in the percentage of the stock held by the shareholder receiving the K-1. Deduction Taxpayer owns 30 percent of the stock of IWI and fills in that number on line A. Matters become a bit more complicated if the shareholder bought or sold his or her interest during the course of the year. A simple way of calculating the shareholder's interest for the year in such a case is to determine the percentage of the year the shareholder owned his or her stock (divide the number of days the stock was owned by 365 to get the percentage), then multiply that number by the percentage of the total stock owned by the shareholder. *Example:* Assume Betty Brown purchased a 30 percent interest in IWI on May 1, 1998. Betty, therefore, owned her stock for 67 percent of the year (245 days of ownership divided by 365). Multiply 30 percent by 67 percent to determine that Betty held a 20 percent ownership interest in IWI in 1994 (.3 times .67 equals .20).

Line B. Fill in the IRS center at which your corporation files its return. *Caution:* If the shareholder and the corporation file their returns with different service centers, fill in the service center at which the corporation files its Form 1120S.

Line C. If your "S" corporation has a tax shelter registration number, supply it on this line.

Line D. Unless you are amending a previously filed form or your corporation went out of business or terminated its "S" status last year, do not check either box.

Pro Rata Share Items (Lines 1 through 23)

In the line items that follow, the numbers to be entered will be percentages of the items reported on Schedule K of Form 1120S. Because Deduction Taxpayer owns a 30 percent interest in IWI, the numbers we will fill in will be 30 percent of the Schedule K figures.

Line 1. IWI's ordinary income, as reported on line 1 of Schedule K, is $39,270. As a 30 percent shareholder, Deduction Taxpayer's share is $11,781.

Lines 2 and 3. Because IWI did not report income or loss from rental activities, it leaves these lines blank. These two lines correspond to lines 2 and 3 on Schedule K. If IWI had reported income or loss on either of those lines, it would report 30 percent of those numbers on either or both lines 2 and 3 of Deduction Taxpayer's Schedule K-1.

Line 4. If your corporation has entries for lines 4a through 4f on Schedule K, it must make corresponding entries on Schedule K-1. IWI reported $1,320 on line 4a and $5,280 on line 4b. Deduction Taxpayer's K-1 shows 30 percent of each of those totals on lines 4a ($396) and 4b ($1,584).

Lines 5 and 6. Because IWI did not show income on lines 5 and 6 of its Schedule K, it has nothing to report on the comparable lines of the K-1. If IWI had reported income or loss on those lines on its Schedule K, it would report 30 percent of those numbers on lines 5 and 6 of Deduction Taxpayer's Schedule K-1.

Lines 7 through 10. Again, look at your corporation's Schedule K and report the appropriate percentages of lines 7 through 10 on the comparable lines of the shareholder's K-1. Because IWI reported $7,920 in charitable contributions on line 7 of its Schedule K, Deduction Taxpayer's K-1 reports 30 percent of that total, or $2,376, on line 7. If IWI had reported deductions on lines 8 and 9 of its Schedule K, it would report 30 percent of those numbers on lines 8 and 9 of Deduction Taxpayer's Schedule K-1.

Line 11. IWI's Schedule K shows $990 on line 11a and $6,600 on line 11b(1). Therefore, Deduction Taxpayer's K-1 reports 30 percent of lines 11a ($297) and 11b(1) ($1,980).

Lines 12 and 13. IWI's Schedule K shows an entry on line 13 ($1,980); therefore, Deduction Taxpayer's K-1 reports 30 percent ($594) on its line 13. If IWI's Schedule K had reported a credit on lines 12a through 12e, the corporation would report 30 percent of those credits on the comparable parts of line 12 of Deduction Taxpayer's Schedule K-1.

Lines 14 and 15. Because IWI's Schedule K did not have entries for adjustments or tax preference items (line 14) or foreign taxes (line 15), Deduction Taxpayer's K-1 has no entries on its lines 14 and 15. If IWI's Schedule K had recorded an entry on those lines, 30 percent of those numbers would be reported on lines 14 and 15 of Deduction Taxpayer's Schedule K-1.

Lines 16 through 22. Again, review Schedule K of Form 1120S. If there are entries on lines 16 through 22, the appropriate percentages of those entries must be reported on lines 16 through 22 of the shareholder's K-1. IWI reported tax-exempt interest income of $1,650 on line 17 of its Schedule K. Deduction Taxpayer's K-1, therefore, reports 30 percent of that amount, or $495, on line 17. Similarly, IWI's Schedule K, at line 19, reported nondeductible expenses of $5,396. Thirty percent of that amount, $1,619, is reported on line 19 of Deduction Taxpayer's K-1. IWI also reported $21,450 in property and cash distributions on line 20 of its Schedule K. Thirty percent of that amount, $6,435, is reported on line 20 of Deduction Taxpayer's K-1.

Line 23. Any supplemental information needed to explain items shown on lines 1 through 22 should be provided on line 23. For the most part, it is unlikely that you will have to supply any supplemental information. If, however, your corporation has filed schedules as required by line 21 of Schedule K, it will have to supply supplemental information on line 23 of its shareholders' K-1 schedules. As indicated when we discussed line 21 of Schedule K, if your corporation engages in any of the specialized activities contemplated by that line, engage the services of a professional to prepare the return.

Form 1120S

U.S. Income Tax Return for an S Corporation

Department of the Treasury
Internal Revenue Service

► Do not file this form unless the corporation has timely filed Form 2553 to elect to be an S corporation.
► See separate instructions.

1998

For calendar year 1998, or tax year beginning		, 1998, and ending	, 19	

A Effective date of election as an S corporation *July 1, 1997*	Use IRS label. Other-wise, please print or type.	Name *International Widgets, Inc.*	**C** Employer identification number *23 : 1234567*
B NEW bus. code no. (see pages 26–28) *339900*		Number, street, and room or suite no. (If a P.O. box, see page 10 of the instructions.) *123 Commercial Road*	**D** Date incorporated *February 3, 1997*
		City or town, state, and ZIP code *Anywhere, PA 19000*	**E** Total assets (see page 10) *$ 231,400 |20*

F Check applicable boxes: **(1)** ☐ Initial return **(2)** ☐ Final return **(3)** ☐ Change in address **(4)** ☐ Amended return
G Enter number of shareholders in the corporation at end of the tax year . . . . ► *3*

Caution: *Include only trade or business income and expenses on lines 1a through 21. See the instructions for more information.*

Income

1a	Gross receipts or sales *510,081 |00*	**b** Less returns and allowances *6,930 |00*	**c** Bal ► **1c**	*503,151*
2	Cost of goods sold (Schedule A, line 8)		**2**	*315,051*
3	Gross profit. Subtract line 2 from line 1c		**3**	*188,100*
4	Net gain (loss) from Form 4797, Part II, line 18 (attach Form 4797)		**4**	
5	Other income (loss) (attach schedule)		**5**	
6	**Total income (loss).** Combine lines 3 through 5 . . . . ►		**6**	*188,100*

Deductions (see page 11 of the instructions for limitations)

7	Compensation of officers		**7**	*56,100*
8	Salaries and wages (less employment credits) . . .		**8**	*45,540*
9	Repairs and maintenance		**9**	*264*
10	Bad debts		**10**	*528*
11	Rents		**11**	*3,036*
12	Taxes and licenses		**12**	*4,950*
13	Interest		**13**	*4,686*
14a	Depreciation (if required, attach Form 4562)	**14a** *5,016*		
b	Depreciation claimed on Schedule A and elsewhere on return .	**14b**		
c	Subtract line 14b from line 14a		**14c**	*5,016*
15	Depletion **(Do not deduct oil and gas depletion.)** . . .		**15**	
16	Advertising		**16**	*2,871*
17	Pension, profit-sharing, etc., plans		**17**	
18	Employee benefit programs		**18**	
19	Other deductions (attach schedule)		**19**	*25,839*
20	**Total deductions.** Add the amounts shown in the far right column for lines 7 through 19 . ►		**20**	*148,830*
21	Ordinary income (loss) from trade or business activities. Subtract line 20 from line 6		**21**	*39,270*

Tax and Payments

22	**Tax: a** Excess net passive income tax (attach schedule) . . .	**22a**		
	b Tax from Schedule D (Form 1120S)	**22b**		
	c Add lines 22a and 22b (see page 14 of the instructions for additional taxes)		**22c**	
23	**Payments: a** 1998 estimated tax payments and amount applied from 1997 return	**23a**		
	b Tax deposited with Form 7004	**23b**		
	c Credit for Federal tax paid on fuels (attach Form 4136) . . .	**23c**		
	d Add lines 23a through 23c		**23d**	
24	Estimated tax penalty. Check if Form 2220 is attached . . . . ►☐		**24**	
25	**Tax due.** If the total of lines 22c and 24 is larger than line 23d, enter amount owed. See page 4 of the instructions for depository method of payment . . . . ►		**25**	
26	**Overpayment.** If line 23d is larger than the total of lines 22c and 24, enter amount overpaid ►		**26**	
27	Enter amount of line 26 you want: **Credited to 1999 estimated tax** ►	**Refunded** ►	**27**	

Please Sign Here

Under penalties of perjury, I declare that I have examined this return, including accompanying schedules and statements, and to the best of my knowledge and belief, it is true, correct, and complete. Declaration of preparer (other than taxpayer) is based on all information of which preparer has any knowledge.

► *Joseph R. Taxpayer*   *3/1/99*   ► *President*
Signature of officer   Date   Title

Paid Preparer's Use Only

Preparer's signature ►		Date	Check if self-employed ► ☐	Preparer's social security number
Firm's name (or yours if self-employed) and address ►			EIN ►
			ZIP code ►

For Paperwork Reduction Act Notice, see the separate instructions.   Cat. No. 11510H   Form **1120S** (1998)

| Schedule A | Cost of Goods Sold (see page 15 of the instructions) |

1	Inventory at beginning of year	1	41,580
2	Purchases.	2	371,943
3	Cost of labor .	3	
4	Additional section 263A costs *(attach schedule)* .	4	
5	Other costs *(attach schedule)*.	5	
6	**Total.** Add lines 1 through 5	6	413,523
7	Inventory at end of year	7	98,472
8	**Cost of goods sold.** Subtract line 7 from line 6. Enter here and on page 1, line 2 .	8	315,051

9a Check all methods used for valuing closing inventory:
  (i) ☐ Cost as described in Regulations section 1.471-3
  (ii) ☑ Lower of cost or market as described in Regulations section 1.471-4
  (iii) ☐ Other (specify method used and attach explanation) ▶ ....
  b Check if there was a writedown of "subnormal" goods as described in Regulations section 1.471-2(c) . . . . ▶ ☐
  c Check if the LIFO inventory method was adopted this tax year for any goods *(if checked, attach Form 970).* . . . . . ▶ ☐
  d If the LIFO inventory method was used for this tax year, enter percentage (or amounts) of closing
     inventory computed under LIFO . | **9d** |
  e Do the rules of section 263A (for property produced or acquired for resale) apply to the corporation? . . . . . ☐ Yes ☑ No
  f Was there any change in determining quantities, cost, or valuations between opening and closing inventory? . . ☐ Yes ☑ No
     If "Yes," attach explanation.

| Schedule B | Other Information |

		Yes	No
1	Check method of accounting: **(a)** ☐ Cash **(b)** ☑ Accrual **(c)** ☐ Other (specify) ▶		
2	Refer to the list on pages 26 through 28 of the instructions and state the corporation's principal:		
	(a) Business activity ▶ *339900 — manufacturer* **(b)** Product or service ▶ *widgets*		
3	Did the corporation at the end of the tax year own, directly or indirectly, 50% or more of the voting stock of a domestic corporation? (For rules of attribution, see section 267(c).) If "Yes," attach a schedule showing: **(a)** name, address, and employer identification number and **(b)** percentage owned.		✓
4	Was the corporation a member of a controlled group subject to the provisions of section 1561?		✓
5	At any time during calendar year 1998, did the corporation have an interest in or a signature or other authority over a financial account in a foreign country (such as a bank account, securities account, or other financial account)? (See page 15 of the instructions for exceptions and filing requirements for Form TD F 90-22.1.)		✓
	If "Yes," enter the name of the foreign country ▶		
6	During the tax year, did the corporation receive a distribution from, or was it the grantor of, or transferor to, a foreign trust? If "Yes," the corporation may have to file Form 3520. See page 15 of the instructions.		✓
7	Check this box if the corporation has filed or is required to file **Form 8264,** Application for Registration of a Tax Shelter .		
	. . . . ▶ ☐		
8	Check this box if the corporation issued publicly offered debt instruments with original issue discount . . ▶ ☐		
	If so, the corporation may have to file **Form 8281,** Information Return for Publicly Offered Original Issue Discount Instruments.		
9	If the corporation: **(a)** filed its election to be an S corporation after 1986, **(b)** was a C corporation before it elected to be an S corporation **or** the corporation acquired an asset with a basis determined by reference to its basis (or the basis of any other property) in the hands of a C corporation, and **(c)** has net unrealized built-in gain (defined in section 1374(d)(1)) in excess of the net recognized built-in gain from prior years, enter the net unrealized built-in gain reduced by net recognized built-in gain from prior years (see page 16 of the instructions) . . . . . ▶ $		
10	Check this box if the corporation had accumulated earnings and profits at the close of the tax year (see page 16 of the instructions) . . . . ▶ ☐		

Schedule K	**Shareholders' Shares of Income, Credits, Deductions, etc.**		
	(a) Pro rata share items		**(b) Total amount**

Income (Loss)

1	Ordinary income (loss) from trade or business activities (page 1, line 21)	**1**	39,270
2	Net income (loss) from rental real estate activities (attach Form 8825)	**2**	
3a	Gross income from other rental activities	**3a**	
b	Expenses from other rental activities (attach schedule). .	**3b**	
c	Net income (loss) from other rental activities. Subtract line 3b from line 3a	**3c**	
4	Portfolio income (loss):		
a	Interest income	**4a**	1,320
b	Ordinary dividends	**4b**	5,280
c	Royalty income	**4c**	
d	Net short-term capital gain (loss) (attach Schedule D (Form 1120S))	**4d**	
e	Net long-term capital gain (loss) (attach Schedule D (Form 1120S)):		
	(1) 28% rate gain (loss) ▶ .... (2) Total for year ▶	**4e(2)**	
f	Other portfolio income (loss) (attach schedule)	**4f**	
5	Net section 1231 gain (loss) (other than due to casualty or theft) (attach Form 4797) . .	**5**	
6	Other income (loss) (attach schedule)	**6**	

Deductions

7	Charitable contributions (attach schedule).	**7**	7,920
8	Section 179 expense deduction (attach Form 4562).	**8**	
9	Deductions related to portfolio income (loss) (itemize)	**9**	
10	Other deductions (attach schedule)	**10**	

Investment Interest

11a	Interest expense on investment debts	**11a**	990
b	(1) Investment income included on lines 4a, 4b, 4c, and 4f above	**11b(1)**	6,600
	(2) Investment expenses included on line 9 above	**11b(2)**	

Credits

12a	Credit for alcohol used as a fuel (attach Form 6478)	**12a**	
b	Low-income housing credit:		
	(1) From partnerships to which section 42(j)(5) applies for property placed in service before 1990	**12b(1)**	
	(2) Other than on line 12b(1) for property placed in service before 1990.	**12b(2)**	
	(3) From partnerships to which section 42(j)(5) applies for property placed in service after 1989	**12b(3)**	
	(4) Other than on line 12b(3) for property placed in service after 1989	**12b(4)**	
c	Qualified rehabilitation expenditures related to rental real estate activities (attach Form 3468) .	**12c**	
d	Credits (other than credits shown on lines 12b and 12c) related to rental real estate activities	**12d**	
e	Credits related to other rental activities	**12e**	
13	Other credits	**13**	1,980

Adjustments and Tax Preference Items

14a	Depreciation adjustment on property placed in service after 1986	**14a**	
b	Adjusted gain or loss	**14b**	
c	Depletion (other than oil and gas)	**14c**	
d	(1) Gross income from oil, gas, or geothermal properties	**14d(1)**	
	(2) Deductions allocable to oil, gas, or geothermal properties	**14d(2)**	
e	Other adjustments and tax preference items (attach schedule)	**14e**	

Foreign Taxes

15a	Type of income ▶		
b	Name of foreign country or U.S. possession		
c	Total gross income from sources outside the United States (attach schedule)	**15c**	
d	Total applicable deductions and losses (attach schedule)	**15d**	
e	Total foreign taxes (check one): ▶ ☐ Paid ☐ Accrued	**15e**	
f	Reduction in taxes available for credit (attach schedule)	**15f**	
g	Other foreign tax information (attach schedule)	**15g**	

Other

16	Section 59(e)(2) expenditures: a Type ▶ .... b Amount ▶	**16b**	
17	Tax-exempt interest income	**17**	1,650
18	Other tax-exempt income	**18**	
19	Nondeductible expenses	**19**	5,396
20	Total property distributions (including cash) other than dividends reported on line 22 below	**20**	21,450
21	Other items and amounts required to be reported separately to shareholders (attach schedule)		
22	Total dividend distributions paid from accumulated earnings and profits	**22**	
23	**Income (loss).** (Required only if Schedule M-1 must be completed.) Combine lines 1 through 6 in column (b). From the result, subtract the sum of lines 7 through 11a, 15e, and 16b	**23**	36,960

SCHEDULE K-1
(Form 1120S)

Department of the Treasury
Internal Revenue Service

Shareholder's Share of Income, Credits, Deductions, etc.

▶ See separate instructions.

For calendar year 1998 or tax year
beginning *January 1*, 1998, and ending *December 31*, 1998

1998

Shareholder's identifying number ▶	Corporation's identifying number ▶
Shareholder's name, address, and ZIP code	Corporation's name, address, and ZIP code
Deduction Shareholder *36 Cheerful Lane* *Somewhere, PA 19000*	*International Widgets, Inc.* *123 Commercial Road* *Anywhere, PA 19000*

A   Shareholder's percentage of stock ownership for tax year (see instructions for Schedule K-1) . . . . . ▶ *30* %
B   Internal Revenue Service Center where corporation filed its return ▶ .... *Philadelphia, PA* ....
C   Tax shelter registration number (see instructions for Schedule K-1) . . . . ▶ ....
D   Check applicable boxes: (1) ☐ Final K-1   (2) ☐ Amended K-1

	(a) Pro rata share items		(b) Amount	(c) Form 1040 filers enter the amount in column (b) on:
Income (Loss)	1 Ordinary income (loss) from trade or business activities . . .	**1**	*11,781*	See pages 4 and 5 of the Shareholder's Instructions for Schedule K-1 (Form 1120S).
	2 Net income (loss) from rental real estate activities	**2**		
	3 Net income (loss) from other rental activities	**3**		
	4 Portfolio income (loss):			
	a Interest	**4a**	*396*	Sch. B, Part I, line 1
	b Ordinary dividends	**4b**	*1,584*	Sch. B, Part II, line 5
	c Royalties	**4c**		Sch. E, Part I, line 4
	d Net short-term capital gain (loss).	**4d**		Sch. D, line 5, col. (f)
	e Net long-term capital gain (loss):			
	(1) 28% rate gain (loss)	**e(1)**		Sch. D, line 12, col. (g)
	(2) Total for year.	**e(2)**		Sch. D, line 12, col. (f)
	f Other portfolio income (loss) *(attach schedule)*	**4f**		*(Enter on applicable line of your return.)*
	5 Net section 1231 gain (loss) (other than due to casualty or theft)	**5**		See Shareholder's Instructions for Schedule K-1 (Form 1120S).
	6 Other income (loss) *(attach schedule)*	**6**		*(Enter on applicable line of your return.)*
Deductions	7 Charitable contributions *(attach schedule)*	**7**	*2,376*	Sch. A, line 15 or 16
	8 Section 179 expense deduction	**8**		See page 6 of the Shareholder's Instructions for Schedule K-1 (Form 1120S).
	9 Deductions related to portfolio income (loss) *(attach schedule)* .	**9**		
	10 Other deductions *(attach schedule)*	**10**		
Investment Interest	11a Interest expense on investment debts	**11a**	*297*	Form 4952, line 1
	b (1) Investment income included on lines 4a, 4b, 4c, and 4f above	**b(1)**	*1,980*	See Shareholder's Instructions for Schedule K-1 (Form 1120S).
	(2) Investment expenses included on line 9 above	**b(2)**		
Credits	12a Credit for alcohol used as fuel	**12a**		Form 6478, line 10
	b Low-income housing credit:			
	(1) From section 42(j)(5) partnerships for property placed in service before 1990.	**b(1)**		
	(2) Other than on line 12b(1) for property placed in service before 1990	**b(2)**		
	(3) From section 42(j)(5) partnerships for property placed in service after 1989	**b(3)**		Form 8586, line 5
	(4) Other than on line 12b(3) for property placed in service after 1989	**b(4)**		
	c Qualified rehabilitation expenditures related to rental real estate activities	**12c**		
	d Credits (other than credits shown on lines 12b and 12c) related to rental real estate activities	**12d**		See page 7 of the Shareholder's Instructions for Schedule K-1 (Form 1120S).
	e Credits related to other rental activities.	**12e**		
	13 Other credits	**13**	*594*	

For Paperwork Reduction Act Notice, see the Instructions for Form 1120S.   Cat. No. 11520D   **Schedule K-1 (Form 1120S) 1998**

	(a) Pro rata share items		(b) Amount	(c) Form 1040 filers enter the amount in column (b) on:
Adjustments and Tax Preference Items	**14a** Depreciation adjustment on property placed in service after 1986	**14a**		See page 7 of the Shareholder's Instructions for Schedule K-1 (Form 1120S) and Instructions for Form 6251
	b Adjusted gain or loss	**14b**		
	c Depletion (other than oil and gas)	**14c**		
	d (1) Gross income from oil, gas, or geothermal properties . . .	**d(1)**		
	(2) Deductions allocable to oil, gas, or geothermal properties .	**d(2)**		
	e Other adjustments and tax preference items *(attach schedule)* .	**14e**		
Foreign Taxes	**15a** Type of income ▶			Form 1116, Check boxes
	b Name of foreign country or U.S. possession ▶			
	c Total gross income from sources outside the United States *(attach schedule)*	**15c**		Form 1116, Part I
	d Total applicable deductions and losses *(attach schedule)* . .	**15d**		
	e Total foreign taxes (check one): ▶ ☐ Paid ☐ Accrued . .	**15e**		Form 1116, Part II
	f Reduction in taxes available for credit *(attach schedule)* . . .	**15f**		Form 1116, Part III
	g Other foreign tax information *(attach schedule)*	**15g**		See Instructions for Form 1116
Other	**16** Section 59(e)(2) expenditures: **a** Type ▶			See Shareholder's Instructions for Schedule K-1 (Form 1120S).
	b Amount	**16b**		
	17 Tax-exempt interest income	**17**	*495*	Form 1040, line 8b
	18 Other tax-exempt income	**18**		
	19 Nondeductible expenses	**19**	*1,619*	See pages 7 and 8 of the Shareholder's Instructions for Schedule K-1 (Form 1120S).
	20 Property distributions (including cash) other than dividend distributions reported to you on Form 1099-DIV . . .	**20**	*6,435*	
	21 Amount of loan repayments for "Loans From Shareholders" . .	**21**		
	22 Recapture of low-income housing credit:			
	a From section 42(j)(5) partnerships	**22a**		Form 8611, line 8
	b Other than on line 22a	**22b**		

23 Supplemental information required to be reported separately to each shareholder *(attach additional schedules if more space is needed)*:

Supplemental Information

Income Tax Forms for an "S" Corporation

Department of the Treasury
Internal Revenue Service

Instructions for Form 1120S

U.S. Income Tax Return for an S Corporation

Section references are to the Internal Revenue Code unless otherwise noted.

Paperwork Reduction Act Notice. We ask for the information on this form to carry out the Internal Revenue laws of the United States. You are required to give us the information. We need it to ensure that you are complying with these laws and to allow us to figure and collect the right amount of tax.

You are not required to provide the information requested on a form that is subject to the Paperwork Reduction Act unless the form displays a valid OMB control number. Books or records relating to a form or its instructions must be retained as long as their contents may become material in the administration of any Internal Revenue law. Generally, tax returns and return information are confidential, as required by section 6103.

The time needed to complete and file this form and related schedules will vary depending on individual circumstances. The estimated average times are:

Form	Recordkeeping	Learning about the law or the form	Preparing the form	Copying, assembling, and sending the form to the IRS
1120S	63 hr., 22 min.	21 hr., 21 min.	39 hr., 9 min.	4 hr., 34 min.
Sch. D (1120S)	10 hr., 31 min.	4 hr., 38 min.	9 hr., 39 min.	1 hr., 20 min.
Sch. K-1 (1120S)	15 hr., 32 min.	10 hr., 25 min.	14 hr., 50 min.	1 hr., 4 min.

If you have comments concerning the accuracy of these time estimates or suggestions for making these forms simpler, we would be happy to hear from you. You can write to the Tax Forms Committee, Western Area Distribution Center, Rancho Cordova, CA 95743-0001. **DO NOT** send the tax form to this address. Instead, see **Where To File** on page 3.

Changes To Note

● The new **Codes for Principal Business Activity** beginning on page 26 are based on the North American Industry Classification System (NAICS), which was developed by the statistical agencies of Canada, Mexico, and the United States in cooperation with the Office of Management and Budget. The NAICS-based codes replace the industry codes previously based on the Standard Industrial Classification (SIC) system.

● For tax years beginning after 1997, exempt organizations described in section 401(a) or 501(c)(3) are permitted to be shareholders.

Unresolved Tax Problems

Most problems can be resolved with one contact either by calling, writing, or visiting an IRS office. But if the corporation has tried unsuccessfully to resolve a problem with the IRS, it should contact the Taxpayer Advocate's Problem Resolution Program (PRP). Someone at PRP will assign the corporation a personal advocate who is in the best position to try to resolve the problem. The Taxpayer Advocate can also offer special help if the corporation has a significant hardship as a result of a tax problem.

Contact the Taxpayer Advocate if:
● The corporation has tried unsuccessfully to resolve a problem with the IRS and has not been contacted by the date promised, or
● The corporation is on its second attempt to resolve a problem.

You may contact a Taxpayer Advocate by calling a new toll-free assistance number, **1-877-777-4778**. Persons who have access to TTY/TDD equipment may call 1-800-828-4059 and ask for the Taxpayer Advocate. If the corporation prefers, it may write to the Taxpayer

Cat. No. 11515K

Advocate at the IRS office that last contacted the corporation.

While Taxpayer Advocates cannot change the tax law or make a technical tax decision, they can clear up problems that resulted from previous contacts and ensure that the corporation's case is given a complete and impartial review. Taxpayer Advocates are working to put service first. For more details, see **Pub. 1546,** The Problem Resolution Program of the Internal Revenue Service.

How To Make a Contribution To Reduce the Public Debt

To make a contribution to reduce the public debt, send a check made payable to "Bureau of the Public Debt" to Bureau of the Public Debt, Department G, Washington, DC 20239-0601. Or, enclose a check with Form 1120S. Contributions to reduce the public debt are deductible, subject to the rules and limitations for charitable contributions.

How To Get Forms and Publications

Personal Computer

Access the IRS's internet web site at **www.irs.ustreas.gov** to do the following:
- Download forms, instructions, and publications.
- See answers to frequently asked tax questions.
- Search publications on-line by topic or keyword.
- Send us comments or request help via e-mail.
- Sign up to receive hot tax issues and news by e-mail from the IRS Digital Dispatch.

You can also reach us using:
- Telnet at **iris.irs.ustreas.gov**
- File transfer protocol at **ftp.irs.ustreas.gov**
- Direct dial (by modem) at **703-321-8020**.

CD-ROM

Order **Pub. 1796,** Federal Tax Products on CD-ROM, and get:
- Current year forms, instructions, and publications.
- Prior year forms and instructions.
- Popular forms that may be filled in electronically, printed out for submission, and saved for recordkeeping.

Buy the CD-ROM on the Internet at **www.irs.ustreas.gov/cdorders** from the National Technical Information Service (NTIS) for $13 (plus a $5 handling fee), and save 35%, or call **1-877-CDFORMS** (1-877-233-6767) toll-free to buy the CD-ROM for $20 (plus a $5 handling fee).

By Phone and in Person

You can order forms and publications 24 hours a day, 7 days a week, by calling **1-800-TAX-FORM** (1-800-829-3676). You

can also get most forms and publications at your local IRS office.

General Instructions

Purpose of Form

Form 1120S is used to report the income, deductions, gains, losses, etc., of a domestic corporation that has elected to be an S corporation by filing **Form 2553,** Election by a Small Business Corporation, and whose election is in effect for the tax year.

Who Must File

A corporation must file Form 1120S if **(a)** it elected to be an S corporation by filing Form 2553, **(b)** the IRS accepted the election, and **(c)** the election remains in effect. **Do not** file Form 1120S for any tax year before the year the election takes effect.

Termination of Election

Once the election is made, it stays in effect until it is terminated. If the election is terminated in a tax year beginning after 1996, the corporation (or a successor corporation) can make another election on Form 2553 only with IRS consent for any tax year before the 5th tax year after the first tax year in which the termination took effect. See Regulations section 1.1362-5 for more details.

An election terminates **automatically** in any of the following cases:

1. The corporation is no longer a small business corporation as defined in section 1361(b). The termination of an election in this manner is effective as of the day on which the corporation no longer meets the definition of a small business corporation. If the election terminates for this reason, attach to Form 1120S for the final year of the S corporation a statement notifying the IRS of the termination and the date it occurred.

2. The corporation, for each of three consecutive tax years, **(a)** has accumulated earnings and profits and **(b)** derives more than 25% of its gross receipts from passive investment income as defined in section 1362(d)(3)(C). The election terminates on the first day of the first tax year beginning after the third consecutive tax year. The corporation must pay a tax for each year it has excess net passive income. See the instructions for line 22a for details on how to figure the tax.

3. The election is revoked. An election may be revoked only with the consent of shareholders who, at the time the revocation is made, hold more than 50% of the number of issued and outstanding shares of stock (including non-voting stock). The revocation may specify an effective revocation date that is on or after the day the revocation is filed. If no date is specified, the revocation is effective at the start of a tax year if the revocation is

made on or before the 15th day of the 3rd month of that tax year. If no date is specified and the revocation is made after the 15th day of the 3rd month of the tax year, the revocation is effective at the start of the next tax year.

To revoke the election, the corporation must file a statement with the service center where it filed its election to be an S corporation. In the statement, the corporation must notify the IRS that it is revoking its election to be an S corporation. The statement must be signed by each shareholder who consents to the revocation and contain the information required by Regulations section 1.1362-6(a)(3). A revocation may be rescinded before it takes effect. See Regulations section 1.1362-6(a)(4) for details.

For rules on allocating income and deductions between an S short year and a C short year and other special rules that apply when an election is terminated, see section 1362(e) and Regulations section 1.1362-3.

If an election was terminated under **1** or **2** above, and the corporation believes the termination was inadvertent, the corporation may request permission from the IRS to continue to be treated as an S corporation. See Regulations section 1.1362-4 for the specific requirements that must be met to qualify for inadvertent termination relief.

When To File

In general, file Form 1120S by the 15th day of the 3rd month following the date the corporation's tax year ended as shown at the top of Form 1120S. For calendar year corporations, the due date is March 15, 1999. If the due date falls on a Saturday, Sunday, or legal holiday, file on the next business day. A business day is any day that is not a Saturday, Sunday, or legal holiday.

If the S election was terminated during the tax year, file Form 1120S for the S short year by the due date (including extensions) of the C short year return.

Private Delivery Services

You can use certain private delivery services designated by the IRS to meet the "timely filing as timely filing/paying" rule for tax returns and payments. The IRS publishes a list of designated private delivery services in September of each year. The list published in September 1998 includes only the following:
- Airborne Express (Airborne): Overnight Air Express Service, Next Afternoon Service, Second Day Service.
- DHL Worldwide Express (DHL): DHL "Same Day" Service, DHL USA Overnight.
- Federal Express (FedEx): FedEx Priority Overnight, FedEx Standard Overnight, FedEx 2Day.
- United Parcel Service (UPS): UPS Next Day Air, UPS Next Day Air Saver, UPS 2nd Day Air, UPS 2nd Day Air A.M.

The private delivery service can tell you how to get written proof of the mailing date.

Extension

Use **Form 7004,** Application for Automatic Extension of Time To File Corporation Income Tax Return, to request an automatic 6-month extension of time to file Form 1120S.

Period Covered

File the 1998 return for calendar year 1998 and fiscal years beginning in 1998 and ending in 1999. If the return is for a fiscal year or a short tax year, fill in the tax year space at the top of the form.

Note: *The 1998 Form 1120S may also be used if (a) the corporation has a tax year of less than 12 months that begins and ends in 1999 and (b) the 1999 Form 1120S is not available by the time the corporation is required to file its return. However, the corporation must show its 1999 tax year on the 1998 Form 1120S and incorporate any tax law changes that are effective for tax years beginning after December 31, 1998.*

Where To File

File your return at the applicable IRS address listed below.

If the corporation's principal business, office, or agency is located in	Use the following Internal Revenue Service Center address
New Jersey, New York (New York City and counties of Nassau, Rockland, Suffolk, and Westchester)	Holtsville, NY 00501-0013
New York (all other counties), Connecticut, Maine, Massachusetts, New Hampshire, Rhode Island, Vermont	Andover, MA 05501-0013
Florida, Georgia, South Carolina	Atlanta, GA 39901-0013
Indiana, Kentucky, Michigan, Ohio, West Virginia	Cincinnati, OH 45999-0013
Kansas, New Mexico, Oklahoma, Texas	Austin, TX 73301-0013
Illinois, Iowa, Minnesota, Missouri, Wisconsin	Kansas City, MO 64999-0013
Alabama, Arkansas, Louisiana, Mississippi, North Carolina, Tennessee	Memphis, TN 37501-0013
Alaska, Arizona, California (counties of Alpine, Amador, Butte, Calaveras, Colusa, Contra Costa, Del Norte, El Dorado, Glenn, Humboldt, Lake, Lassen, Marin, Mendocino, Modoc, Napa, Nevada, Placer, Plumas, Sacramento, San Joaquin, Shasta, Sierra, Siskiyou, Solano, Sonoma, Sutter, Tehama, Trinity, Yolo, and Yuba), Colorado, Idaho, Montana, Nebraska, Nevada, North Dakota, Oregon, South Dakota, Utah, Washington, Wyoming	Ogden, UT 84201-0013
California (all other counties), Hawaii	Fresno, CA 93888-0013
Delaware, District of Columbia, Maryland, Pennsylvania, Virginia	Philadelphia, PA 19255-0013

Who Must Sign

The return must be signed and dated by the president, vice president, treasurer, assistant treasurer, chief accounting officer, or any other corporate officer (such as a tax officer) authorized to sign. A receiver, trustee, or assignee must sign and date any return he or she is required to file on behalf of a corporation.

If a corporate officer filled in Form 1120S, the Paid Preparer's space under "Signature of officer" should remain blank. If someone prepares Form 1120S and does not charge the corporation, that person should not sign the return. Certain others who prepare Form 1120S should not sign. For example, a regular, full-time employee of the corporation such as a clerk, secretary, etc., should not sign.

Generally, anyone paid to prepare Form 1120S must sign the return and fill in the other blanks in the Paid Preparer's Use Only area of the return.

The preparer required to sign the return MUST complete the required preparer information and:

● Sign it, by hand, in the space provided for the preparer's signature. (Signature stamps or labels are not acceptable.)

● Give a copy of Form 1120S to the taxpayer in addition to the copy filed with the IRS.

Accounting Methods

Figure ordinary income using the method of accounting regularly used in keeping the corporation's books and records. Generally, permissible methods include:

● Cash,

● Accrual, or

● Any other method permitted by the Internal Revenue Code.

In all cases, the method adopted must clearly reflect income.

Generally, an S corporation may not use the cash method of accounting if the corporation is a tax shelter (as defined in section 448(d)(3)). See section 448 for details.

Under the accrual method, an amount is includible in income when:

● All the events have occurred that fix the right to receive the income, and

● The amount can be determined with reasonable accuracy.

See Regulations section 1.451-1(a) for details.

Generally, an accrual basis taxpayer can deduct accrued expenses in the tax year in which:

● All events that determine liability have occurred,

● The amount of the liability can be figured with reasonable accuracy, and

● Economic performance takes place with respect to the expense. There are exceptions for certain items, including recurring expenses. See section 461(h) and the related regulations for the rules for determining when economic performance takes place.

Except for certain home construction contracts and other real property small construction contracts, long-term contracts must generally be accounted for using the percentage of completion method described in section 460.

Mark-to-Market Accounting Method for Dealers in Securities

Dealers in securities must use the "mark-to-market" accounting method described in section 475. Under this method, any security that is inventory to the dealer must be included in inventory at its fair market value. Any security that is not inventory and that is held at the close of the tax year is treated as sold at its fair market value on the last business day of the tax year, and any gain or loss must be taken into account in determining gross income. The gain or loss taken into account is generally treated as ordinary gain or loss. For details, including exceptions, see section 475 and the related regulations.

Note: *Dealers in commodities, and traders in securities and commodities, may make an election to use the mark-to-market accounting method. See sections 475(e) and (f) for details.*

Change in Accounting Method

Generally, the corporation may change its method of accounting used to report taxable income (for income as a whole or for any material item) only by getting consent on **Form 3115,** Application for Change in Accounting Method. For more information, see **Pub. 538,** Accounting Periods and Methods.

Accounting Periods

Generally, an S corporation may not change its accounting period to a tax year that is not a permitted year. A "permitted year" is a calendar year or any other accounting period for which the corporation can establish to the satisfaction of the IRS that there is a business purpose for the tax year.

To change an accounting period, see Regulations section 1.442-1 and **Form 1128,** Application To Adopt, Change, or Retain a Tax Year. Also see Pub. 538.

Election of a Tax Year Other Than a Required Year

Under the provisions of section 444, an S corporation may elect to have a tax year other than a permitted year, but only if the deferral period of the tax year is not longer than the shorter of 3 months or the deferral period of the tax year being changed. This election is made by filing **Form 8716,** Election To Have a Tax Year Other Than a Required Tax Year.

An S corporation may not make or continue an election under section 444 if it is a member of a tiered structure, other than a tiered structure that consists entirely of partnerships and S corporations that have the same tax year. For the S corporation to have a section 444 election in effect, it must make the payments required by section 7519 and file **Form 8752,** Required Payment or Refund Under Section 7519.

A section 444 election ends if an S corporation changes its accounting period to a calendar year or some other permitted year; it is penalized for willfully failing to comply with the requirements of section 7519; or its S election is terminated (unless it immediately becomes a personal service corporation). If the termination results in a short tax year, type or legibly print at the top of the first page of Form 1120S for the short tax year, "SECTION 444 ELECTION TERMINATED."

Rounding Off to Whole Dollars

You may round off cents to whole dollars on your return and accompanying schedules. To do so, drop amounts under 50 cents and increase amounts from 50 to 99 cents to the next higher dollar.

Recordkeeping

The corporation's records must be kept as long as they may be needed for the administration of any provision of the Internal Revenue Code. Usually, records that support an item of income, deduction, or credit on the corporation's return must be kept for 3 years from the date each shareholder's return is due or is filed, whichever is later. Keep records that verify the corporation's basis in property for as long as they are needed to figure the basis of the original or replacement property.

The corporation should also keep copies of any returns it has filed. They help in preparing future returns and in making computations when filing an amended return.

Depository Method of Tax Payment

The corporation must pay the tax due in full no later than the 15th day of the 3rd month after the end of the tax year. Some corporations (described below) are required to electronically deposit all depository taxes, including corporation income tax payments.

Electronic Deposit Requirement

The corporation must make electronic deposits of all depository tax liabilities that occur after 1998 if:
- It was required to electronically deposit taxes in prior years,
- It deposited more than $50,000 in social security, Medicare, and withheld income taxes in 1997, or
- It **did not** deposit social security, Medicare, or withheld income taxes in 1997, but deposited more than $50,000 in other taxes under section 6302 (such as corporate income taxes) in 1997.

For details, see Regulations section 31.6302-1(h).

The Electronic Federal Tax Payment System (EFTPS) must be used to make electronic deposits. If the corporation is required to make electronic deposits and fails to do so, it may be subject to a 10% penalty.

Note: *A penalty will not be imposed for tax liabilities that occur prior to July 1, 1999, if the corporation was first required to use EFTPS on or after July 1, 1997.*

Corporations that are not required to make electronic deposits may voluntarily participate in EFTPS. To enroll in EFTPS, call 1-800-945-8400 or 1-800-555-4477. For general information on EFTPS, call 1-800-829-1040.

Deposits With Form 8109

If the corporation does not use EFTPS, deposit corporation income tax payments (and estimated tax payments) with **Form 8109,** Federal Tax Deposit Coupon. Do not send deposits directly to an IRS office; otherwise, the corporation may have to pay a penalty. Mail or deliver the completed Form 8109 with the payment to a qualified depositary for Federal taxes or to the Federal Reserve bank (FRB) servicing the corporation's geographic area. Make checks or money orders payable to that depositary or FRB.

To help ensure proper crediting, write the corporation's employer identification number, the tax period to which the deposit applies, and "Form 1120S" on the check or money order. Be sure to darken the "1120" box on the coupon. Records of these deposits will be sent to the IRS.

For more information on deposits, see the instructions in the coupon booklet (Form 8109) and **Pub. 583,** Starting a Business and Keeping Records.

Estimated Tax

Generally, the corporation must make estimated tax payments for the following taxes if the total of these taxes is $500 or more: **(a)** the tax on certain capital gains, **(b)** the tax on built-in gains, **(c)** the excess net passive income tax, and **(d)** the investment credit recapture tax.

The amount of estimated tax required to be paid annually is the smaller of **(a)** the total of the above taxes shown on the return for the tax year (or if no return is filed, the total of these taxes for the year) or **(b)** the sum of *(i)* the investment credit recapture tax and the built-in gains tax (or the tax on certain capital gains) shown on the return for the tax year (or if no return is filed, the total of these taxes for the year), and *(ii)* any excess net passive income tax shown on the corporation's return for the preceding tax year. If the preceding tax year was less than 12 months, the estimated tax must be determined under **(a).**

The estimated tax is generally payable in four equal installments. However, the corporation may be able to lower the amount of one or more installments by using the annualized income installment method or adjusted seasonal installment method under section 6655(e).

For a calendar year corporation, the payments are due for 1999 by April 15, June 15, September 15, and December 15. For a fiscal year corporation, they are due by the 15th day of the 4th, 6th, 9th, and 12th months of the fiscal year.

The corporation must make the payments using the depository method described above.

Interest and Penalties

Interest

Interest is charged on taxes not paid by the due date, even if an extension of time to file is granted. Interest is also charged from the due date (including extensions) to the date of payment on the failure to file penalty, the accuracy-related penalty, and the fraud penalty. The interest charge is figured at a rate determined under section 6621.

Late Filing of Return

A corporation that does not file its tax return by the due date, including extensions, may have to pay a penalty of 5% a month, or part of a month, up to a maximum of 25%, for each month the return is not filed. The penalty is imposed on the net amount due. The minimum penalty for filing a return more than 60 days late is the smaller of the tax due or $100. The penalty will not be imposed if the corporation can show that the failure to file on time was due to reasonable cause. If the failure is due to reasonable cause, attach an explanation to the return.

Late Payment of Tax

A corporation that does not pay the tax when due generally may have to pay a penalty of ½ of 1% a month or part of a month, up to a maximum of 25%, for each month the tax is not paid. The penalty is imposed on the net amount due.

The penalty will not be imposed if the corporation can show that failure to pay on time was due to reasonable cause.

Failure To Furnish Information Timely

Section 6037(b) requires an S corporation to furnish to each shareholder a copy of the information shown on Schedule K-1 (Form 1120S) that is attached to Form 1120S. Provide Schedule K-1 to each shareholder on or before the day on which the corporation files Form 1120S.

For each failure to furnish Schedule K-1 to a shareholder when due and each failure to include on Schedule K-1 all the information required to be shown (or the inclusion of incorrect information), a $50 penalty may be imposed with regard to each Schedule K-1 for which a failure occurs. If the requirement to report correct information is intentionally disregarded, each $50 penalty is increased to $100 or, if greater, 10% of the aggregate amount of items required to be reported. See sections 6722 and 6724 for more information.

The penalty will not be imposed if the corporation can show that not furnishing information timely was due to reasonable cause and not due to willful neglect.

Trust Fund Recovery Penalty

This penalty may apply if certain excise, income, social security, and Medicare taxes that must be collected or withheld are not collected or withheld, or these taxes are not paid to the IRS. These taxes are generally reported on Forms 720, 941, 943, or 945. The trust fund recovery penalty may be imposed on all persons who are determined by the IRS to have been **responsible** for collecting, accounting for, and paying over these taxes, and who acted willfully in not doing so. The penalty is equal to the unpaid trust fund tax. See the instructions for Form 720, **Pub. 15 (Circular E)**, Employer's Tax Guide, or **Pub. 51 (Circular A)**, Agricultural Employer's Tax Guide, for more details, including the definition of responsible persons.

Other Forms and Statements That May Be Required

• **Forms W-2** and **W-3**, Wage and Tax Statement; and Transmittal of Wage and Tax Statements.
• **Form 720**, Quarterly Federal Excise Tax Return. Use Form 720 to report environmental excise taxes, communications and air transportation taxes, fuel taxes, luxury tax on passenger vehicles, manufacturers' taxes, ship passenger tax, and certain other excise taxes.
Caution: *See Trust Fund Recovery Penalty above.*
• **Form 926**, Return by a U.S. Transferor of Property to a Foreign Corporation. Use this form to report certain information required under section 6038B.
• **Form 940** or **Form 940-EZ**, Employer's Annual Federal Unemployment (FUTA) Tax Return. The corporation may be liable for FUTA tax and may have to file Form 940 or 940-EZ if it paid wages of $1,500 or more in any calendar quarter during the calendar year (or the preceding calendar year) or one or more employees worked for the corporation for some part of a day in any 20 different weeks during the calendar year (or the preceding calendar year). A corporate officer who performs substantial services is considered an employee. Except as provided in section 3306(a), reasonable compensation for these services is subject to FUTA tax, no matter what the corporation calls the payments.
• **Form 941**, Employer's Quarterly Federal Tax Return. Employers must file this form quarterly to report income tax withheld on wages and employer and employee social security and Medicare taxes. A corporate officer who performs substantial services is considered an employee. Except as provided in sections 3121(a) and 3401(a), reasonable compensation for these services is

subject to employer and employee social security and Medicare taxes and income tax withholding, no matter what the corporation calls the payments. Agricultural employers must file **Form 943**, Employer's Annual Tax Return for Agricultural Employees, instead of Form 941, to report income tax withheld and employer and employee social security and Medicare taxes on farmworkers.
Caution: *See Trust Fund Recovery Penalty above.*
• **Form 945**, Annual Return of Withheld Federal Income Tax. Use this form to report income tax withheld from nonpayroll payments, including pensions, annuities, IRAs, gambling winnings, and backup withholding.
Caution: *See Trust Fund Recovery Penalty above.*
• **Form 966**, Corporate Dissolution or Liquidation.
• **Forms 1042** and **1042-S**, Annual Withholding Tax Return for U.S. Source Income of Foreign Persons; and Foreign Person's U.S. Source Income Subject to Withholding. Use these forms to report and transmit withheld tax on payments made to nonresident alien individuals, foreign partnerships, or foreign corporations to the extent such payments constitute gross income from sources within the United States (see sections 861 through 865). For more information, see sections 1441 and 1442, and **Pub. 515**, Withholding of Tax on Nonresident Aliens and Foreign Corporations.
• **Form 1096**, Annual Summary and Transmittal of U.S. Information Returns.
• **Form 1098**, Mortgage Interest Statement. Use this form to report the receipt from any individual of $600 or more of mortgage interest and points in the course of the corporation's trade or business.
• **Forms 1099-A, B, C, DIV, INT, LTC, MISC, MSA, OID, PATR, R,** and **S.** You may have to file these information returns to report acquisitions or abandonments of secured property; proceeds from broker and barter exchange transactions; cancellation of debt; certain dividends and distributions; interest payments; payments of long-term care and accelerated death benefits; miscellaneous income payments; distributions from a medical savings account; original issue discount; distributions from cooperatives to their patrons; distributions from pensions, annuities, retirement or profit-sharing plans, IRAs, insurance contracts, etc.; and proceeds from real estate transactions. Also use certain of these returns to report amounts that were received as a nominee on behalf of another person.

Use Form 1099-DIV to report actual dividends paid by the corporation. Only distributions from accumulated earnings and profits are classified as dividends. **Do not** issue Form 1099-DIV for dividends received by the corporation that are allocated to shareholders on line 4b of Schedule K-1.

For more information, see the Instructions for Forms 1099, 1098, 5498, and W-2G.
Note: *Every corporation must file Forms 1099-MISC if it makes payments of rents, commissions, or other fixed or determinable income (see section 6041) totaling $600 or more to any one person in the course of its trade or business during the calendar year.*
• **Form 5471**, Information Return of U.S. Persons With Respect to Certain Foreign Corporations. A corporation may have to file Form 5471 if any of the following apply:
   1. It controls a foreign corporation.
   2. It acquires, disposes of, or owns 5% or more in value of the outstanding stock of a foreign corporation.
   3. It owns stock in a corporation that is a controlled foreign corporation for an uninterrupted period of 30 days or more during any tax year of the foreign corporation, and it owned that stock on the last day of that year.
• **Form 5713**, International Boycott Report. Every corporation that had operations in, or related to, a "boycotting" country, company, or national of a country must file Form 5713 to report those operations and figure the loss of certain tax benefits.
• **Form 8264**, Application for Registration of a Tax Shelter. Tax shelter organizers must file Form 8264 to register tax shelters with the IRS for the purpose of receiving a tax shelter registration number.
• **Form 8271**, Investor Reporting of Tax Shelter Registration Number. Corporations that have acquired an interest in a tax shelter that is required to be registered use Form 8271 to report the tax shelter's registration number. Attach Form 8271 to any return on which a deduction, credit, loss, or other tax benefit attributable to a tax shelter is taken or any income attributable to a tax shelter is reported.
• **Form 8275**, Disclosure Statement. File Form 8275 to disclose items or positions, except those contrary to a regulation, that are not otherwise adequately disclosed on a tax return. The disclosure is made to avoid the parts of the accuracy-related penalty imposed for disregard of rules or substantial understatement of tax. Form 8275 is also used for disclosures relating to preparer penalties for understatements due to unrealistic positions or disregard of rules.
• **Form 8275-R**, Regulation Disclosure Statement, is used to disclose any item on a tax return for which a position has been taken that is contrary to Treasury regulations.
• **Form 8281**, Information Return for Publicly Offered Original Issue Discount Instruments. This form is used by issuers of publicly offered debt instruments having OID to provide the information required by section 1275(c).
• **Forms 8288** and **8288-A**, U.S. Withholding Tax Return for Dispositions

Instructions for Form 1120S

Page 5

by Foreign Persons of U.S. Real Property Interests; and Statement of Withholding on Dispositions by Foreign Persons of U.S. Real Property Interests. Use these forms to report and transmit withheld tax on the sale of U.S. real property by a foreign person. See section 1445 and the related regulations for additional information.

• **Form 8300,** Report of Cash Payments Over $10,000 Received in a Trade or Business. File this form to report the receipt of more than $10,000 in cash or foreign currency in one transaction (or a series of related transactions).

• **Form 8594,** Asset Acquisition Statement. Both the purchaser and seller of a group of assets constituting a trade or business must file this form if section 197 intangibles attach, or could attach, to such assets and if the purchaser's basis in the assets is determined only by the amount paid for the assets.

• **Form 8697,** Interest Computation Under the Look-Back Method for Completed Long-Term Contracts. Certain S corporations that are not closely held may have to file Form 8697. Form 8697 is used to figure the interest due or to be refunded under the look-back method of section 460(b)(2) on certain long-term contracts that are accounted for under either the percentage of completion-capitalized cost method or the percentage of completion method. Closely held corporations should see the instructions on page 23 for line 23, item 10, of Schedule K-1 for details on the Form 8697 information they must provide to their shareholders.

• **Form 8866,** Interest Computation Under the Look-Back Method for Property Depreciated Under the Income Forecast Method. Certain S corporations that are not closely held may have to file Form 8866. Form 8866 is used to figure the interest due or to be refunded under the look-back method of section 167(g)(2) for certain property placed in service after September 13, 1995, and depreciated under the income forecast method. Closely held corporations should see the instructions on page 24 for line 23, item 17, of Schedule K-1 for details on the Form 8666 information they must provide to their shareholders.

Statements

Stock ownership in foreign corporations. If the corporation owned at least 5% in value of the outstanding stock of a foreign personal holding company, and the corporation was required to include in its gross income any undistributed foreign personal holding company income, attach the statement required by section 551(c).

Transfers to a corporation controlled by the transferor. If a person receives stock of a corporation in exchange for property, and no gain or loss is recognized under section 351, the transferor and transferee must each attach to their tax returns the information required by Regulations section 1.351-3.

Attachments

Attach **Form 4136,** Credit for Federal Tax Paid on Fuels, after page 4, Form 1120S. Attach schedules in alphabetical order and other forms in numerical order after Form 4136.

To assist us in processing the return, **please complete every applicable entry space on Form 1120S and Schedule K-1.** If you attach statements, do not write "See attached" instead of completing the entry spaces on Form 1120S and Schedule K-1.

If you need more space on the forms or schedules, attach separate sheets. Use the same size and format as on the printed forms. **But show the totals on the printed forms.** Attach these separate sheets after all the schedules and forms. Be sure to put the corporation's name and employer identification number (EIN) on each sheet.

Amended Return

To correct an error on a Form 1120S already filed, file an amended Form 1120S and check box F(4). If the amended return results in a change to income, or a change in the distribution of any income or other information provided any shareholder, an amended Schedule K-1 (Form 1120S) must also be filed with the amended Form 1120S and given to that shareholder. Be sure to check box D(2) on each Schedule K-1 to indicate that it is an amended Schedule K-1.

A change to the corporation's Federal return may affect its state return. This includes changes made as the result of an IRS examination of Form 1120S. For more information, contact the state tax agency for the state in which the corporation's return was filed.

Passive Activity Limitations

In general, section 469 limits the amount of losses, deductions, and credits that shareholders may claim from "passive activities." The passive activity limitations do not apply to the corporation. Instead, they apply to each shareholder's share of any income or loss and credit attributable to a passive activity. Because the treatment of each shareholder's share of corporate income or loss and credit depends upon the nature of the activity that generated it, the corporation must report income or loss and credits separately for each activity.

The instructions below (pages 6 through 10) and the instructions for Schedules K and K-1 (pages 16 through 24) explain the applicable passive activity limitation rules and specify the type of information the corporation must provide to its shareholders for each activity. If the corporation had more than one activity, it must report information for each activity on an attachment to Schedules K and K-1.

Generally, passive activities include **(a)** activities that involve the conduct of a trade or business in which the shareholder does not materially participate and **(b)** any rental activity (defined on page 7) even if the shareholder materially participates. For exceptions, see **Activities That Are Not Passive Activities** below. The level of each shareholder's participation in an activity must be determined by the shareholder.

The passive activity rules provide that losses and credits from passive activities can generally be applied only against income and tax from passive activities. Thus, passive losses and credits cannot be applied against income from salaries, wages, professional fees, or a business in which the shareholder materially participates; against "portfolio income" (defined on page 8); or against the tax related to any of these types of income.

Special rules require that net income from certain activities that would otherwise be treated as passive income must be recharacterized as nonpassive income for purposes of the passive activity limitations.

To allow each shareholder to apply the passive activity limitations at the individual level, the corporation must report income or loss and credits separately for each of the following: trade or business activities, rental real estate activities, rental activities other than rental real estate, and portfolio income.

Activities That Are Not Passive Activities

Passive activities do not include:

1. Trade or business activities in which the shareholder materially participated for the tax year.

2. Any rental real estate activity in which the shareholder materially participated and met both of the following conditions for the tax year:

a. More than half of the personal services the shareholder performed in trades or businesses were performed in real property trades or businesses in which he or she materially participated, and

b. The shareholder performed more than 750 hours of services in real property trades or businesses in which he or she materially participated.

For purposes of this rule, each interest in rental real estate is a separate activity unless the shareholder elects to treat all interests in rental real estate as one activity.

If the shareholder is married filing jointly, either the shareholder or his or her spouse must separately meet both of the above conditions, without taking into account services performed by the other spouse.

A real property trade or business is any real property development, redevelopment, construction, reconstruction, acquisition, conversion, rental, operation, management, leasing,

Page 6

or brokerage trade or business. Services the shareholder performed as an employee are not treated as performed in a real property trade or business unless he or she owned more than 5% of the stock in the employer.

3. The rental of a dwelling unit used by a shareholder for personal purposes during the year for more than the greater of 14 days or 10% of the number of days that the residence was rented at fair rental value.

4. An activity of trading personal property for the account of owners of interests in the activity. See Temporary Regulations section 1.469-1T(e)(6).

Note: *The section 469(c)(3) exception for a working interest in oil and gas properties does not apply to an S corporation because state law generally limits the liability of corporate shareholders.*

Trade or Business Activities

A trade or business activity is an activity (other than a rental activity or an activity treated as incidental to an activity of holding property for investment) that—

1. Involves the conduct of a trade or business (within the meaning of section 162),

2. Is conducted in anticipation of starting a trade or business, or

3. Involves research or experimental expenditures deductible under section 174 (or that would be if you chose to deduct rather than capitalize them).

If the shareholder does not materially participate in the activity, a trade or business activity of the corporation is a passive activity for the shareholder.

Each shareholder must determine if he or she materially participated in an activity. As a result, while the corporation's overall trade or business income (loss) is reported on page 1 of Form 1120S, the specific income and deductions from each separate trade or business activity must be reported on attachments to Form 1120S. Similarly, while each shareholder's allocable share of the corporation's overall trade or business income (loss) is reported on line 1 of Schedule K-1, each shareholder's allocable share of the income and deductions from each trade or business activity must be reported on attachments to each Schedule K-1. See **Passive Activity Reporting Requirements** on page 9 for more information.

Rental Activities

Generally, except as noted below, if the gross income from an activity consists of amounts paid principally for the use of real or personal tangible property held by the corporation, the activity is a rental activity.

There are several exceptions to this general rule. Under these exceptions, an activity involving the use of real or personal tangible property is not a rental activity if any of the following apply:

● The average period of customer use (defined below) for such property is 7 days or less.

● The average period of customer use for such property is 30 days or less and significant personal services (defined below) are provided by or on behalf of the corporation.

● Extraordinary personal services (defined below) are provided by or on behalf of the corporation.

● Rental of the property is treated as incidental to a nonrental activity of the corporation under Temporary Regulations section 1.469-1T(e)(3)(vi) and Regulations section 1.469-1(e)(3)(vi).

● The corporation customarily makes the property available during defined business hours for nonexclusive use by various customers.

● The corporation provides property for use in a nonrental activity of a partnership in its capacity as an owner of an interest in such partnership. Whether the corporation provides property used in an activity of a partnership in the corporation's capacity as an owner of an interest in the partnership is based on all the facts and circumstances.

In addition, a guaranteed payment described in section 707(c) is not income from a rental activity under any circumstances.

Average period of customer use. Figure the average period of customer use of property by dividing the total number of days in all rental periods by the number of rentals during the tax year. If the activity involves renting more than one class of property, multiply the average period of customer use of each class by the ratio of the gross rental income from that class to the activity's total gross rental income. The activity's average period of customer use equals the sum of these class-by-class average periods weighted by gross income. See Regulations section 1.469-1(e)(3)(iii).

Significant personal services. Personal services include only services performed by individuals. In determining whether personal services are significant personal services, consider all of the relevant facts and circumstances. Relevant facts and circumstances include how often the services are provided, the type and amount of labor required to perform the services, and the value of the services in relation to the amount charged for the use of the property.

The following services are not considered in determining whether personal services are significant:

● Services necessary to permit the lawful use of the rental property.

● Services performed in connection with improvements or repairs to the rental property that extend the useful life of the property substantially beyond the average rental period.

● Services provided in connection with the use of any improved real property that are similar to those commonly provided in connection with long-term rentals of high-grade commercial or residential property. Examples include cleaning and maintenance of common areas, routine repairs, trash collection, elevator service, and security at entrances.

Extraordinary personal services. Services provided in connection with making rental property available for customer use are extraordinary personal services only if the services are performed by individuals and the customers' use of the rental property is incidental to their receipt of the services. For example, a patient's use of a hospital room generally is incidental to the care that the patient receives from the hospital's medical staff. Similarly, a student's use of a dormitory room in a boarding school is incidental to the personal services provided by the school's teaching staff.

Rental property incidental to a nonrental activity. An activity is not a rental activity if the rental of the property is incidental to a nonrental activity, such as the activity of holding property for investment, a trade or business activity, or the activity of dealing in property.

Rental of property is incidental to an activity of holding property for investment if both of the following apply:

● The main purpose for holding the property is to realize a gain from the appreciation of the property.

● The gross rental income from such property for the tax year is less than 2% of the smaller of the property's unadjusted basis or its fair market value.

Rental of property is incidental to a trade or business activity if all of the following apply:

● The corporation owns an interest in the trade or business at all times during the year.

● The rental property was mainly used in the trade or business activity during the tax year or during at least 2 of the 5 preceding tax years.

● The gross rental income from the property is less than 2% of the smaller of the property's unadjusted basis or its fair market value.

The sale or exchange of property that is also rented during the tax year (where the gain or loss is recognized) is treated as incidental to the activity of dealing in property if, at the time of the sale or exchange, the property was held primarily for sale to customers in the ordinary course of the corporation's trade or business.

See Temporary Regulations section 1.469-1T(e)(3) and Regulations section 1.469-1(e)(3) for more information on the definition of rental activities for purposes of the passive activity limitations.

Reporting of rental activities. In reporting the corporation's income or losses and credits from rental activities, the corporation must separately report **(a)** rental real estate activities and **(b)** rental activities other than rental real estate activities.

Shareholders who actively participate in a rental real estate activity may be able to deduct part or all of their rental real estate losses (and the deduction equivalent of rental real estate credits) against income (or tax) from nonpassive activities. Generally, the combined amount of rental real estate losses and the deduction equivalent of rental real estate credits from all sources (including rental real estate activities not held through the corporation) that may be claimed is limited to $25,000.

Report rental real estate activity income (loss) on **Form 8825,** Rental Real Estate Income and Expenses of a Partnership or an S Corporation, and on line 2 of Schedules K and K-1 rather than on page 1 of Form 1120S. Report credits related to rental real estate activities on lines 12c and 12d and low-income housing credits on line 12b of Schedules K and K-1.

Report income (loss) from rental activities other than rental real estate on line 3 and credits related to rental activities other than rental real estate on line 12e of Schedules K and K-1.

Portfolio Income

Generally, portfolio income includes all gross income, other than income derived in the ordinary course of a trade or business, that is attributable to interest; dividends; royalties; income from a real estate investment trust, a regulated investment company, a real estate mortgage investment conduit, a common trust fund, a controlled foreign corporation, a qualified electing fund, or a cooperative; income from the disposition of property that produces income of a type defined as portfolio income; and income from the disposition of property held for investment.

Solely for purposes of the preceding paragraph, gross income derived in the ordinary course of a trade or business includes **(and portfolio income, therefore, does not include)** only the following types of income:

● Interest income on loans and investments made in the ordinary course of a trade or business of lending money.

● Interest on accounts receivable arising from the performance of services or the sale of property in the ordinary course of a trade or business of performing such services or selling such property, but only if credit is customarily offered to customers of the business.

● Income from investments made in the ordinary course of a trade or business of furnishing insurance or annuity contracts or reinsuring risks underwritten by insurance companies.

● Income or gain derived in the ordinary course of an activity of trading or dealing in any property if such activity constitutes a trade or business (unless the dealer held the property for investment at any time before such income or gain is recognized).

● Royalties derived by the taxpayer in the ordinary course of a trade or business of licensing intangible property.

● Amounts included in the gross income of a patron of a cooperative by reason of any payment or allocation to the patron based on patronage occurring with respect to a trade or business of the patron.

● Other income identified by the IRS as income derived by the taxpayer in the ordinary course of a trade or business.

See Temporary Regulations section 1.469-2T(c)(3) for more information on portfolio income.

Report portfolio income on line 4 of Schedules K and K-1, rather than on page 1 of Form 1120S.

Report deductions related to portfolio income on line 9 of Schedules K and K-1.

Grouping Activities

Generally, one or more trade or business activities or rental activities may be treated as a single activity if the activities make up an appropriate economic unit for measurement of gain or loss under the passive activity rules. Whether activities make up an appropriate economic unit depends on all the relevant facts and circumstances. The factors given the greatest weight in determining whether activities make up an appropriate economic unit are—

1. Similarities and differences in types of trades or businesses,

2. The extent of common control,

3. The extent of common ownership,

4. Geographical location, and

5. Reliance between or among the activities.

Example: The corporation has a significant ownership interest in a bakery and a movie theater in Baltimore and in a bakery and a movie theater in Philadelphia. Depending on the relevant facts and circumstances, there may be more than one reasonable method for grouping the corporation's activities. For instance, the following groupings may or may not be permissible: a single activity, a movie theater activity and a bakery activity, a Baltimore activity and a Philadelphia activity, or four separate activities.

Once the corporation chooses a grouping under these rules, it must continue using that grouping in later tax years unless a material change in the facts and circumstances makes it clearly inappropriate.

The IRS may regroup the corporation's activities if the corporation's grouping fails to reflect one or more appropriate economic units and one of the primary purposes for the grouping is to avoid the passive activity limitations.

Limitation on grouping certain activities. The following activities may not be grouped together:

1. A rental activity with a trade or business activity unless the activities being grouped together make up an appropriate economic unit, and

a. The rental activity is insubstantial relative to the trade or business activity or vice versa, or

b. Each owner of the trade or business activity has the same proportionate ownership interest in the rental activity. If so, the portion of the rental activity involving the rental of property to be used in the trade or business activity may be grouped with the trade or business activity.

2. An activity involving the rental of real property with an activity involving the rental of personal property (except for personal property provided in connection with real property), or vice versa.

3. Any activity with another activity in a different type of business and in which the corporation holds an interest as a limited partner or as a limited entrepreneur (as defined in section 464(e)(2)) if that other activity engages in holding, producing, or distributing motion picture films or videotapes; farming; leasing section 1245 property; or exploring for (or exploiting) oil and gas resources or geothermal deposits.

Activities conducted through partnerships. Once a partnership determines its activities under these rules, the corporation as a partner may use these rules to group those activities with each other, with activities conducted directly by the corporation, and with activities conducted through other partnerships. The corporation may not treat as separate activities those activities grouped together by the partnership.

Recharacterization of Passive Income

Under Temporary Regulations section 1.469-2T(f) and Regulations section 1.469-2(f), net passive income from certain passive activities must be treated as nonpassive income. Net passive income is the excess of an activity's passive activity gross income over its passive activity deductions (current year deductions and prior year unallowed losses).

Income from the following six sources is subject to recharacterization. Note that any net passive income recharacterized as nonpassive income is treated as investment income for purposes of figuring investment interest expense limitations if it is from **(a)** an activity of renting substantially nondepreciable property from an equity-financed lending activity or **(b)** an activity related to an interest in a pass-through entity that licenses intangible property.

1. **Significant participation passive activities.** A significant participation passive activity is any trade or business activity in which the shareholder both participates for more than 100 hours during the tax year and does not materially participate. Because each shareholder must determine his or her level of participation, the corporation will

not be able to identify significant participation passive activities.

2. Certain nondepreciable rental property activities. Net passive income from a rental activity is nonpassive income if less than 30% of the unadjusted basis of the property used or held for use by customers in the activity is subject to depreciation under section 167.

3. Passive equity-financed lending activities. If the corporation has net income from a passive equity-financed lending activity, the smaller of the net passive income or equity-financed interest income from the activity is nonpassive income.

Note: *The amount of income from the activities in items 1 through 3 above that any shareholder will be required to recharacterize as nonpassive income may be limited under Temporary Regulations section 1.469-2T(f)(8). Because the corporation will not have information regarding all of a shareholder's activities, it must identify all corporate activities meeting the definitions in items 2 and 3 as activities that may be subject to recharacterization.*

4. Rental activities incidental to a development activity. Net rental activity income (defined below) is nonpassive income for a shareholder if all of the following apply: **(a)** the corporation recognizes gain from the sale, exchange, or other disposition of the rental property during the tax year; **(b)** the use of the item of property in the rental activity started less than 12 months before the date of disposition (the use of an item of rental property begins on the first day on which *(i)* the corporation owns an interest in the property, *(ii)* substantially all of the property is either rented or held out for rent and ready to be rented, and *(iii)* no significant value-enhancing services remain to be performed); and **(c)** the shareholder materially participated or significantly participated for any tax year in an activity that involved the performance of services for the purpose of enhancing the value of the property (or any other item of property, if the basis of the property disposed of is determined in whole or in part by reference to the basis of that item of property).

Net rental activity income is the excess of passive activity gross income from renting or disposing of property over passive activity deductions (current year deductions and prior year unallowed losses) that are reasonably allocable to the rented property.

Because the corporation cannot determine a shareholder's level of participation, the corporation must identify net income from property described in items **4(a)** and **4(b)** as income that may be subject to recharacterization.

5. Activities involving property rented to a nonpassive activity. If a taxpayer rents property to a trade or business activity in which the taxpayer materially participates, the taxpayer's net rental activity income (defined in item 4) from the property is nonpassive income.

6. Acquisition of an interest in a pass-through entity that licenses intangible property. Generally, net royalty income from intangible property is nonpassive income if the taxpayer acquired an interest in the pass-through entity after it created the intangible property or performed substantial services or incurred substantial costs in developing or marketing the intangible property.

Net royalty income is the excess of passive activity gross income from licensing or transferring any right in intangible property over passive activity deductions (current year deductions and prior year unallowed losses) that are reasonably allocable to the intangible property.

See Temporary Regulations section 1.469-2T(f)(7)(iii) for exceptions to this rule.

Passive Activity Reporting Requirements

To allow shareholders to correctly apply the passive activity loss and credit limitation rules, any corporation that carries on more than one activity must:

1. Provide an attachment for each activity conducted through the corporation that identifies the type of activity conducted (trade or business, rental real estate, rental activity other than rental real estate, or investment).

2. On the attachment for each activity, provide a schedule, using the same line numbers as shown on Schedule K-1, detailing the net income (loss), credits, and all items required to be separately stated under section 1366(a)(1) from each trade or business activity, from each rental real estate activity, from each rental activity other than a rental real estate activity, and from investments.

3. Identify the net income (loss) and the shareholder's share of corporation interest expense from each activity of renting a dwelling unit that any shareholder uses for personal purposes during the year for more than the greater of 14 days or 10% of the number of days that the residence is rented at fair rental value.

4. Identify the net income (loss) and the shareholder's share of interest expense from each activity of trading personal property conducted through the corporation.

5. For any gain (loss) from the disposition of an interest in an activity or of an interest in property used in an activity (including dispositions before 1987 from which gain is being recognized after 1986):

a. Identify the activity in which the property was used at the time of disposition;

b. If the property was used in more than one activity during the 12 months preceding the disposition, identify the activities in which the property was used

and the adjusted basis allocated to each activity; and

c. For gains only, if the property was substantially appreciated at the time of the disposition and the applicable holding period specified in Regulations section 1.469-2(c)(2)(iii)(A) was not satisfied, identify the amount of the nonpassive gain and indicate whether or not the gain is investment income under Regulations section 1.469-2(c)(2)(iii)(F).

6. Specify the amount of gross portfolio income, the interest expense properly allocable to portfolio income, and expenses other than interest expense that are clearly and directly allocable to portfolio income.

7. Identify the ratable portion of any section 481 adjustment (whether a net positive or a net negative adjustment) allocable to each corporate activity.

8. Identify any gross income from sources specifically excluded from passive activity gross income, including:

a. Income from intangible property, if the shareholder is an individual whose personal efforts significantly contributed to the creation of the property;

b. Income from state, local, or foreign income tax refunds; and

c. Income from a covenant not to compete, if the shareholder is an individual who contributed the covenant to the corporation.

9. Identify any deductions that are not passive activity deductions.

10. If the corporation makes a full or partial disposition of its interest in another entity, identify the gain (loss) allocable to each activity conducted through the entity, and the gain allocable to a passive activity that would have been recharacterized as nonpassive gain had the corporation disposed of its interest in property used in the activity (because the property was substantially appreciated at the time of the disposition, and the gain represented more than 10% of the shareholder's total gain from the disposition).

11. Identify the following items that may be subject to the recharacterization rules under Temporary Regulations section 1.469-2T(f) and Regulations section 1.469-2(f):

a. Net income from an activity of renting substantially nondepreciable property;

b. The smaller of equity-financed interest income or net passive income from an equity-financed lending activity;

c. Net rental activity income from property developed (by the shareholder or the corporation), rented, and sold within 12 months after the rental of the property commenced;

d. Net rental activity income from the rental of property by the corporation to a trade or business activity in which the shareholder had an interest (either directly or indirectly); and

e. Net royalty income from intangible property if the shareholder acquired the shareholder's interest in the corporation after the corporation created the intangible property or performed substantial services or incurred substantial costs in developing or marketing the intangible property.

12. Identify separately the credits from each activity conducted by or through the corporation.

Specific Instructions

General Information

Name, Address, and Employer Identification Number

Use the label that was mailed to the corporation. Cross out any errors and print the correct information on the label.

Name. If the corporation did not receive a label, print or type the corporation's true name (as set forth in the corporate charter or other legal document creating it).

Address. Include the suite, room, or other unit number after the street address. If a preaddressed label is used, please include the information on the label. If the Post Office does not deliver to the street address and the corporation has a P.O. box, show the box number instead of the street address.

If the corporation changes its mailing address after filing its return, it can notify the IRS by filing **Form 8822,** Change of Address.

Employer identification number (EIN). Show the correct EIN in item C on page 1 of Form 1120S.

Item B—Business Code No.

See the new **Codes for Principal Business Activity** on pages 26 through 28 of these instructions.

Item E—Total Assets

Enter the corporation's total assets at the end of the tax year, as determined by the accounting method regularly used in maintaining the corporation's books and records. If there were no assets at the end of the tax year, enter the total assets as of the beginning of the tax year. If the S election terminated during the tax year, see the instructions for Schedule L on page 24 for special rules that may apply when figuring the corporation's year-end assets.

Item F—Initial Return, Final Return, Change in Address, and Amended Return

If this is the corporation's first return, check box F(1). If the corporation has ceased to exist, check box F(2). Also check box D(1) on each Schedule K-1 to indicate that it is a final Schedule K-1. Indicate a change in address by checking box F(3). If this amends a previously filed return, check box F(4). If Schedules K-1 are also being amended, check box D(2) on each Schedule K-1.

Income

Caution: *Report only trade or business activity income or loss on lines 1a through 6.* **Do not report rental activity income or portfolio income or loss on these lines.** *(See* **Passive Activity Limitations** *beginning on page 6 for definitions of rental income and portfolio income.) Rental activity income and portfolio income are reported on Schedules K and K-1 (rental real estate activities are also reported on Form 8825).*

Do not include any tax-exempt income on lines 1 through 5. A corporation that receives any exempt income other than interest, or holds any property or engages in an activity that produces exempt income, reports this income on line 18 of Schedules K and K-1.

Report tax-exempt interest income, including exempt-interest dividends received as a shareholder in a mutual fund or other regulated investment company, on line 17 of Schedules K and K-1.

See **Deductions** beginning on page 11 for information on how to report expenses related to tax-exempt income.

If the S corporation has had debt discharged resulting from a title 11 bankruptcy proceeding, or while insolvent, see **Form 982,** Reduction of Tax Attributes Due to Discharge of Indebtedness, and **Pub. 908,** Bankruptcy Tax Guide.

Line 1—Gross Receipts or Sales

Enter gross receipts or sales from all trade or business operations except those you report on lines 4 and 5. For reporting advance payments, see Regulations section 1.451-5. To report income from long-term contracts, see section 460.

Installment sales. Generally, the installment method cannot be used for dealer dispositions of property. A dealer disposition is any disposition of personal property by a person who regularly sells or otherwise disposes of property of the same type on the installment plan or any disposition of real property held for sale to customers in the ordinary course of the taxpayer's trade or business. The disposition of property used or produced in the farming business is not included as a dealer disposition. See section 453(l) for details and exceptions.

Enter on line 1a the gross profit on collections from installment sales for any of the following:

● Dealer dispositions of property before March 1, 1986.

● Dispositions of property used or produced in the trade or business of farming.

● Certain dispositions of timeshares and residential lots reported under the installment method.

Attach a schedule showing the following information for the current and the 3 preceding years:

● Gross sales.

● Cost of goods sold.

● Gross profits.

● Percentage of gross profits to gross sales.

● Amount collected.

● Gross profit on the amount collected.

Line 2—Cost of Goods Sold

See the instructions for Schedule A on page 15.

Line 4—Net Gain (Loss) From Form 4797

Caution: *Include only ordinary gains or losses from the sale, exchange, or involuntary conversion of assets used in a trade or business activity. Ordinary gains or losses from the sale, exchange, or involuntary conversions of assets used in rental activities are reported separately on Schedule K as part of the net income (loss) from the rental activity in which the property was used.*

A corporation that is a partner in a partnership must include on **Form 4797,** Sales of Business Property, its share of ordinary gains (losses) from sales, exchanges, or involuntary or compulsory conversions (other than casualties or thefts) of the partnership's trade or business assets.

Do not include any recapture of the section 179 expense deduction. See the instructions on page 23 for Schedule K-1, line 23, item 3, and the Instructions for Form 4797 for more information.

Line 5—Other Income (Loss)

Enter on line 5 trade or business income (loss) that is not included on lines 1a through 4. Examples of such income include:

1. Interest income derived in the ordinary course of the corporation's trade or business, such as interest charged on receivable balances;

2. Recoveries of bad debts deducted in earlier years under the specific charge-off method;

3. Taxable income from insurance proceeds;

4. The amount of credit figured on **Form 6478,** Credit for Alcohol Used as Fuel;

5. All section 481 income adjustments resulting from changes in accounting methods (show the computation on an attached schedule); and

6. Ordinary income (loss) from trade or business activities of a partnership (from Schedule K-1 (Form 1065), line 1).

The corporation must include as other income the recapture amount for section 280F if the business use of listed property drops to 50% or less. To figure the recapture amount, the corporation must complete Part IV of Form 4797.

The corporation must also include in other income the amount of any deduction previously taken under section 179A that is subject to recapture. The S corporation may have to recapture the benefit of any allowable deduction for qualified clean-fuel vehicle property (or clean-fuel vehicle refueling property), if the property later ceases to qualify for the deduction. See **Pub. 535,** Business Expenses, for details on how to figure the recapture.

Do not include items requiring separate computations by shareholders that must be reported on Schedules K and K-1. See the instructions for Schedules K and K-1 beginning on page 16.

If "other income" consists of only one item, identify it by showing the account caption in parentheses on line 5. A separate schedule need not be attached to the return in this case.

Do not net any expense item (such as interest) with a similar income item. Report all trade or business expenses on lines 7 through 19.

Deductions

Caution: *Report **only** trade or business activity expenses on lines 7 through 19.*

Do not report rental activity expenses or deductions allocable to portfolio income on these lines. Rental activity expenses are separately reported on Form 8825 or line 3 of Schedules K and K-1. Deductions allocable to portfolio income are separately reported on line 9 of Schedules K and K-1. See **Passive Activity Limitations** beginning on page 6 for more information on rental activities and portfolio income.

Do not report any nondeductible amounts (such as expenses connected with the production of tax-exempt income) on lines 7 through 19. Instead, report nondeductible expenses on line 19 of Schedules K and K-1. If an expense is connected with both taxable income and nontaxable income, allocate a reasonable part of the expense to each kind of income.

Limitations on Deductions

Section 263A uniform capitalization rules. The uniform capitalization rules of section 263A require corporations to capitalize or include in inventory certain costs incurred in connection with:

● The production of real and tangible personal property held in inventory or held for sale in the ordinary course of business.

● Personal property (tangible and intangible) acquired for resale.

● The production of property constructed or improved by a corporation for use in its trade or business or in an activity engaged in for profit.

The costs required to be capitalized under section 263A are not deductible until the property to which the costs relate is sold, used, or otherwise disposed of by the corporation.

Exceptions. Section 263A **does not** apply to:

● Personal property acquired for resale if the taxpayer's average annual gross receipts for the 3 prior tax years are $10 million or less.

● Timber.

● Most property produced under a long-term contract.

● Certain property produced in a farming business. See below.

The corporation must report the following costs separately to the shareholders for purposes of determinations under section 59(e):

● Research and experimental costs under section 174.

● Intangible drilling costs for oil, gas, and geothermal property.

● Mining exploration and development costs.

Tangible personal property produced by a corporation includes a film, sound recording, video tape, book, or similar property.

Corporations subject to the rules are required to capitalize not only direct costs but an allocable portion of most indirect costs (including taxes) that benefit the assets produced or acquired for resale.

For inventory, some of the ***indirect costs*** that must be capitalized are:

● Administration expenses.

● Taxes.

● Depreciation.

● Insurance.

● Compensation paid to officers attributable to services.

● Rework labor.

● Contributions to pension, stock bonus, and certain profit-sharing, annuity, or deferred compensation plans.

Regulations section 1.263A-1(e)(3) specifies other indirect costs that relate to production or resale activities that must be capitalized and those that may be currently deducted.

Interest expense paid or incurred during the production period of certain property must be capitalized and is governed by special rules. For more details, see Regulations sections 1.263A-8 through 1.263A-15.

For more details on the uniform capitalization rules, see Regulations sections 1.263A-1 through 1.263A-3.

Special rules for certain corporations engaged in farming. For S corporations not required to use the accrual method of accounting, the rules of section 263A **do not** apply to expenses of raising any—

● Animal or

● Plant that has a preproductive period of 2 years or less.

Shareholders of S corporations not required to use the accrual method of accounting may elect to currently deduct the preproductive period expenses of certain plants that have a preproductive period of more than 2 years. Because each shareholder makes the election to deduct these expenses, the corporation should not capitalize them. Instead, the corporation should report the expenses separately on line 21 of Schedule K and each shareholder's pro rata share on line 23 of Schedule K-1.

See sections 263A(d) and (e) and Temporary Regulations section 1.263A-4T for definitions and other details.

Transactions between related taxpayers. Generally, an accrual basis S corporation may deduct business expenses and interest owed to a related party (including any shareholder) **only** in the tax year of the corporation that includes the day on which the payment is includible in the income of the related party. See section 267 for details.

Section 291 limitations. If the S corporation was a C corporation for any of the 3 immediately preceding years, the corporation may be required to adjust deductions allowed to the corporation for depletion of iron ore and coal, and the amortizable basis of pollution control facilities. See section 291 to determine the amount of the adjustment.

Business start-up expenses. Business start-up expenses must be capitalized. An election may be made to amortize them over a period of not less than 60 months. See section 195.

Reducing certain expenses for which credits are allowable. For each credit listed below, the corporation must reduce the otherwise allowable deductions for expenses used to figure the credit by the amount of the current year credit.

1. The work opportunity credit,

2. The welfare-to-work credit,

3. The credit for increasing research activities,

4. The enhanced oil recovery credit,

5. The disabled access credit,

6. The empowerment zone employment credit,

7. The Indian employment credit,

8. The credit for employer social security and Medicare taxes paid on certain employee tips, and

9. The orphan drug credit.

If the corporation has any of these credits, be sure to figure each current year credit before figuring the deductions for expenses on which the credit is based.

Line 7—Compensation of Officers

Enter on line 7 the total compensation of all officers paid or incurred in the trade or business activities of the corporation, including fringe benefit expenditures made on behalf of officers owning more than 2% of the corporation's stock. Also report these fringe benefits as wages in box 1 of Form W-2. Do not include on line 7 amounts paid or incurred for fringe benefits of officers owning 2% or less of the corporation's stock. These amounts are reported on line 18, page 1, of Form 1120S. See the instructions for that line for information on the types of expenditures that are treated as fringe benefits and for the stock ownership rules.

Report amounts paid for health insurance coverage for a more than 2% shareholder (including that shareholder's spouse and dependents) as an information item in box 14 of that shareholder's Form W-2. For 1998, a more than 2% shareholder may be allowed to deduct up to 45% of such amounts on Form 1040, line 28.

Do not include on line 7 compensation reported elsewhere on the return, such as amounts included in cost of goods sold, elective contributions to a section 401(k) cash or deferred arrangement, or amounts contributed under a salary reduction SEP agreement.

Line 8—Salaries and Wages

Enter on line 8 the amount of salaries and wages paid or incurred for the tax year, reduced by any applicable employment credits from **Form 5884,** Work Opportunity Credit, **Form 8861,** Welfare-to-Work Credit, **Form 8844,** Empowerment Zone Employment Credit, and **Form 8845,** Indian Employment Credit. See the instructions for these forms for more information. Include fringe benefit expenditures made on behalf of employees (other than officers) owning more than 2% of the corporation's stock. Also report these fringe benefits as wages in box 1 of Form W-2. Do not include on line 8 amounts paid or incurred for fringe benefits of employees owning 2% or less of the corporation's stock. These amounts are reported on line 18, page 1, of Form 1120S. See the instructions for that line for information on the types of expenditures that are treated as fringe benefits and for the stock ownership rules.

Report amounts paid for health insurance coverage for a more than 2% shareholder (including that shareholder's spouse and dependents) as an information item in box 14 of that shareholder's Form W-2. For 1998, a more than 2% shareholder may be allowed to deduct up to 45% of such amounts on Form 1040, line 28.

Do not include on line 8 salaries and wages reported elsewhere on the return, such as amounts included in cost of goods sold, elective contributions to a section 401(k) cash or deferred arrangement, or amounts contributed under a salary reduction SEP agreement.

If a shareholder or a member of the family of one or more shareholders of the corporation renders services or furnishes capital to the corporation for which reasonable compensation is not paid, the IRS may make adjustments in the items taken into account by such individuals and the value of such services or capital. See section 1366(e).

Line 9—Repairs and Maintenance

Enter the costs of incidental repairs and maintenance, such as labor and supplies, that do not add to the value of the property or appreciably prolong its life, but only to the extent that such costs relate to a trade or business activity and are not claimed elsewhere on the return. New buildings, machinery, or permanent improvements that increase the value of the property are not deductible. They are chargeable to capital accounts and may be depreciated or amortized.

Line 10—Bad Debts

Enter the total debts that became worthless in whole or in part during the year, but only to the extent such debts relate to a trade or business activity. Report deductible nonbusiness bad debts as a short-term capital loss on Schedule D (Form 1120S).

Caution: *Cash method taxpayers cannot take a bad debt deduction unless the amount was previously included in income.*

Line 11—Rents

If the corporation rented or leased a vehicle, enter the total annual rent or lease expense paid or incurred in the trade or business activities of the corporation. Also complete Part V of **Form 4562,** Depreciation and Amortization. If the corporation leased a vehicle for a term of 30 days or more, the deduction for vehicle lease expense may have to be reduced by an amount called the **inclusion amount.** The corporation may have an inclusion amount if—

The lease term began:	And the vehicle's fair market value on the first day of the lease exceeded:
After 12/31/96	$15,800
After 12/31/94 but before 1/1/97	$15,500
After 12/31/93 but before 1/1/95	$14,600
After 12/31/92 but before 1/1/94	$14,300

If the lease term began before January 1, 1993, see **Pub. 463,** Travel, Entertainment, Gift, and Car Expenses, to find out if the corporation has an inclusion amount.

See Pub. 463 for instructions on figuring the inclusion amount.

Line 12—Taxes and Licenses

Enter taxes and licenses paid or incurred in the trade or business activities of the corporation, if not reflected in cost of goods sold. Federal import duties and Federal excise and stamp taxes are deductible only if paid or incurred in carrying on the trade or business of the corporation.

Do not deduct the following taxes on line 12:

- State and local sales taxes paid or incurred in connection with the acquisition or disposition of business property. These taxes must be added to the cost of the property, or in the case of a disposition, subtracted from the amount realized.
- Taxes assessed against local benefits that increase the value of the property assessed, such as for paving, etc.
- Federal income taxes, or taxes reported elsewhere on the return.
- Section 901 foreign taxes. Report these taxes separately on line 15e, Schedule K.
- Taxes allocable to a rental activity. Taxes allocable to a rental real estate activity are reported on Form 8825. Taxes allocable to a rental activity other than a rental real estate activity are reported on line 3b of Schedule K.
- Taxes allocable to portfolio income. Report these taxes separately on line 9 of Schedules K and K-1.
- Taxes paid or incurred for the production or collection of income, or for the management, conservation, or maintenance of property held to produce income. Report these taxes separately on line 10 of Schedules K and K-1.

See section 263A(a) for information on capitalization of allocable costs (including taxes) for any property.

Line 13—Interest

Include on line 13 only interest incurred in the trade or business activities of the corporation that is not claimed elsewhere on the return.

Do not include interest expense on debt used to purchase rental property or debt used in a rental activity. Interest allocable to a rental real estate activity is reported on Form 8825 and is used in arriving at net income (loss) from rental real estate activities on line 2 of Schedules K and K-1. Interest allocable to a rental activity other than a rental real estate activity is included on line 3b of Schedule K and is used in arriving at net income (loss) from a rental activity (other than a rental real estate activity) is reported on line 3c of Schedule K and line 3 of Schedule K-1.

Do not include interest expense clearly and directly allocable to portfolio or investment income. This interest expense is reported separately on line 11a of Schedule K.

Do not include interest on debt proceeds allocated to distributions made to shareholders during the tax year. Instead, report such interest on line 10 of Schedules K and K-1. To determine the amount to allocate to distributions to shareholders, see Notice 89-35, 1989-1 C.B. 675.

Do not include interest expense on debt required to be allocated to the production of qualified property. Interest allocable to certain property produced by an S corporation for its own use or for sale must be capitalized. The corporation must also capitalize any interest on debt that is allocable to an asset used to produce the above property. A shareholder may have to capitalize interest that the shareholder incurs during the tax year for the production expenditures of the S corporation. Similarly, interest incurred by an S corporation may have to be capitalized by a shareholder for the shareholder's own production expenditures. The information required by the shareholder to properly capitalize interest for this purpose must be provided by the corporation on an attachment for line 23 of Schedule K-1. See section 263A(f) and Regulations sections 1.263A-8 through 1.263A-15 for additional information.

Temporary Regulations section 1.163-8T gives rules for allocating interest expense among activities so that the limitations on passive activity losses, investment interest, and personal interest can be properly figured. Generally, interest expense is allocated in the same manner as debt is allocated. Debt is allocated by tracing disbursements of the debt proceeds to specific expenditures. These regulations give rules for tracing debt proceeds to expenditures.

Generally, prepaid interest can only be deducted over the period to which the prepayment applies. See section 461(g) for details.

Note: *The deduction for interest is limited when the corporation is a policyholder or beneficiary with respect to a life insurance, endowment, or annuity contract issued after June 8, 1997. For details, see section 264. Attach a statement showing the computation of the deduction disallowed under section 264.*

Line 14—Depreciation

Enter on line 14a only the depreciation claimed on assets used in a trade or business activity. See the Instructions for Form 4562 or **Pub. 946,** How To Depreciate Property, to figure the amount of depreciation to enter on this line. Complete and attach Form 4562 only if the corporation placed property in service during 1998 or claims depreciation on any car or other listed property.

Do not include any section 179 expense deduction on this line. This amount is not deductible by the corporation. Instead, it is passed through to the shareholders on line 8 of Schedule K-1.

Line 15—Depletion

If the corporation claims a deduction for timber depletion, complete and attach **Form T,** Forest Activities Schedules.

Caution: *Do not deduct depletion for oil and gas properties. Each shareholder figures depletion on these properties under section 613A(c)(11). See the instructions on page 23 for Schedule K-1, line 23, item 2, for information on oil and gas depletion that must be supplied to the shareholders by the corporation.*

Line 17—Pension, Profit-Sharing, etc., Plans

Enter the deductible contributions not claimed elsewhere on the return made by the corporation for its employees under a qualified pension, profit-sharing, annuity, or simplified employee pension (SEP) or SIMPLE plan, and under any other deferred compensation plan.

If the corporation contributes to an individual retirement arrangement (IRA) for employees, include the contribution in salaries and wages on page 1, line 8, or Schedule A, line 3, and not on line 17.

Employers who maintain a pension, profit-sharing, or other funded deferred compensation plan, whether or not qualified under the Internal Revenue

Code and whether or not a deduction is claimed for the current tax year, generally must file one of the forms listed below:

Form 5500, Annual Return/Report of Employee Benefit Plan (With 100 or more participants).

Form 5500-C/R, Return/Report of Employee Benefit Plan (With fewer than 100 participants).

Form 5500-EZ, Annual Return of One-Participant (Owners and Their Spouses) Retirement Plan.

There are penalties for failure to file these forms on time and for overstating the pension plan deduction.

Line 18—Employee Benefit Programs

Enter amounts for fringe benefits paid or incurred on behalf of employees owning 2% or less of the corporation's stock. These fringe benefits include **(a)** employer contributions to certain accident and health plans, **(b)** the cost of up to $50,000 of group-term life insurance on an employee's life, and **(c)** meals and lodging furnished for the employer's convenience.

Do not deduct amounts that are an incidental part of a pension, profit-sharing, etc., plan included on line 17 or amounts reported elsewhere on the return.

Report amounts paid on behalf of more than 2% shareholders on line 7 or 8, whichever applies. A shareholder is considered to own more than 2% of the corporation's stock if that person owns on any day during the tax year more than 2% of the outstanding stock of the corporation or stock possessing more than 2% of the combined voting power of all stock of the corporation. See section 318 for attribution rules.

Line 19—Other Deductions

Attach your own schedule listing by type and amount all allowable deductions related to a trade or business activity for which there is no separate line on page 1 of Form 1120S. Enter the total on this line. Do not include items that must be reported separately on Schedules K and K-1.

An S corporation may not take the deduction for net operating losses provided by section 172 or the special deductions in sections 241 through 249 (except the election to amortize organizational expenditures under section 248). Subject to limitations, the corporation's net operating loss is allowed as a deduction from the shareholders' gross income. See section 1366.

Do not include qualified expenditures to which an election under section 59(e) may apply. See the instructions on page 22 for lines 16a and 16b of Schedule K-1 for details on treatment of these items.

Include on line 19 the deduction taken for amortization. See the Instructions for Form 4562 for more information. Complete and attach Form 4562 if the corporation is claiming amortization of costs that began during its 1998 tax year.

Section 464(f) limits the deduction for certain expenditures of S corporations engaged in farming that use the cash method of accounting, and whose prepaid farm supplies are more than 50% of other deductible farming expenses. Prepaid farm supplies include expenses for feed, seed, fertilizer, and similar farm supplies not used or consumed during the year. They also include the cost of poultry that would be allowable as a deduction in a later tax year if the corporation were to **(a)** capitalize the cost of poultry bought for use in its farm business and deduct it ratably over the lesser of 12 months or the useful life of the poultry and **(b)** deduct the cost of poultry bought for resale in the year it sells or otherwise disposes of it. If the limit applies, the corporation can deduct prepaid farm supplies that do not exceed 50% of its other deductible farm expenses in the year of payment. The excess is deductible only in the year the corporation uses or consumes the supplies (other than poultry, which is deductible as explained above). For exceptions and more details on these rules, see **Pub. 225,** Farmer's Tax Guide.

Do not deduct amounts paid or incurred to participate or intervene in any political campaign on behalf of a candidate for public office, or to influence the general public regarding legislative matters, elections, or referendums. In addition, corporations generally cannot deduct expenses paid or incurred to influence Federal or state legislation, or to influence the actions or positions of certain Federal executive branch officials. However, certain in-house lobbying expenditures that do not exceed $2,000 are deductible. See section 162(e) for more details.

Do not deduct fines or penalties paid to a government for violating any law.

A deduction is allowed for part of the cost of qualified clean-fuel vehicle property and qualified clean-fuel vehicle refueling property. For more details, see section 179A.

Travel, meals, and entertainment. Subject to limitations and restrictions discussed below, a corporation can deduct ordinary and necessary travel, meals, and entertainment expenses paid or incurred in its trade or business. Special rules apply to deductions for gifts, skybox rentals, luxury water travel, convention expenses, and entertainment tickets. See section 274 and Pub. 463 for more details.

Travel. The corporation cannot deduct travel expenses of any individual accompanying a corporate officer or employee, including a spouse or dependent of the officer or employee, unless:

● That individual is an employee of the corporation, and

● His or her travel is for a bona fide business purpose and would otherwise be deductible by that individual.

Meals and entertainment. Generally, the corporation can deduct only 50% of the amount otherwise allowable for meals and entertainment expenses. In addition (subject to exceptions under section 274(k)(2)):

● Meals must not be lavish or extravagant,

● A bona fide business discussion must occur during, immediately before, or immediately after the meal; and

● An employee of the corporation must be present at the meal.

Membership dues. The corporation may deduct amounts paid or incurred for membership dues in civic or public service organizations, professional organizations (such as bar and medical associations), business leagues, trade associations, chambers of commerce, boards of trade, and real estate boards. However, no deduction is allowed if a principal purpose of the organization is to entertain, or provide entertainment facilities for, members or their guests. In addition, corporations may not deduct membership dues in any club organized for business, pleasure, recreation, or other social purpose. This includes country clubs, golf and athletic clubs, airline and hotel clubs, and clubs operated to provide meals under conditions favorable to business discussion.

Entertainment facilities. The corporation cannot deduct an expense paid or incurred for a facility (such as a yacht or hunting lodge) used for an activity usually considered entertainment, amusement, or recreation.

Note: *The corporation may be able to deduct otherwise nondeductible meals, travel, and entertainment expenses if the amounts are treated as compensation and reported on Form W-2 for an employee or on Form 1099-MISC for an independent contractor.*

Line 21—Ordinary Income (Loss)

Enter this income or loss on line 1 of Schedule K. Line 21 income is not used in figuring the tax on line 22a or 22b. See the instructions for line 22a for figuring taxable income for purposes of line 22a or 22b tax.

Tax and Payments

Line 22a—Excess Net Passive Income Tax

If the corporation has always been an S corporation, the excess net passive income tax does not apply. If the corporation has accumulated earnings and profits (E&P) at the close of its tax year, has passive investment income for the tax year that is in excess of 25% of gross receipts, **and** has taxable income at year-end, the corporation must pay a tax on the excess net passive income. Complete lines 1 through 3 and line 9 of the worksheet below to make this determination. If line 2 is greater than line 3 and the corporation has taxable income (see instructions for line 9 of worksheet), it must pay the tax. Complete a separate schedule using the format of lines 1 through 11 of the worksheet below to figure the tax. Enter the tax on line 22a, page 1, Form 1120S, and attach the computation schedule to Form 1120S.

Reduce each item of passive income passed through to shareholders by its portion of tax on line 22a. See section 1366(f)(3).

Line 22b—Tax From Schedule D (Form 1120S)

If the corporation elected to be an S corporation before 1987 (or elected to be an S corporation during 1987 or 1988 and qualifies for transitional relief from the built-in gains tax), see instructions for Part III of Schedule D (Form 1120S) to determine if the corporation is liable for the capital gains tax.

If the corporation made its election to be an S corporation after 1986, see the instructions for Part IV of Schedule D to determine if the corporation is liable for the built-in gains tax.

Note: *For purposes of line 20 of Part III and line 26 of Part IV of Schedule D, taxable income is defined in section 1375(b)(1)(B) and is generally figured in the same manner as taxable income for line 9 of the line 22a worksheet below.*

Line 22c

Include in the total for line 22c the following:

Investment credit recapture tax. The corporation is liable for investment credit recapture attributable to credits allowed for tax years for which the corporation was not an S corporation. Figure the corporation's investment credit recapture tax by completing **Form 4255,** Recapture of Investment Credit.

To the left of the line 22c total, enter the amount of recapture tax and "Tax From Form 4255." Attach Form 4255 to Form 1120S.

LIFO recapture tax. The corporation may be liable for the additional tax due to LIFO recapture under Regulations section 1.1363-2 if—

● The corporation used the LIFO inventory pricing method for its last tax year as a C corporation, or

● A C corporation transferred LIFO inventory to the corporation in a nonrecognition transaction in which those assets were transferred basis property.

The additional tax due to LIFO recapture is figured for the corporation's last tax year as a C corporation or for the tax year of the transfer, whichever applies. See the Instructions for Forms 1120 and 1120-A to figure the tax. The tax is paid in four equal installments. The C corporation must pay the first installment by the due date (not including extensions) of Form 1120 for the corporation's last tax year as a C corporation or for the tax year of the transfer, whichever applies. The S corporation must pay each of the remaining installments by the due date (not including extensions) of Form 1120S for the 3 succeeding tax years. Include this year's installment in the total amount to be entered on line 22c. To the left of the total on line 22c, enter the installment amount and "LIFO tax."

Interest due under the look-back method for completed long-term contracts. If the corporation owes interest, attach **Form 8697,** Interest Computation Under the Look-Back Method for Completed Long-Term Contracts. To the left of the total on line

---

Worksheet for Line 22a

1. Enter gross receipts for the tax year (see section 1362(d)(3)(B) for gross receipts from the sale of capital assets)* . . . . _____

2. Enter passive investment income as defined in section 1362(d)(3)(C)* . . _____

3. Enter 25% of line 1 (If line 2 is less than line 3, stop here. You are not liable for this tax.) . . . . _____

4. Excess passive investment income— Subtract line 3 from line 2 . . _____

5. Enter deductions directly connected with the production of income on line 2 (see section 1375(b)(2))* . . _____

6. Net passive income—Subtract line 5 from line 2 . . . . _____

7. Divide amount on line 4 by amount on line 2 . . . . _____ %

8. Excess net passive income—Multiply line 6 by line 7 . . . . . _____

9. Enter taxable income (see instructions for taxable income below) . . _____

10. Enter smaller of line 8 or line 9 . _____

11. Excess net passive income tax—Enter 35% of line 10. Enter here and on line 22a, page 1, Form 1120S . . . _____

*Income and deductions on lines 1, 2, and 5 are from total operations for the tax year. This includes applicable income and expenses from page 1, Form 1120S, as well as those reported separately on Schedule K. See section 1375(b)(4) for an exception regarding lines 2 and 5.

Line 9 of Worksheet—Taxable income

Line 9 taxable income is defined in Regulations section 1.1374-1(d). Figure this income by completing lines 1 through 28 of **Form 1120,** U.S. Corporation Income Tax Return. Include the Form 1120 computation with the worksheet computation you attach to Form 1120S. You do not have to attach the schedules, etc., called for on Form 1120. However, you may want to complete certain Form 1120 schedules, such as Schedule D (Form 1120) if you have capital gains or losses.

22c, enter the amount owed and "From Form 8697."

Interest due under the look-back method for property depreciated under the income forecast method. If the corporation owes interest, attach **Form 8866,** Interest Computation Under the Look-Back Method for Property Depreciated Under the Income Forecast Method. To the left of the total on line 22c, enter the amount owed and "From Form 8866."

Line 23d

If the S corporation is a beneficiary of a trust and the trust makes a section 643(g) election to credit its estimated tax payments to its beneficiaries, include the corporation's share of the payment (reported to the corporation on Schedule K-1 (Form 1041)) in the total amount entered on line 23d. Also, to the left of line 23d, enter "T" and the amount of the payment.

Line 24—Estimated Tax Penalty

A corporation that fails to make estimated tax payments when due may be subject to an underpayment penalty for the period of underpayment. Use **Form 2220,** Underpayment of Estimated Tax by Corporations, to see if the corporation owes a penalty and to figure the amount of the penalty. If you attach Form 2220 to Form 1120S, be sure to check the box on line 24 and enter the amount of any penalty on this line.

Schedule A—Cost of Goods Sold

Inventories are required at the beginning and end of each tax year if the production, purchase, or sale of merchandise is an income-producing factor. See Regulations section 1.471-1.

Section 263A Uniform Capitalization Rules

The uniform capitalization rules of section 263A are discussed under **Limitations on Deductions** starting on page 11. See those instructions before completing Schedule A.

Line 4—Additional Section 263A Costs

An entry is required on this line only for corporations that have elected a simplified method of accounting.

For corporations that have elected the simplified production method, additional section 263A costs are generally those costs, other than interest, that were not capitalized under the corporation's method of accounting immediately prior to the effective date of section 263A that are required to be capitalized under section 263A. For new corporations, additional section 263A costs are the costs, other than interest, that must be capitalized under section 263A, but which the corporation would not have been required to capitalize if it had existed before the

effective date of section 263A. For more details, see Regulations section 1.263A-2(b).

For corporations that have elected the simplified resale method, additional section 263A costs are generally those costs incurred with respect to the following categories:

- Off-site storage or warehousing.
- Purchasing.
- Handling, processing, assembly, and repackaging.
- General and administrative costs (mixed service costs).

For more details, see Regulations section 1.263A-3(d).

Enter on line 4 the balance of section 263A costs paid or incurred during the tax year not included on lines 2, 3, and 5.

Line 5—Other Costs

Enter on line 5 any other inventoriable costs paid or incurred during the tax year not entered on lines 2 through 4.

Line 7—Inventory at End of Year

See Regulations sections 1.263A-1 through 1.263A-3 for details on figuring the costs to be included in ending inventory.

Lines 9a Through 9e—Inventory Valuation Methods

Inventories can be valued at:
- Cost.
- Cost or market value (whichever is lower).
- Any other method approved by the IRS that conforms to the requirements of the applicable regulations.

The average cost (rolling average) method of valuing inventories generally does not conform to the requirements of the regulations. See Rev. Rul. 71-234, 1971-1 C.B. 148.

Corporations that use erroneous valuation methods must change to a method permitted for Federal income tax purposes. To make this change, use Form 3115.

On line 9a, check the method(s) used for valuing inventories. Under "lower of cost or market," *market* (for normal goods) means the current bid price prevailing on the inventory valuation date for the particular merchandise in the volume usually purchased by the taxpayer. For a manufacturer, market applies to the basic elements of cost—raw materials, labor, and burden. If section 263A applies to the taxpayer, the basic elements of cost must reflect the current bid price of all direct costs and all indirect costs properly allocable to goods on hand at the inventory date.

Inventory may be valued below cost when the merchandise is unsalable at normal prices or unusable in the normal way because the goods are "subnormal" due to damage, imperfections, shop wear, etc., within the meaning of Regulations section 1.471-2(c). These goods may be valued at a current bona fide selling price

minus direct cost of disposition (but not less than scrap value) if such a price can be established.

If this is the first year the last-in, first-out (LIFO) inventory method was either adopted or extended to inventory goods not previously valued under the LIFO method provided in section 472, attach **Form 970,** Application To Use LIFO Inventory Method, or a statement with the information required by Form 970. Also check the LIFO box on line 9c. On line 9d, enter the amount or the percent of total closing inventories covered under section 472. Estimates are acceptable.

If the corporation has changed or extended its inventory method to LIFO and has had to "write up" its opening inventory to cost in the year of election, report the effect of this write-up as income (line 5, page 1) proportionately over a 3-year period that begins with the tax year of the election (section 472(d)).

See Pub. 538 for more information on inventory valuation methods.

Schedule B—Other Information

Be sure to answer the questions and provide other information in items 1 through 10.

Line 5—Foreign Financial Accounts

Answer "Yes" to question 5 if either **1** or **2** below applies to the corporation. Otherwise, check the "No" box.

1. At any time during calendar year 1998, the corporation had an interest in or signature or other authority over a bank account, securities account, or other financial account in a foreign country; AND

- The combined value of the accounts was more than $10,000 during the calendar year; AND
- The accounts were NOT with a U.S. military banking facility operated by a U.S. financial institution.

2. The corporation owns more than 50% of the stock in any corporation that would answer the question "Yes" based on item **1** above.

Get **Form TD F 90-22.1,** Report of Foreign Bank and Financial Accounts, to see if the corporation is considered to have an interest in or signature or other authority over a bank account, securities account, or other financial account in a foreign country.

If you answered "Yes" to question 5, file Form TD F 90-22.1 by June 30, 1999, with the Department of the Treasury at the address shown on the form. Form TD F 90-22.1 is not a tax return, so do not file it with Form 1120S. Form TD F 90-22.1 may be ordered by calling 1-800-TAX-FORM (1-800-829-3676).

Line 6

The corporation may be required to file **Form 3520,** Annual Return To Report

Transactions With Foreign Trusts and Receipt of Certain Foreign Gifts, if it—

• Directly or indirectly transferred property or money to a foreign trust. For this purpose, any U.S. person who created a foreign trust is considered a transferor.

• Is treated as the owner of any part of the assets of a foreign trust under the grantor trust rules.

• Received a distribution from a foreign trust.

For more information, see the Instructions for Form 3520.

Note: *An owner of a foreign trust must ensure that the trust files an annual information return on* **Form 3520-A,** *Annual Information Return of Foreign Trust With a U.S. Owner.*

Line 9

Complete line 9 if the corporation **(a)** filed its election to be an S corporation after 1986; **(b)** was a C corporation before it elected to be an S corporation **or** the corporation acquired an asset with a basis determined by reference to its basis (or the basis of any other property) in the hands of a C corporation; and **(c)** has net unrealized built-in gain (defined below) in excess of the net recognized built-in gain from prior years.

The corporation is liable for section 1374 tax if **(a)**, **(b)**, and **(c)** above apply and it has a net recognized built-in gain (section 1374(d)(2)) for its tax year.

Section 633(d)(8) of the Tax Reform Act of 1986 provides transitional relief from the built-in gains tax for certain corporations that elected to be S corporations in 1987 or 1988. See the instructions for Part IV of Schedule D (Form 1120S) for more information.

The corporation's net unrealized built-in gain is the amount, if any, by which the fair market value of the assets of the corporation at the beginning of its first S corporation year (or as of the date the assets were acquired, for any asset with a basis determined by reference to its basis (or the basis of any other property) in the hands of a C corporation) exceeds the aggregate adjusted basis of such assets at that time.

Enter on line 9 the corporation's net unrealized built-in gain reduced by the net recognized built-in gain for prior years. See sections 1374(c)(2) and (d)(1).

Line 10

Check the box on line 10 if the corporation was a C corporation in a prior year and has accumulated earnings and profits (E&P) at the close of its 1998 tax year. For details on figuring accumulated E&P, see section 312. If the corporation has accumulated E&P, it may be liable for tax imposed on excess net passive income. See the instructions for line 22a, page 1, of Form 1120S for details on this tax.

General Instructions for Schedules K and K-1— Shareholders' Shares of Income, Credits, Deductions, etc.

Purpose of Schedules

The corporation is liable for taxes on lines 22a, 22b, and 22c, page 1, Form 1120S. Shareholders are liable for income tax on their shares of the corporation's income (reduced by any taxes paid by the corporation on income) and must include their share of the income on their tax return whether or not it is distributed to them. Unlike most partnership income, S corporation income is **not** self-employment income and is not subject to self-employment tax.

Schedule K is a summary schedule of all the shareholders' shares of the corporation's income, deductions, credits, etc. Schedule K-1 shows each shareholder's separate share. Attach a copy of each shareholder's Schedule K-1 to the Form 1120S filed with the IRS. Keep a copy as a part of the corporation's records, and give each shareholder a separate copy.

The total pro rata share items (column (b)) of all Schedules K-1 should equal the amount reported on the same line of Schedule K. Lines 1 through 20 of Schedule K correspond to lines 1 through 20 of Schedule K-1. Other lines do not correspond, but instructions explain the differences.

Be sure to give each shareholder a copy of the Shareholder's Instructions for Schedule K-1 (Form 1120S). These instructions are available separately from Schedule K-1 at most IRS offices.

Note: *Instructions that apply only to line items reported on Schedule K-1 may be prepared and given to each shareholder instead of the instructions printed by the IRS.*

Substitute Forms

The corporation **does not** need IRS approval to use a substitute Schedule K-1 if it is an exact copy of the IRS schedule, **or** if it contains only those lines the taxpayer is required to use, and the lines have the same numbers and titles and are in the same order as on the IRS Schedule K-1. In either case, the substitute schedule must include the OMB number and either **(a)** the Shareholder's Instructions for Schedule K-1 (Form 1120S) or **(b)** instructions that apply to the items reported on Schedule K-1 (Form 1120S).

The corporation must request IRS approval to use other substitute Schedules K-1. To request approval, write to Internal Revenue Service, Attention: Substitute Forms Program Coordinator, OP:FS:FP:F:CD, 1111 Constitution Avenue, N.W., Washington, DC 20224.

The corporation may be subject to a penalty if it files a substitute Schedule K-1 that does not conform to the specifications of Rev. Proc. 97-54, 1997-2 C.B. 529.

Shareholder's Pro Rata Share Items

General Rule

Items of income, loss, deductions, etc., are allocated to a shareholder on a daily basis, according to the number of shares of stock held by the shareholder on each day during the tax year of the corporation. See the instructions for item A.

A shareholder who disposes of stock is treated as the shareholder for the day of disposition. A shareholder who dies is treated as the shareholder for the day of the shareholder's death.

Special Rules

Termination of shareholder's interest. If a shareholder terminates his or her interest in a corporation during the tax year, the corporation, with the consent of all affected shareholders (including the one whose interest is terminated), may elect to allocate income and expenses, etc., as if the corporation's tax year consisted of 2 separate tax years, the first of which ends on the date of the shareholder's termination.

To make the election, the corporation must attach a statement to a timely filed original or amended Form 1120S for the tax year for which the election is made. In the statement, the corporation must state that it is electing under section 1377(a)(2) and Regulations section 1.1377-1(b) to treat the tax year as if it consisted of 2 separate tax years. The statement must also explain how the shareholder's entire interest was terminated (e.g., sale or gift), and state that the corporation and each affected shareholder consent to the corporation making the election. A corporate officer must sign the statement under penalties of perjury on behalf of the corporation. A single statement may be filed for all terminating elections made for the tax year. If the election is made, write "Section 1377(a)(2) Election Made" at the top of each affected shareholder's Schedule K-1.

For more details on the election, see Regulations section 1.1377-1(b).

Qualifying dispositions. If a qualifying disposition takes place during the tax year, the corporation may make an irrevocable election to allocate income and expenses, etc., as if the corporation's tax year consisted of 2 tax years, the first of which ends on the close of the day on which the qualifying disposition occurs. A qualifying disposition is:

1. A disposition by a shareholder of at least 20% of the corporation's outstanding stock in one or more transactions in any 30-day period during the tax year,

2. A redemption treated as an exchange under section 302(a) or 303(a) of at least 20% of the corporation's outstanding stock in one or more transactions in any 30-day period during the tax year, or

3. An issuance of stock that equals at least 25% of the previously outstanding stock to one or more new shareholders in any 30-day period during the tax year.

To make the election, the corporation must attach a statement to a timely filed original or amended Form 1120S for the tax year for which the election is made. In the statement, the corporation must state that it is electing under Regulations section 1.1368-1(g)(2)(i) to treat the tax year as if it consisted of separate tax years. The statement must also give the facts relating to the qualifying disposition (e.g., sale, gift, stock issuance, or redemption), and state that each shareholder who held stock in the corporation during the tax year consents to the election. A corporate officer must sign the statement under penalties of perjury on behalf of the corporation. A single election statement may be filed for all elections made under this special rule for the tax year.

For more details on the election, see Regulations section 1.1368-1(g)(2).

Specific Instructions (Schedule K Only)

Enter the total pro rata share amount for each applicable line item on Schedule K.

Specific Instructions (Schedule K-1 Only)

General Information

On each Schedule K-1, complete the date spaces at the top; enter the names, addresses, and identifying numbers of the shareholder and corporation; complete items A through D; and enter the shareholder's pro rata share of each item. **Schedule K-1 must be prepared and given to each shareholder on or before the day on which Form 1120S is filed.**
Note: *Space has been provided on line 23 (Supplemental Information) of Schedule K-1 for the corporation to provide additional information to shareholders. This space, if sufficient, should be used in place of any attached schedules required for any lines on Schedule K-1, or other amounts not shown on lines 1 through 22 of Schedule K-1. Please be sure to identify the applicable line number next to the information entered below line 23.*

Special Reporting Requirements for Corporations With Multiple Activities

If items of income, loss, deduction, or credit from more than one activity (determined for purposes of the passive activity loss and credit limitations) are reported on lines 1, 2, or 3 of Schedule K-1, the corporation must provide information for each activity to its shareholders. See **Passive Activity**

Instructions for Form 1120S

Reporting Requirements on page 9 for details on the reporting requirements.

Special Reporting Requirements for At-Risk Activities

If the corporation is involved in one or more at-risk activities for which a loss is reported on Schedule K-1, the corporation must report information separately for each at-risk activity. See section 465(c) for a definition of at-risk activities.

For each at-risk activity, the following information must be provided on an attachment to Schedule K-1:

1. A statement that the information is a breakdown of at-risk activity loss amounts.

2. The identity of the at-risk activity; the loss amount for the activity; other income and deductions; and other information that relates to the activity.

Specific Items

Item A

If there was no change in shareholders or in the relative interest in stock the shareholders owned during the tax year, enter the percentage of total stock owned by each shareholder during the tax year. For example, if shareholders X and Y each owned 50% for the entire tax year, enter 50% in item A for each shareholder. Each shareholder's pro rata share items (lines 1 through 20 of Schedule K-1) are figured by multiplying the Schedule K amount on the corresponding line of Schedule K by the percentage in item A.

If there was a change in shareholders or in the relative interest in stock the shareholders owned during the tax year, each shareholder's percentage of ownership is weighted for the number of days in the tax year that stock was owned. For example, A and B each held 50% for half the tax year and A, B, and C held 40%, 40%, and 20%, respectively, for the remaining half of the tax year. The percentage of ownership for the year for A, B, and C is figured as follows and is then entered in item A.

	a	b	c (a × b)
	% of total stock owned	% of tax year held	% of ownership for the year
A	50 40	50 50	25 +20	45
B	50 40	50 50	25 +20	45
C	20	50	10	10
Total	. . . .		.100%

If there was a change in shareholders or in the relative interest in stock the shareholders owned during the tax year, each shareholder's pro rata share items generally are figured by multiplying the Schedule K amount by the percentage in item A. However, if a shareholder terminated his or her entire interest in the corporation during the year or a qualifying disposition took place, the corporation may elect to allocate income and

expenses, etc., as if the tax year consisted of 2 tax years, the first of which ends on the day of the termination or qualifying disposition. See **Special Rules** starting on page 16 for more details. Each shareholder's pro rata share items are figured separately for each period on a daily basis, based on the percentage of stock held by the shareholder on each day.

Item B

Enter the Internal Revenue Service Center address where the Form 1120S, to which a copy of this K-1 was attached, was or will be filed.

Item C

If the corporation is a registration-required tax shelter or has invested in a registration-required tax shelter, it must enter its tax shelter registration number in item C. Also, a corporation that has invested in a registration-required shelter must furnish a copy of its Form 8271 to its shareholders. See Form 8271 for more details.

Specific Instructions (Schedules K and K-1, Except as Noted)

Income (Loss)

Reminder: Before entering income items on Schedule K or K-1, be sure to reduce the items of income for the following:

1. Built-in gains tax (Schedule D, Part IV, line 32). Each recognized built-in gain item (within the meaning of section 1374(d)(3)) is reduced by its proportionate share of the built-in gains tax.

2. Capital gains tax (Schedule D, Part III, line 24). The section 1231 gain included on line 5 or 6 of Schedule K is reduced by this tax.

3. Excess net passive income tax (line 22a, page 1, Form 1120S). Each item of passive investment income (within the meaning of section 1362(d)(3)(C)) is reduced by its proportionate share of the net passive income tax.

Line 1—Ordinary Income (Loss) From Trade or Business Activities

Enter the amount from line 21, page 1. Enter the income or loss without reference to **(a)** shareholders' basis in the stock of the corporation and in any indebtedness of the corporation to the shareholders (section 1366(d)), **(b)** shareholders' at-risk limitations, and **(c)** shareholders' passive activity limitations. These limitations, if applicable, are determined at the shareholder level.

If the corporation is involved in more than one trade or business activity, see **Passive Activity Reporting Requirements** on page 9 for details on the information to be reported for each activity. If an at-risk activity loss is reported on line 1, see **Special Reporting Requirements for At-Risk Activities** on page 17.

Page 17

Line 2—Net Income (Loss) From Rental Real Estate Activities

Enter the net income or loss from rental real estate activities of the corporation from **Form 8825,** Rental Real Estate Income and Expenses of a Partnership or an S Corporation. Each Form 8825 has space for reporting the income and expenses of up to eight properties.

If the corporation has income or loss from more than one rental real estate activity reported on line 2, see **Passive Activity Reporting Requirements** on page 9 for details on the information to be reported for each activity. If an at-risk activity loss is reported on line 2, see **Special Reporting Requirements for At-Risk Activities** on page 17.

Line 3—Income and Expenses of Other Rental Activities

Enter on lines 3a and 3b of Schedule K (line 3 of Schedule K-1) the income and expenses of rental activities other than the income and expenses reported on Form 8825. If the corporation has more than one rental activity reported on line 3, see **Passive Activity Reporting Requirements** on page 9 for details on the information to be reported for each activity. If an at-risk activity loss is reported on line 3, see **Special Reporting Requirements for At-Risk Activities** on page 17. Also see **Rental activities** on page 7 for a definition and other details on other rental activities.

Lines 4a Through 4f—Portfolio Income (Loss)

Enter portfolio income (loss) on lines 4a through 4f. See **Portfolio income** on page 8 for the definition of portfolio income. Do not reduce portfolio income by deductions allocated to it. Report such deductions (other than interest expense) on line 9 of Schedules K and K-1. Interest expense allocable to portfolio income is generally investment interest expense and is reported on line 11a of Schedules K and K-1.

Lines 4a and 4b. Enter only taxable interest and ordinary dividends that are portfolio income. Interest income derived in the ordinary course of the corporation's trade or business, such as interest charged on receivable balances, is reported on line 5, page 1, Form 1120S. See Temporary Regulations section 1.469-2T(c)(3).

Lines 4d, 4e(1), and 4e(2). Enter on line 4d the gain or loss that is portfolio income (loss) from Schedule D (Form 1120S), line 6. Enter on line 4e(1) the gain or loss that is portfolio income (loss) from Schedule D (Form 1120S), line 12. Enter on line 4e(2) the gain or loss that is portfolio income (loss) from Schedule D (Form 1120S), line 13.

If any gain or loss from lines 6, 12, and 13 of Schedule D is not portfolio income (e.g., gain or loss from the disposition of nondepreciable personal property used in a trade or business), do not report this income or loss on lines 4d(2), 4e(1), and

4e(2). Instead, report it on line 6 of Schedules K and K-1. If the income or loss is attributable to more than one activity, report the income or loss amount separately for each activity on an attachment to Schedule K-1 and identify the activity to which the income or loss relates.

Line 4f. Enter any other portfolio income not reported on lines 4a through 4e.

If the corporation holds a residual interest in a REMIC, report on an attachment for line 4f each shareholder's share of taxable income (net loss) from the REMIC (line 1b of Schedule Q (Form 1066)); excess inclusion (line 2c of Schedule Q (Form 1066)); and section 212 expenses (line 3b of Schedule Q (Form 1066)). Because Schedule Q (Form 1066) is a quarterly statement, the corporation must follow the Schedule Q (Form 1066) Instructions for Residual Interest Holder to figure the amounts to report to shareholders for the corporation's tax year.

Line 5—Net Section 1231 Gain (Loss) (Other Than Due to Casualty or Theft)

Enter the net section 1231 gain (loss) (excluding net gain from involuntary conversions due to casualty or theft) from Form 4797, line 7, column (g). Report net gain or loss from involuntary conversions due to casualty or theft on line 6.

If the corporation is involved in more than one trade or business or rental activity, see **Passive Activity Reporting Requirements** on page 9 for details on the information to be reported for each activity. If an at-risk activity loss is reported on line 5, see **Special Reporting Requirements for At-Risk Activities** on page 17.

Note: *If the corporation was a partner in a 1997–98 fiscal year partnership and has a net section 1231 gain (loss) figured using only 28% rate gains and losses shown on Form 4797, line 7, column (h), see the instructions on page 24 for line 23, item 18.*

Line 6—Other Income (Loss)

Enter any other item of income or loss not included on lines 1 through 5. Items to be reported on line 6 include:
- Recoveries of tax benefit items (section 111).
- Gambling gains and losses (section 165(d)).
- Net gain (loss) from involuntary conversions due to casualty or theft. The amount for this item is shown on **Form 4684,** Casualties and Thefts, line 38a or 38b. Also, separately report the 28% rate gain (loss), if any, from involuntary conversions due to casualty or theft.
- Any net gain or loss from section 1256 contracts from **Form 6781,** Gains and Losses From Section 1256 Contracts and Straddles.
- Gain from the sale or exchange of qualified small business stock (as defined in the Instructions for Schedule D) that is eligible for the 50% section 1202

exclusion. To be eligible for the section 1202 exclusion, the stock must have been held by the corporation for more than 5 years and sold after August 11, 1998. Corporate shareholders are not eligible for the section 1202 exclusion. Additional limitations apply at the shareholder level. Report each shareholder's share of section 1202 gain on Schedule K-1. Each shareholder will determine if he or she qualifies for the section 1202 exclusion. Report on an attachment to Schedule K-1 for each sale or exchange the name of the qualified small business that issued the stock, the shareholder's share of the corporation's adjusted basis and sales price of the stock, and the dates the stock was bought and sold.
- Gain eligible for section 1045 rollover (replacement stock purchased by the corporation). Include only gain from the sale or exchange of qualified small business stock (as defined in the Instructions for Schedule D) that was deferred by the corporation under section 1045 and reported on Schedule D. See the Instructions for Schedule D for more details. Corporate shareholders are not eligible for the section 1045 rollover. Additional limitations apply at the shareholder level. Report each shareholder's share of the gain eligible for section 1045 rollover on Schedule K-1. Each shareholder will determine if he or she qualifies for the rollover. Report on an attachment to Schedule K-1 for each sale or exchange the name of the qualified small business that issued the stock, the shareholder's share of the corporation's adjusted basis and sales price of the stock, and the dates the stock was bought and sold.
- Gain eligible for section 1045 rollover (replacement stock not purchased by the corporation). Include only gain from the sale or exchange of qualified small business stock (as defined in the Instructions for Schedule D) the corporation held for more than 6 months but that **was not** deferred by the corporation under section 1045. See the Instructions for Schedule D for more details. A shareholder (other than a corporation) may be eligible to defer his or her pro rata share of this gain under section 1045 if he or she purchases other qualified small business stock during the 60-day period that began on the date the stock was sold by the corporation. Additional limitations apply at the shareholder level. Report on an attachment to Schedule K-1 for each sale or exchange the name of the qualified small business that issued the stock, the shareholder's share of the corporation's adjusted basis and sales price of the stock, and the dates the stock was bought and sold.

If the corporation is involved in more than one trade or business or rental activity, see **Passive Activity Reporting Requirements** on page 9 for details on the information to be reported for each activity. If an at-risk activity loss is reported on line 6, see **Special Reporting**

Requirements for At-Risk Activities on page 17.

Deductions

Line 7—Charitable Contributions

Enter the amount of charitable contributions paid by the corporation during its tax year. On an attachment to Schedules K and K-1, show separately the dollar amount of contributions subject to each of the 50%, 30%, and 20% of adjusted gross income limits. For additional information, see **Pub. 526,** Charitable Contributions.

Generally, no deduction is allowed for any contribution of $250 or more unless the corporation obtains a written acknowledgment from the charitable organization that shows the amount of cash contributed, describes any property contributed, and gives an estimate of the value of any goods or services provided in return for the contribution. The acknowledgment must be obtained by the due date (including extensions) of the corporation's return, or if earlier, the date the corporation files its return. Do not attach the acknowledgment to the tax return, but keep it with the corporation's records. These rules apply in addition to the filing requirements for Form 8283 described below.

Certain contributions made to an organization conducting lobbying activities are not deductible. See section 170(f)(9) for more details.

If the corporation contributes property other than cash and the deduction claimed for such property exceeds $500, complete **Form 8283,** Noncash Charitable Contributions, and attach it to Form 1120S. The corporation must give a copy of its Form 8283 to every shareholder if the deduction for any item or group of similar items of contributed property exceeds $5,000, even if the amount allocated to any shareholder is $5,000 or less.

If the deduction for an item or group of similar items of contributed property is $5,000 or less, the corporation must report each shareholder's pro rata share of the amount of noncash contributions to enable individual shareholders to complete their own Forms 8283. See the Instructions for Form 8283 for more information.

If the corporation made a qualified conservation contribution under section 170(h), also include the fair market value of the underlying property before and after the donation, as well as the type of legal interest contributed, and describe the conservation purpose furthered by the donation. Give a copy of this information to each shareholder.

Line 8—Section 179 Expense Deduction

An S corporation may elect to expense part of the cost of certain tangible property that the corporation purchased during the tax year for use in its trade or business or certain rental activities. See the Instructions for Form 4562 for more information.

Complete Part I of Form 4562 to figure the corporation's section 179 expense deduction. The corporation does not claim the deduction itself, but instead passes it through to the shareholders. Attach Form 4562 to Form 1120S and show the total section 179 expense deduction on Schedule K, line 8. Report each individual shareholder's pro rata share on Schedule K-1, line 8. Do not complete line 8 of Schedule K-1 for any shareholder that is an estate or trust.

If the corporation is an enterprise zone business, also report on an attachment to Schedules K and K-1 the cost of section 179 property placed in service during the year that is qualified zone property.

See the instructions for line 23 of Schedule K-1, item 3, for any recapture of a section 179 amount.

Line 9—Deductions Related to Portfolio Income (Loss)

Enter on line 9 the deductions clearly and directly allocable to portfolio income (other than interest expense). Interest expense related to portfolio income is investment interest expense and is reported on line 11a of Schedules K and K-1. Generally, the line 9 expenses are section 212 expenses and are subject to section 212 limitations at the shareholder level.

Note: *No deduction is allowed under section 212 for expenses allocable to a convention, seminar, or similar meeting. Because these expenses are not deductible by shareholders, the corporation does not report these expenses on line 9 or line 10. The expenses are nondeductible and are reported as such on line 19 of Schedules K and K-1.*

Line 10—Other Deductions

Enter any other deductions not included on lines 7, 8, 9, and 15e. On an attachment, identify the deduction and amount, and if the corporation has more than one activity, the activity to which the deduction relates.

Examples of items to be reported on an attachment to line 10 include:

● Amounts (other than investment interest required to be reported on line 11a of Schedules K and K-1) paid by the corporation that would be allowed as itemized deductions on a shareholder's income tax return if they were paid directly by a shareholder for the same purpose. These amounts include, but are not limited to, expenses under section 212 for the production of income other than from the corporation's trade or business.

● Any penalty on early withdrawal of savings not reported on line 9 because the corporation withdrew funds from its time savings deposit before its maturity.

● Soil and water conservation expenditures (section 175).

● Expenditures paid or incurred for the removal of architectural and transportation barriers to the elderly and disabled that the corporation has elected to treat as a current expense. See section 190.

● Contributions to a capital construction fund.

● Interest expense allocated to debt-financed distributions. See Notice 89-35, 1989-1 C.B. 675, for more information.

● If there was a gain (loss) from a casualty or theft to property not used in a trade or business or for income producing purposes, provide each shareholder with the needed information to complete Form 4684.

Investment Interest

Lines 11a and 11b must be completed for all shareholders.

Line 11a—Investment Interest Expense

Include on this line the interest properly allocable to debt on property held for investment purposes. Property held for investment includes property that produces income (unless derived in the ordinary course of a trade or business) from interest, dividends, annuities, or royalties; and gains from the disposition of property that produces those types of income or is held for investment.

Investment interest expense **does not** include interest expense allocable to a passive activity.

Report investment interest expense only on line 11a of Schedules K and K-1.

The amount on line 11a will be deducted by individual shareholders on Schedule A (Form 1040), line 13, after applying the investment interest expense limitations of section 163(d).

For more information, see **Form 4952,** Investment Interest Expense Deduction.

Lines 11b(1) and 11b(2)—Investment Income and Expenses

Enter on line 11b(1) only the investment income included on lines 4a, b, c, and f of Schedule K-1. Do not include other portfolio gains or losses on this line.

Enter on line 11b(2) only the investment expense included on line 9 of Schedule K-1.

If there are other items of investment income or expense included in the amounts that are required to be passed through separately to the shareholders on Schedule K-1, such as net short-term capital gain or loss, net long-term capital gain or loss, and other portfolio gains or losses, give each shareholder a schedule identifying these amounts.

Investment income includes gross income from property held for investment, the excess of net gain attributable to the disposition of property held for investment over net capital gain from the disposition of property held for investment, and any net capital gain from the disposition of property held for investment that each shareholder elects to include in investment income under section 163(d)(4)(B)(iii). Generally, investment income and investment expenses do not include any income or expenses from a passive activity. See Regulations section 1.469-2(f)(10) for exceptions.

Property subject to a net lease is not treated as investment property because it is subject to the passive loss rules. Do not reduce investment income by losses from passive activities.

Investment expenses are deductible expenses (other than interest) directly connected with the production of investment income. See the Instructions for Form 4952 for more information on investment income and expenses.

Credits

Note: *If the corporation has credits from more than one trade or business activity on line 12a or 13, or from more than one rental activity on line 12b, 12c, 12d, or 12e, it must report separately on an attachment to Schedule K-1, the amount of each credit and provide any other applicable activity information listed in* **Passive Activity Reporting Requirements** *on page 9.*

Line 12a—Credit for Alcohol Used as Fuel

Enter on line 12a of Schedule K the credit for alcohol used as fuel attributable to trade or business activities. Enter on line 12d or 12e the credit for alcohol used as fuel attributable to rental activities. Figure the credit on **Form 6478,** Credit for Alcohol Used as Fuel, and attach it to Form 1120S. The credit must be included in income on page 1, line 5, of Form 1120S. See section 40(f) for an election the corporation can make to have the credit not apply.

Enter each shareholder's share of the credit for alcohol used as fuel on line 12a, 12d, or 12e of Schedule K-1.

If this credit includes the small ethanol producer credit, identify on a statement attached to each Schedule K-1 **(a)** the amount of the small producer credit included in the total credit allocated to the shareholder, **(b)** the number of gallons of qualified ethanol fuel production allocated to the shareholder, and **(c)** the shareholder's pro rata share, in gallons, of the corporation's productive capacity for alcohol.

Line 12b—Low-Income Housing Credit

Section 42 provides for a credit that may be claimed by owners of low-income residential rental buildings. If shareholders are eligible to claim the low-income housing credit, complete the applicable parts of **Form 8586,** Low-Income Housing Credit, and attach it to Form 1120S. Enter the credit figured by the corporation on Form 8586, and any low-income housing credit received from other entities in which the corporation is allowed to invest, on the applicable line as explained below. The corporation must also complete and attach **Form 8609,** Low-Income Housing Credit Allocation Certification, and **Schedule A**

(Form 8609), Annual Statement, to Form 1120S. See the Instructions for Form 8586 and Form 8609 for information on completing these forms.

Line 12b(1). If the corporation invested in a partnership to which the provisions of section 42(j)(5) apply, report on line 12b(1) the credit the partnership reported to the corporation on line 12a(1) of Schedule K-1 (Form 1065). If the corporation invested **before 1990** in a section 42(j)(5) partnership, also include on this line any credit the partnership reported to the corporation on line 12a(3) of Schedule K-1 (Form 1065).

Line 12b(2). Report on line 12b(2) any low-income housing credit for property placed in service before 1990 and not reported on line 12b(1). This includes any credit from a building placed in service before 1990 in a project owned by the corporation and any credit from a partnership reported to the corporation on line 12a(2) of Schedule K-1 (Form 1065). Also include on this line any credit from a partnership reported to the corporation on line 12a(4) of Schedule K-1 (Form 1065), if the corporation invested in that partnership **before 1990.**

Line 12b(3). If the corporation invested **after 1989** in a partnership to which the provisions of section 42(j)(5) apply, report on line 12b(3) the credit the partnership reported to the corporation on line 12a(3) of Schedule K-1 (Form 1065).

Line 12b(4). Report on line 12b(4) any low-income housing credit for property placed in service after 1989 and not reported on any other line. This includes any credit from a building placed in service after 1989 in a project owned by the corporation and any credit from a partnership reported to the corporation on line 12a(4) of Schedule K-1 (Form 1065), if the corporation invested in that partnership **after 1989.**

Line 12c—Qualified Rehabilitation Expenditures Related to Rental Real Estate Activities

Enter total qualified rehabilitation expenditures related to rental real estate activities of the corporation. For line 12c of Schedule K, complete the applicable lines of **Form 3468,** Investment Credit, that apply to qualified rehabilitation expenditures for property related to rental real estate activities of the corporation for which income or loss is reported on line 2 of Schedule K. See Form 3468 for details on qualified rehabilitation expenditures. Attach Form 3468 to Form 1120S.

For line 12c of Schedule K-1, enter each shareholder's pro rata share of the expenditures. On the dotted line to the left of the entry space for line 12c, enter the line number of Form 3468 on which the shareholder should report the expenditures. If there is more than one type of expenditure, or the expenditures are from more than one line 2 activity, report this information separately for each expenditure or activity on an attachment to Schedules K and K-1.

Note: *Qualified rehabilitation expenditures* **not** *related to rental real estate activities must be listed separately on line 23 of Schedule K-1.*

Line 12d—Credits (Other Than Credits Shown on Lines 12b and 12c) Related to Rental Real Estate Activities

Enter on line 12d any other credit (other than credits on lines 12b and 12c) related to rental real estate activities. On the dotted line to the left of the entry space for line 12d, identify the type of credit. If there is more than one type of credit or the credit is from more than one line 2 activity, report this information separately for each credit or activity on an attachment to Schedules K and K-1. These credits may include any type of credit listed in the instructions for line 13.

Line 12e—Credits Related to Other Rental Activities

Enter on line 12e any credit related to other rental activities for which income or loss is reported on line 3 of Schedules K and K-1. On the dotted line to the left of the entry space for line 12e, identify the type of credit. If there is more than one type of credit or the credit is from more than one line 3 activity, report this information separately for each credit or activity on an attachment to Schedules K and K-1. These credits may include any type of credit listed in the instructions for line 13.

Line 13—Other Credits

Enter on line 13 any other credit, except credits or expenditures shown or listed for lines 12a through 12e of Schedules K and K-1 or the credit for Federal tax paid on fuels (which is reported on line 23 of page 1). On the dotted line to the left of the entry space for line 13, identify the type of credit. If there is more than one type of credit or the credit is from more than one activity, report this information separately for each credit or activity on an attachment to Schedules K and K-1.

The credits to be reported on line 13 and other required attachments follow.

● Credit for backup withholding on dividends, interest, or patronage dividends.

● Nonconventional source fuel credit. Figure this credit on a separate schedule and attach it to Form 1120S. See section 29 for rules on figuring the credit.

● Qualified electric vehicle credit (Form 8834).

● Unused investment credit from cooperatives. If the corporation is a member of a cooperative that passes an unused investment credit through to its members, the credit is in turn passed through to the corporation's shareholders.

● Work opportunity credit (Form 5884).

● Welfare-to-work credit (Form 8861).

● Credit for increasing research activities (Form 6765).

● Enhanced oil recovery credit (Form 8830).

● Disabled access credit (Form 8826).

- Renewable electricity production credit (Form 8835).
- Empowerment zone employment credit (Form 8844).
- Indian employment credit (Form 8845).
- Credit for employer social security and Medicare taxes paid on certain employee tips (Form 8846).
- Orphan drug credit (Form 8820).
- Credit for contributions to selected community development corporations (Form 8847).
- General credits from an electing large partnership.

See the instructions on page 23 for line 21 (Schedule K) and line 23 (Schedule K-1) to report expenditures qualifying for the **(a)** rehabilitation credit not related to rental real estate activities, **(b)** energy credit, or **(c)** reforestation credit.

Adjustments and Tax Preference Items

Lines 14a through 14e must be completed for all shareholders.

Enter items of income and deductions that are adjustments or tax preference items. See **Form 6251,** Alternative Minimum Tax—Individuals, or Schedule I of **Form 1041,** U.S. Income Tax Return for Estates and Trusts, to determine the amounts to enter and for other information.

Do not include as a tax preference item any qualified expenditures to which an election under section 59(e) may apply. Because these expenditures are subject to an election by each shareholder, the corporation cannot figure the amount of any tax preference related to them. Instead, the corporation must pass through to each shareholder on lines 16a and 16b of Schedule K-1 the information needed to figure the deduction.

Line 14a—Depreciation Adjustment on Property Placed in Service After 1986

Figure the adjustment for line 14a based only on tangible property placed in service after 1986 (and tangible property placed in service after July 31, 1986, and before 1987 for which the corporation elected to use the general depreciation system). **Do not** make an adjustment for motion picture films, videotapes, sound recordings, certain public utility property (as defined in section 168(f)(2)), or property depreciated under the unit-of-production method (or any other method not expressed in a term of years).

Using the same convention the corporation used for regular tax purposes, refigure depreciation as follows:
- For property that is neither real property nor property depreciated using the straight-line method, use the 150% declining balance method over the property's class life (instead of the recovery period), switching to straight line for the first tax year that method gives a better result. See Pub. 946 for a table of class lives. For property having no class life, use 12 years.

- For property depreciated using the straight-line method (other than real property), use the straight-line method over the property's class life (instead of the recovery period). For property having no class life, use 12 years.
- For residential rental and nonresidential real property, use the straight-line method over 40 years.

Determine the depreciation adjustment by subtracting the refigured depreciation from the depreciation claimed on Form 4562. If the refigured depreciation exceeds the depreciation claimed on Form 4562, enter the difference as a negative amount. See the Instructions for Form 6251 and Form 4562 for more information.

Note to fiscal year 1998–99 filers: *For certain property placed in service after December 31, 1998, the depreciation adjustment is eliminated. This includes residential rental and nonresidential real property and any other property depreciated using the straight line or 150% declining balance method for regular tax purposes.*

An AMT depreciation adjustment will still have to be computed on MACRS property depreciated using the 200% declining balance method for regular tax purposes. However, the adjustment will equal the difference between the depreciation claimed for regular tax purposes and the depreciation that would have been claimed using the 150% declining balance method. This is because the use of alternative depreciation system (ADS) recovery periods to compute AMT depreciation has been repealed for property placed in service after December 31, 1998.

Line 14b—Adjusted Gain or Loss

If the corporation disposed of any tangible property placed in service after 1986 (or after July 31, 1986, if an election was made to use the General Depreciation System), or if it disposed of a certified pollution control facility placed in service after 1986, refigure the gain or loss from the disposition using the adjusted basis for the AMT. The property's adjusted basis for the AMT is its cost or other basis minus all depreciation or amortization deductions allowed or allowable for the AMT during the current tax year and previous tax years. Enter on this line the difference between the regular tax gain (loss) and the AMT gain (loss). If the AMT gain is less than the regular tax gain, OR the AMT loss is more than the regular tax loss, OR there is an AMT loss and a regular tax gain, enter the difference as a negative amount.

If any part of the adjustment is allocable to net short-term capital gain (loss), net long-term capital gain (loss), or net section 1231 gain (loss), attach a schedule that identifies the amount of the adjustment allocable to each type of gain or loss. For a net long-term capital gain (loss) or net section 1231 gain (loss), also identify the amount of adjustment that is

28% rate gain (loss) and unrecaptured section 1250 gain. No schedule is required if the adjustment is allocable solely to ordinary gain (loss).

Line 14c—Depletion (Other Than Oil and Gas)

Do not include any depletion on oil and gas wells. The shareholders must figure their depletion deductions and preference items separately under section 613A.

Refigure the depletion deduction under section 611 for mines, wells (other than oil and gas wells), and other natural deposits for the AMT. Percentage depletion is limited to 50% of the taxable income from the property as figured under section 613(a), using only income and deductions for the AMT. Also, the deduction is limited to the property's adjusted basis at the end of the year, as refigured for the AMT. Figure this limit separately for each property. When refiguring the property's adjusted basis, take into account any AMT adjustments made this year or in previous years that affect basis (other than the current year's depletion).

Enter the difference between the regular tax and AMT deduction. If the AMT deduction is greater, enter the difference as a negative amount.

Lines 14d(1) and 14d(2)

Generally, the amounts to be entered on these lines are only the income and deductions for oil, gas, and geothermal properties that are used to figure the amount on line 21, page 1, Form 1120S.

If there are any items of income or deductions for oil, gas, and geothermal properties included in the amounts that are required to be passed through separately to the shareholders on Schedule K-1, give each shareholder a schedule that shows, for the line on which the income or deduction is included, the amount of income or deductions included in the total amount for that line. Do not include any of these direct pass-through amounts on line 14d(1) or 14d(2). The shareholder is told in the Shareholder's Instructions for Schedule K-1 (Form 1120S) to adjust the amounts on lines 14d(1) and 14d(2) for any other income or deductions from oil, gas, or geothermal properties included on lines 2 through 10 and 23 of Schedule K-1 in order to determine the total income and deductions from oil, gas, and geothermal properties for the corporation.

Figure the amounts for lines 14d(1) and 14d(2) separately for oil and gas properties that are not geothermal deposits and for all properties that are geothermal deposits.

Give the shareholders a schedule that shows the separate amounts included in the computation of the amounts on lines 14d(1) and 14d(2).

Line 14d(1)—Gross income from oil, gas, and geothermal properties. Enter the total amount of gross income (within the meaning of section 613(a)) from all oil, gas, and geothermal properties received or accrued during the tax year and included on page 1, Form 1120S.

Line 14d(2)—Deductions allocable to oil, gas, and geothermal properties. Enter the amount of any deductions allowed for the AMT that are allocable to oil, gas, and geothermal properties.

Line 14e—Other Adjustments and Tax Preference Items

Attach a schedule that shows each shareholder's share of other items not shown on lines 14a through 14d(2) that are adjustments or tax preference items or that the shareholder needs to complete Form 6251 or Schedule I of Form 1041. See these forms and their instructions to determine the amount to enter. Other adjustments or tax preference items include the following:

- Accelerated depreciation of real property under pre-1987 rules.
- Accelerated depreciation of leased personal property under pre-1987 rules.
- Long-term contracts entered into after February 28, 1986. Except for certain home construction contracts, the taxable income from these contracts must be figured using the percentage of completion method of accounting for the AMT.
- Losses from tax shelter farm activities. No loss from any tax shelter farm activity is allowed for the AMT.

Foreign Taxes

Lines 15a through 15g must be completed whether or not a shareholder is eligible for the foreign tax credit, if the corporation has foreign income, deductions, or losses, or has paid or accrued foreign taxes.

In addition to the instructions below, see **Form 1116,** Foreign Tax Credit (Individual, Estate, Trust, or Nonresident Alien Individual), and the related instructions.

Line 15a—Type of Income

Enter the type of income from outside the United States as follows:

- Passive income.
- High withholding tax interest.
- Financial services income.
- Shipping income.
- Dividends from a DISC or former DISC.
- Certain distributions from a foreign sales corporation (FSC) or former FSC.
- Dividends from each noncontrolled section 902 corporation.
- Taxable income attributable to foreign trade income (within the meaning of section 923(b)).
- General limitation income (all other income from sources outside the United States, including income from sources within U.S. possessions).

If, for the country or U.S. possession shown on line 15b, the corporation had more than one type of income, enter "See attached" and attach a schedule for each type of income for lines 15c through 15g.

Line 15b—Foreign Country or U.S. Possession

Enter the name of the foreign country or U.S. possession. If, for the type of income shown on line 15a, the corporation had income from, or paid taxes to, more than one foreign country or U.S. possession, enter "See attached" and attach a schedule for each country for lines 15a and 15c through 15g.

Line 15c—Total Gross Income From Sources Outside the United States

Enter in U.S. dollars the total gross income from sources outside the United States. Attach a schedule that shows each type of income listed in the instructions for line 15a.

Line 15d—Total Applicable Deductions and Losses

Enter in U.S. dollars the total applicable deductions and losses attributable to income on line 15c. Attach a schedule that shows each type of deduction or loss as follows:

- Expenses directly allocable to each type of income listed above.
- Pro rata share of all other deductions not directly allocable to specific items of income.
- Pro rata share of losses from other separate limitation categories.

Line 15e—Total Foreign Taxes

Enter in U.S. dollars the total foreign taxes (described in section 901) paid or accrued by the corporation to foreign countries or U.S. possessions. Translate the foreign amounts into U.S. dollars by using the rules in section 986. Attach a schedule that shows the dates the taxes were paid or accrued, the amount in both foreign currency and in U.S. dollars, and the conversion rate for:

- Taxes withheld at source on dividends.
- Taxes withheld at source on rents and royalties.
- Other foreign taxes paid or accrued.

Line 15f—Reduction in Taxes Available for Credit

Enter in U.S. dollars the total reduction in taxes available for credit. Attach a schedule that shows separately the reduction for:

- Foreign mineral income.
- Failure to furnish returns required under section 6038.
- Taxes attributable to boycott operations (section 908).
- Foreign oil and gas extraction income (section 907(a)).
- Any other items (specify).

Line 15g—Other Foreign Tax Information

Enter in U.S. dollars any items not covered on lines 15c through 15f that shareholders need to complete Form 1116 (e.g., gross income from all sources).

Other

Lines 16a and 16b—Section 59(e)(2) Expenditures

Generally, section 59(e) allows each shareholder to make an election to deduct the shareholder's pro rata share of the corporation's otherwise deductible qualified expenditures ratably over 10 years (3 years for circulation expenditures), beginning with the tax year in which the expenditures were made (or for intangible drilling and development costs, over the 60-month period beginning with the month in which such costs were paid or incurred). The term "qualified expenditures" includes only the following types of expenditures paid or incurred during the tax year:

- Circulation expenditures.
- Research and experimental expenditures.
- Intangible drilling and development costs.
- Mining exploration and development costs.

If a shareholder makes the election, the above items are not treated as tax preference items.

Because the shareholders are generally allowed to make this election, the corporation cannot deduct these amounts or include them as adjustments or tax preference items on Schedule K-1. Instead, on lines 16a and 16b of Schedule K-1, the corporation passes through the information the shareholders need to figure their separate deductions.

On line 16a, enter the type of expenditures claimed on line 16b. Enter on line 16b the qualified expenditures paid or incurred during the tax year to which an election under section 59(e) may apply. Enter this amount for all shareholders whether or not any shareholder makes an election under section 59(e). If the expenditures are for intangible drilling and development costs, enter the month in which the expenditures were paid or incurred (after the type of expenditures on line 16a). If there is more than one type of expenditure included in the total shown on line 16b (or intangible drilling and development costs were paid or incurred for more than 1 month), report this information separately for each type of expenditure (or month) on an attachment to Schedules K and K-1.

Line 17—Tax-Exempt Interest Income

Enter on line 17 tax-exempt interest income, including any exempt-interest dividends received from a mutual fund or other regulated investment company. This information must be reported by individuals on line 8b of Form 1040. Generally, the basis of the shareholder's stock is increased by the amount shown on this line under section 1367(a)(1)(A).

Line 18—Other Tax-Exempt Income

Enter on line 18 all income of the corporation exempt from tax other than tax-exempt interest (e.g., life insurance proceeds). Generally, the basis of the shareholder's stock is increased by the amount shown on this line under section 1367(a)(1)(A).

Line 19—Nondeductible Expenses

Enter on line 19 nondeductible expenses paid or incurred by the corporation. Do not include separately stated deductions shown elsewhere on Schedules K and K-1, capital expenditures, or items for which the deduction is deferred to a later tax year. Generally, the basis of the shareholder's stock is decreased by the amount shown on this line under section 1367(a)(2)(D).

Line 20

Enter total distributions made to each shareholder other than dividends reported on line 22 of Schedule K. Noncash distributions of appreciated property are valued at fair market value. See **Distributions** on page 25 for the ordering rules on distributions.

Line 21 (Schedule K Only)

Attach a statement to Schedule K to report the corporation's total income, expenditures, or other information for items 1 through 19 of the line 23 (Schedule K-1 Only) instruction below.

Line 22 (Schedule K Only)

Enter total dividends paid to shareholders from accumulated earnings and profits. Report these dividends to shareholders on Form 1099-DIV. Do not report them on Schedule K-1.

Lines 22a and 22b (Schedule K-1 Only)—Recapture of Low-Income Housing Credit

If recapture of part or all of the low-income housing credit is required because **(a)** prior year qualified basis of a building decreased or **(b)** the corporation disposed of a building or part of its interest in a building, see **Form 8611,** Recapture of Low-Income Housing Credit. The instructions for Form 8611 indicate when Form 8611 is completed by the corporation and what information is provided to shareholders when recapture is required.

Note: *If a shareholder's ownership interest in a building decreased because of a transaction at the shareholder level, the corporation must provide the necessary information to the shareholder to enable the shareholder to figure the recapture.*

If the corporation filed **Form 8693,** Low-Income Housing Credit Disposition Bond, to avoid recapture of the low-income housing credit, no entry should be made on line 22 of Schedule K-1.

See Form 8586, Form 8611, and section 42 for more information.

Supplemental Information

Line 23 (Schedule K-1 Only)

Enter in the line 23 Supplemental Information space of Schedule K-1, or on an attached schedule if more space is needed, each shareholder's share of any information asked for on lines 1 through 22 that is required to be reported in detail, and items **1** through **19** below. Please identify the applicable line number next to the information entered in the Supplemental Information space. Show income or gains as a positive number. Show losses in parentheses.

1. Taxes paid on undistributed capital gains by a regulated investment company or a real estate investment trust (REIT). As a shareholder of a regulated investment company or a REIT, the corporation will receive notice on **Form 2439,** Notice to Shareholder of Undistributed Long-Term Capital Gains, of the amount of tax paid on undistributed capital gains.

2. Gross income and other information relating to oil and gas well properties that are reported to shareholders to allow them to figure the depletion deduction for oil and gas well properties. See section 613A(c)(11) for details.

The corporation cannot deduct depletion on oil and gas wells. Each shareholder must determine the allowable amount to report on his or her return. See Pub. 535 for more information.

3. Recapture of section 179 expense deduction. For property placed in service after 1986, the section 179 deduction is recaptured at any time the business use of property drops to 50% or less. Enter the amount originally passed through and the corporation's tax year in which it was passed through. Inform the shareholder if the recapture amount was caused by the disposition of the section 179 property. See section 179(d)(10) for more information. Do not include this amount on line 4 or 5, page 1, Form 1120S.

4. Recapture of certain mining exploration expenditures (section 617).

5. Any information or statements the corporation is required to furnish to shareholders to allow them to comply with requirements under section 6111 (registration of tax shelters) or section 6662(d)(2)(B)(ii) (regarding adequate disclosure of items that may cause an understatement of income tax).

6. If the corporation is involved in farming or fishing activities, report the gross income from these activities to shareholders.

7. Any information needed by a shareholder to compute the interest due under section 453(l)(3). If the corporation elected to report the dispositions of certain timeshares and residential lots on the installment method, each shareholder's tax liability must be increased by the shareholder's pro rata share of the interest on tax attributable to the installment payments received during the tax year.

8. Any information needed by a shareholder to compute the interest due under section 453A(c). If an obligation arising from the disposition of property to which section 453A applies is outstanding at the close of the year, each shareholder's tax liability must be increased by the tax due under section 453A(c) on the shareholder's pro rata share of the tax deferred under the installment method.

9. Any information needed by a shareholder to properly capitalize interest as required by section 263A(f). See **Section 263A uniform capitalization rules** on page 11 for more information.

10. If the corporation is a closely held S corporation (defined in section 460(b)) and it entered into any long-term contracts after February 28, 1986, that are accounted for under either the percentage of completion-capitalized cost method or the percentage of completion method, it must attach a schedule to Form 1120S showing the information required in items (a) and (b) of the instructions for lines 1 and 3 of Part II for **Form 8697,** Interest Computation Under the Look-Back Method for Completed Long-Term Contracts. It must also report the amounts for Part II, lines 1 and 3, to its shareholders. See the Instructions for Form 8697 for more information.

11. Expenditures qualifying for the **(a)** rehabilitation credit not related to rental real estate activities, **(b)** energy credit, or **(c)** reforestation credit. Complete and attach Form 3468 to Form 1120S. See Form 3468 and related instructions for information on eligible property and the lines on Form 3468 to complete. Do not include that part of the cost of the property the corporation has elected to expense under section 179. Attach to each Schedule K-1 a separate schedule in a format similar to that shown on Form 3468 detailing each shareholder's pro rata share of qualified expenditures. Also indicate the lines of Form 3468 on which the shareholders should report these amounts.

12. Recapture of investment credit. Complete and attach **Form 4255,** Recapture of Investment Credit, when investment credit property is disposed of, or it no longer qualifies for the credit, before the end of the recapture period or the useful life applicable to the property. State the type of property at the top of Form 4255, and complete lines 2, 4, and 5, whether or not any shareholder is subject to recapture of the credit. Attach to each Schedule K-1 a separate schedule providing the information the corporation is required to show on Form 4255, but list only the shareholder's pro rata share of the cost of the property subject to recapture. Also indicate the lines of Form 4255 on which the shareholders should report these amounts.

The corporation itself is liable for investment credit recapture in certain cases. See the instructions for line 22c, page 1, Form 1120S, for details.

13. Any information needed by a shareholder to compute the recapture of the qualified electric vehicle credit. See Pub. 535 for more information.

14. Any information a shareholder may need to figure recapture of the Indian employment credit. Generally, if the corporation terminates a qualified employee less than 1 year after the date of initial employment, any Indian employment credit allowed for a prior tax year by reason of wages paid or incurred to that employee must be recaptured. For details, see section 45A(d).

15. Nonqualified withdrawals by the corporation from a capital construction fund.

16. Unrecaptured section 1250 gain. Figure this amount for each section 1250 property in Part III of Form 4797 for which you had an entry in column (g), but not in column (h), of Part I of Form 4797 by subtracting line 26g of Form 4797 from the **smaller** of line 22 or line 24 of Form 4797. Figure the total of these amounts for all section 1250 properties. Report each shareholder's pro rata share of the total amount as "Unrecaptured section 1250 gain."

If the corporation also received a Schedule K-1 or Form 1099-DIV from an estate, a trust, a REIT, or a mutual fund reporting "unrecaptured section 1250 gain," **do not** add it to the corporation's own unrecaptured section 1250 gain. Instead, report it as a separate amount. For example, if the corporation received a Form 1099-DIV from a REIT with unrecaptured section 1250 gain, report it as "Unrecaptured section 1250 gain from a REIT."

17. If the corporation is a closely held S corporation (defined in section 460(b)(4)) and it depreciated certain property placed in service after September 13, 1995, under the income forecast method, it must attach to Form 1120S the information specified in the instructions for Form 8866, line 2, for the 3rd and 10th tax years beginning after the tax year the property was placed in service. It must also report the line 2 amounts to its shareholders. See the Instructions for Form 8866 for more details.

18. For a corporation that was a partner in a 1997–1998 fiscal year partnership, each shareholder's share of the net section 1231 gain (loss) figured using only 28% rate gains and losses from Form 4797, line 7, column (h).

19. Any other information the shareholders need to prepare their tax returns.

Specific Instructions

Schedule L—Balance Sheets per Books

The balance sheets should agree with the corporation's books and records. Include certificates of deposit as cash on line 1 of Schedule L.

If the S election terminated during the tax year, the year-end balance sheet generally should agree with the books and records at the end of the C short year. However, if the corporation elected under section 1362(e)(3) to have items assigned to each short year under normal tax accounting rules, the year-end balance sheet should agree with the books and records at the end of the S short year.

Line 5—Tax-Exempt Securities

Include on this line—

1. State and local government obligations, the interest on which is excludible from gross income under section 103(a), and

2. Stock in a mutual fund or other regulated investment company that distributed exempt-interest dividends during the tax year of the corporation.

Line 24—Retained Earnings

If the corporation maintains separate accounts for appropriated and unappropriated retained earnings, it may want to continue such accounting for purposes of preparing its financial balance sheet. Also, if the corporation converts to C corporation status in a subsequent year, it will be required to report its appropriated and unappropriated retained earnings on separate lines of Schedule L of Form 1120.

Schedule M-1—Reconciliation of Income (Loss) per Books With Income (Loss) per Return

Line 3b—Travel and Entertainment

Include on this line 50% of meals and entertainment not allowed under section 274(n); expenses for the use of an entertainment facility; the part of business gifts over $25; expenses of an individual allocable to conventions on cruise ships over $2,000; employee achievement awards over $400; the part of the cost of entertainment tickets that exceeds face value (also subject to 50% disallowance); the part of the cost of skyboxes that exceeds the face value of nonluxury box seat tickets; the part of the cost of luxury water travel not allowed under section 274(m); expenses for travel as a form of education; nondeductible club dues; and other travel and entertainment expenses not allowed as a deduction.

Schedule M-2—Analysis of Accumulated Adjustments Account, Other Adjustments Account, and Shareholders' Undistributed Taxable Income Previously Taxed

Column (a)—Accumulated Adjustments Account

The accumulated adjustments account (AAA) is an account of the S corporation that generally reflects the accumulated undistributed net income of the corporation for the corporation's

post-1982 years. S corporations with accumulated E&P must maintain the AAA to determine the tax effect of distributions during S years and the post-termination transition period. An S corporation without accumulated E&P does not need to maintain the AAA in order to determine the tax effect of distributions. Nevertheless, if an S corporation without accumulated E&P engages in certain transactions to which section 381(a) applies, such as a merger into an S corporation with accumulated E&P, the S corporation must be able to calculate its AAA at the time of the merger for purposes of determining the tax effect of post-merger distributions. Therefore, it is recommended that the AAA be maintained by all S corporations.

At the end of the tax year, the AAA is determined by taking into account the taxable income, deductible losses and expenses, and nondeductible losses and expenses for the tax year (other than expenses related to tax-exempt income and Federal taxes attributable to a C corporation tax year). See Regulations section 1.1368-2. After the year-end income and expense adjustments are made, the AAA is reduced by distributions made during the tax year. See **Distributions** on page 25 for distribution rules. For adjustments to the AAA for redemptions, reorganizations, and corporate separations, see Regulations section 1.1368-2(d).

Note: *The AAA may have a negative balance at year end. See section 1368(e).*

Column (b)—Other Adjustments Account

The other adjustments account is adjusted for tax-exempt income (and related expenses) and Federal taxes attributable to a C corporation tax year. After these adjustments are made, the account is reduced for any distributions made during the year. See **Distributions** on page 25.

Column (c)—Shareholders' Undistributed Taxable Income Previously Taxed

The shareholders' undistributed taxable income previously taxed account, also called previously taxed income (PTI), is maintained only if the corporation had a balance in this account at the start of its 1998 tax year. If there is a beginning balance for the 1998 tax year, no adjustments are made to the account except to reduce the account for distributions made under section 1375(d) (as in effect before the enactment of the Subchapter S Revision Act of 1982). See **Distributions** on page 25 for the order of distributions from the account.

Each shareholder's right to nontaxable distributions from PTI is personal and cannot be transferred to another person. The corporation is required to keep records of each shareholder's net share of PTI.

Distributions

General rule. Unless the corporation makes one of the elections described below, property distributions (including cash) are applied in the following order to reduce accounts of the S corporation that are used to figure the tax effect of distributions made by the corporation to its shareholders:

1. Reduce the AAA determined without regard to any net negative adjustment for the tax year (but not below zero). If distributions during the tax year exceed the AAA at the close of the tax year determined without regard to any net negative adjustment for the tax year, the AAA is allocated pro rata to each distribution made during the tax year. See section 1368(c). The term "net negative adjustment" means the excess, if any, of the reductions in the AAA for the tax year (other than distributions) over the increases in the AAA for the tax year.

2. Reduce shareholders' PTI account for any section 1375(d) (as in effect before 1983) distributions. A distribution from the PTI account is tax free to the extent of a shareholder's basis in his or her stock in the corporation.

3. Reduce accumulated E&P. Generally, the S corporation has accumulated E&P only if it has not distributed E&P accumulated in prior years when the S corporation was a C corporation (section 1361(a)(2)). See section 312 for information on E&P. The only adjustments that can be made to the accumulated E&P of an S corporation are **(a)** reductions for dividend distributions; **(b)** adjustments for redemptions, liquidations, reorganizations, etc.; and **(c)** reductions for investment credit recapture tax for which the corporation is liable. See sections 1371(c) and (d)(3).

4. Reduce the other adjustments account.

5. Reduce any remaining shareholders' equity accounts.

Elections relating to source of distributions. The corporation may modify the above ordering rules by making one or more of the following elections:

1. *Election to distribute accumulated E&P first.* If the corporation has accumulated E&P and wants to distribute this E&P before making distributions from the AAA, it may elect to do so with the consent of all its affected shareholders (section 1368(e)(3)(B)). This election is irrevocable and applies only for the tax year for which it is made. For details on making the election, see **Statement regarding elections** below.

2. *Election to make a deemed dividend.* If the corporation wants to distribute all or part of its accumulated E&P through a deemed dividend, it may elect to do so with the consent of all its affected shareholders (section 1368(e)(3)(B)). Under this election, the corporation will be treated as also having made the election to distribute accumulated E&P first. The amount of the deemed dividend cannot exceed the accumulated E&P at the end of the tax year, reduced by any actual distributions of accumulated E&P made during the tax year. A deemed dividend is treated as if it were a pro rata distribution of money to the shareholders, received by the shareholders, and immediately contributed back to the corporation, all on the last day of the tax year. This election is irrevocable and applies only for the tax year for which it is made. For details on making the election, see **Statement regarding elections** below.

3. *Election to forego PTI.* If the corporation wants to forego distributions of PTI, it may elect to do so with the consent of all its affected shareholders (section 1368(e)(3)(B)). Under this election, paragraph 2 under the **General rule** above does not apply to any distribution made during the tax year. This election is irrevocable and applies only for the tax year for which it is made. For details on making the election, see **Statement regarding elections** below.

Statement regarding elections. To make any of the above elections, the corporation must attach a statement to a timely filed original or amended Form 1120S for the tax year for which the election is made. In the statement, the corporation must identify the election it is making and must state that each

shareholder consents to the election. A corporate officer must sign the statement under penalties of perjury on behalf of the corporation. The statement of election to make a deemed dividend must include the amount of the deemed dividend distributed to each shareholder.

Example

The following example shows how the Schedule M-2 accounts are adjusted for items of income (loss), deductions, and distributions reported on Form 1120S.

Items per return are:

1. Page 1, line 21 income—$219,000

2. Schedule K, line 2 loss—($3,000)

3. Schedule K, line 4a income—$4,000

4. Schedule K, line 4b income—$16,000

5. Schedule K, line 7 deduction—$24,000

6. Schedule K, line 8 deduction—$3,000

7. Schedule K, line 13 work opportunity credit—$6,000

8. Schedule K, line 17 tax-exempt interest—$5,000

9. Schedule K, line 19 nondeductible expenses—$6,000 (reduction in salaries and wages for work opportunity credit), and

10. Schedule K, line 20 distributions—$65,000.

Based on return items 1 through 10 and starting balances of zero, the columns for the AAA and the other adjustments account are completed as shown in the Schedule M-2 Worksheet below.

Note: *For the AAA account, the worksheet line 3—$20,000 amount is the total of the Schedule K, lines 4a and 4b incomes of $4,000 and $16,000. The worksheet line 5—$36,000 amount is the total of the Schedule K, line 2 loss of ($3,000), line 7 deduction of $24,000, line 8 deduction of $3,000, and the line 19 nondeductible expenses of $6,000. For the other adjustments account, the worksheet line 3 amount is the Schedule K, line 17, tax-exempt interest income of $5,000. Other worksheet amounts are self-explanatory.*

Schedule M-2 Worksheet

		(a) Accumulated adjustments account	(b) Other adjustments account	(c) Shareholders' undistributed taxable income previously taxed
1	Balance at beginning of tax year	-0-	-0-	
2	Ordinary income from page 1, line 21	219,000		
3	Other additions	20,000	5,000	
4	Loss from page 1, line 21	( )		
5	Other reductions	(36,000)	( )	
6	Combine lines 1 through 5	203,000	5,000	
7	Distributions other than dividend distributions	65,000	-0-	
8	Balance at end of tax year. Subtract line 7 from line 6	138,000	5,000	

Codes for Principal Business Activity

This list of principal business activities and their associated codes is designed to classify an enterprise by the type of activity in which it is engaged to facilitate the administration of the Internal Revenue Code. For tax years beginning after 1997, these principal business activity codes are based on the North American Industry Classification System.

Using the list of activities and codes below, determine from which activity the company derives the largest percentage of its "total receipts." Total receipts is defined as the sum of gross receipts or sales (page 1, line 1a), all other income (page 1, lines 4 and 5), income (receipts only) reported on Schedule K, lines 3a and 4a through 4f, and income (receipts only) reported on Form 8825, lines 2, 19, and 20a. If the company purchases raw materials and supplies them to a subcontractor to produce the finished product, but retains title to the product, the company is considered a manufacturer and must use one of the manufacturing codes (311110-339900).

Once the principal business activity is determined, enter the six-digit code from the list below on page 1, item B. Also enter a brief description of the business activity on page 2, Schedule B, line 2(a) and the principal product or service of the business on line 2(b).

Agriculture, Forestry, Fishing and Hunting

Code

Crop Production
111100 Oilseed & Grain Farming
111210 Vegetable & Melon Farming (including potatoes & yams)
111300 Fruit & Tree Nut Farming
111400 Greenhouse, Nursery, & Floriculture Production
111900 Other Crop Farming (including tobacco, cotton, sugarcane, hay, peanut, sugar beet & all other crop farming)

Animal Production
112111 Beef Cattle Ranching & Farming
112112 Cattle Feedlots
112120 Dairy Cattle & Milk Production
112210 Hog & Pig Farming
112300 Poultry & Egg Production
112400 Sheep & Goat Farming
112510 Animal Aquaculture (including shellfish & finfish farms & hatcheries)
112900 Other Animal Production

Forestry and Logging
113110 Timber Tract Operations
113210 Forest Nurseries & Gathering of Forest Products
113310 Logging

Fishing, Hunting and Trapping
114110 Fishing
114210 Hunting & Trapping

Support Activities for Agriculture and Forestry
115110 Support Activities for Crop Production (including cotton ginning, soil preparation, planting, & cultivating)
115210 Support Activities for Animal Production
115310 Support Activities For Forestry

Mining
211110 Oil & Gas Extraction
212110 Coal Mining
212200 Metal Ore Mining
212310 Stone Mining & Quarrying
212320 Sand, Gravel, Clay, & Ceramic & Refractory Minerals Mining & Quarrying
212390 Other Nonmetallic Mineral Mining & Quarrying
213110 Support Activities for Mining

Utilities
221100 Electric Power Generation, Transmission & Distribution
221210 Natural Gas Distribution
221300 Water, Sewage & Other Systems

Construction

Code

Building, Developing, and General Contracting
233110 Land Subdivision & Land Development
233200 Residential Building Construction
233300 Nonresidential Building Construction

Heavy Construction
234100 Highway, Street, Bridge, & Tunnel Construction
234900 Other Heavy Construction

Special Trade Contractors
235110 Plumbing, Heating, & Air-Conditioning Contractors
235210 Painting & Wall Covering Contractors
235310 Electrical Contractors
235400 Masonry, Drywall, Insulation, & Tile Contractors
235500 Carpentry & Floor Contractors
235610 Roofing, Siding, & Sheet Metal Contractors
235710 Concrete Contractors
235810 Water Well Drilling Contractors
235900 Other Special Trade Contractors

Manufacturing

Food Manufacturing
311100 Animal Food Mfg
311200 Grain & Oilseed Milling
311300 Sugar & Confectionery Product Mfg
311400 Fruit & Vegetable Preserving & Specialty Food Mfg
311500 Dairy Product Mfg
311610 Animal Slaughtering and Processing
311710 Seafood Product Preparation & Packaging
311800 Bakeries & Tortilla Mfg
311900 Other Food Mfg (including coffee, tea, flavorings & seasonings)

Beverage and Tobacco Product Manufacturing
312110 Soft Drink & Ice Mfg
312120 Breweries
312130 Wineries
312140 Distilleries
312200 Tobacco Manufacturing

Textile Mills and Textile Product Mills
313000 Textile Mills
314000 Textile Product Mills

Apparel Manufacturing
315100 Apparel Knitting Mills
315210 Cut & Sew Apparel Contractors
315220 Men's & Boys' Cut & Sew Apparel Mfg
315230 Women's & Girls' Cut & Sew Apparel Mfg

Code
315290 Other Cut & Sew Apparel Mfg
315990 Apparel Accessories & Other Apparel Mfg

Leather and Allied Product Manufacturing
316110 Leather & Hide Tanning & Finishing
316210 Footwear Mfg (including rubber & plastics)
316990 Other Leather & Allied Product Mfg

Wood Product Manufacturing
321110 Sawmills & Wood Preservation
321210 Veneer, Plywood, & Engineered Wood Product Mfg
321900 Other Wood Product Mfg

Paper Manufacturing
322100 Pulp, Paper, & Paperboard Mills
322200 Converted Paper Product Mfg

Printing and Related Support Activities
323100 Printing & Related Support Activities

Petroleum and Coal Products Manufacturing
324110 Petroleum Refineries (including integrated)
324120 Asphalt Paving, Roofing, & Saturated Materials Mfg
324190 Other Petroleum & Coal Products Mfg

Chemical Manufacturing
325100 Basic Chemical Mfg
325200 Resin, Synthetic Rubber, & Artificial & Synthetic Fibers & Filaments Mfg
325300 Pesticide, Fertilizer, & Other Agricultural Chemical Mfg
325410 Pharmaceutical & Medicine Mfg
325500 Paint, Coating, & Adhesive Mfg
325600 Soap, Cleaning Compound, & Toilet Preparation Mfg
325900 Other Chemical Product & Preparation Mfg

Plastics and Rubber Products Manufacturing
326100 Plastics Product Mfg
326200 Rubber Product Mfg

Nonmetallic Mineral Product Manufacturing
327100 Clay Product & Refractory Mfg
327210 Glass & Glass Product Mfg
327300 Cement & Concrete Product Mfg
327400 Lime & Gypsum Product Mfg
327900 Other Nonmetallic Mineral Product Mfg

Primary Metal Manufacturing
331110 Iron & Steel Mills & Ferroalloy Mfg
331200 Steel Product Mfg from Purchased Steel
331310 Alumina & Aluminum Production & Processing
331400 Nonferrous Metal (except Aluminum) Production & Processing
331500 Foundries

Fabricated Metal Product Manufacturing
332110 Forging & Stamping
332210 Cutlery & Handtool Mfg
332300 Architectural & Structural Metals Mfg
332400 Boiler, Tank, & Shipping Container Mfg
332510 Hardware Mfg
332610 Spring & Wire Product Mfg
332700 Machine Shops; Turned Product; & Screw, Nut, & Bolt Mfg
332810 Coating, Engraving, Heat Treating, & Allied Activities
332900 Other Fabricated Metal Product Mfg

Code

Machinery Manufacturing
333100 Agriculture, Construction, & Mining Machinery Mfg
333200 Industrial Machinery Mfg
333310 Commercial & Service Industry Machinery Mfg
333410 Ventilation, Heating, Air-Conditioning, & Commercial Refrigeration Equipment Mfg
333510 Metalworking Machinery Mfg
333610 Engine, Turbine & Power Transmission Equipment Mfg
333900 Other General Purpose Machinery Mfg

Computer and Electronic Product Manufacturing
334110 Computer & Peripheral Equipment Mfg
334200 Communications Equipment Mfg
334310 Audio & Video Equipment Mfg
334410 Semiconductor & Other Electronic Component Mfg
334500 Navigational, Measuring, Electromedical, & Control Instruments Mfg
334610 Manufacturing & Reproducing Magnetic & Optical Media

Electrical Equipment, Appliance, and Component Manufacturing
335100 Electric Lighting Equipment Mfg
335200 Household Appliance Mfg
335310 Electrical Equipment Mfg
335900 Other Electrical Equipment & Component Mfg

Transportation Equipment Manufacturing
336100 Motor Vehicle Mfg
336210 Motor Vehicle Body & Trailer Mfg
336300 Motor Vehicle Parts Mfg
336410 Aerospace Product & Parts Mfg
336510 Railroad Rolling Stock Mfg
336610 Ship & Boat Building
336990 Other Transportation Equipment Mfg

Furniture and Related Product Manufacturing
337000 Furniture & Related Product Manufacturing

Miscellaneous Manufacturing
339110 Medical Equipment & Supplies Mfg
339900 Other Miscellaneous Manufacturing

Wholesale Trade

Wholesale Trade, Durable Goods
421100 Motor Vehicle & Motor Vehicle Parts & Supplies Wholesalers
421200 Furniture & Home Furnishing Wholesalers
421300 Lumber & Other Construction Materials Wholesalers
421400 Professional & Commercial Equipment & Supplies Wholesalers
421500 Metal & Mineral (except Petroleum) Wholesalers
421600 Electrical Goods Wholesalers
421700 Hardware, & Plumbing & Heating Equipment & Supplies Wholesalers
421800 Machinery, Equipment, & Supplies Wholesalers
421910 Sporting & Recreational Goods & Supplies Wholesalers
421920 Toy & Hobby Goods & Supplies Wholesalers
421930 Recyclable Material Wholesalers
421940 Jewelry, Watch, Precious Stone, & Precious Metal Wholesalers
421990 Other Miscellaneous Durable Goods Wholesalers

Code		Code		Code		Code	

Wholesale Trade, Nondurable Goods

422100 Paper & Paper Product Wholesalers
422210 Drugs & Druggists' Sundries Wholesalers
422300 Apparel, Piece Goods, & Notions Wholesalers
422400 Grocery & Related Product Wholesalers
422500 Farm Product Raw Material Wholesalers
422600 Chemical & Allied Products Wholesalers
422700 Petroleum & Petroleum Products Wholesalers
422800 Beer, Wine, & Distilled Alcoholic Beverage Wholesalers
422910 Farm Supplies Wholesalers
422920 Book, Periodical, & Newspaper Wholesalers
422930 Flower, Nursery Stock, & Florists' Supplies Wholesalers
422940 Tobacco & Tobacco Product Wholesalers
422950 Paint, Varnish, & Supplies Wholesalers
422990 Other Miscellaneous Nondurable Goods Wholesalers

Retail Trade

Motor Vehicle and Parts Dealers

441110 New Car Dealers
441120 Used Car Dealers
441210 Recreational Vehicle Dealers
441221 Motorcycle Dealers
441222 Boat Dealers
441229 All Other Motor Vehicle Dealers
441300 Automotive Parts, Accessories, & Tire Stores

Furniture and Home Furnishings Stores

442110 Furniture Stores
442210 Floor Covering Stores
442291 Window Treatment Stores
442299 All Other Home Furnishings Stores

Electronics and Appliance Stores

443111 Household Appliance Stores
443112 Radio, Television, & Other Electronics Stores
443120 Computer & Software Stores
443130 Camera & Photographic Supplies Stores

Building Material and Garden Equipment and Supplies Dealers

444110 Home Centers
444120 Paint & Wallpaper Stores
444130 Hardware Stores
444190 Other Building Material Dealers
444200 Lawn & Garden Equipment & Supplies Stores

Food and Beverage Stores

445110 Supermarkets and Other Grocery (except Convenience) Stores
445120 Convenience Stores
445210 Meat Markets
445220 Fish & Seafood Markets
445230 Fruit & Vegetable Markets
445291 Baked Goods Stores
445292 Confectionery & Nut Stores
445299 All Other Specialty Food Stores
445310 Beer, Wine, & Liquor Stores

Health and Personal Care Stores

446110 Pharmacies & Drug Stores
446120 Cosmetics, Beauty Supplies, & Perfume Stores
446130 Optical Goods Stores
446190 Other Health & Personal Care Stores

Gasoline Stations

447100 Gasoline Stations (including convenience stores with gas)

Clothing and Clothing Accessories Stores

448110 Men's Clothing Stores
448120 Women's Clothing Stores
448130 Children's & Infants' Clothing Stores
448140 Family Clothing Stores
448150 Clothing Accessories Stores
448190 Other Clothing Stores
448210 Shoe Stores
448310 Jewelry Stores
448320 Luggage & Leather Goods Stores

Sporting Goods, Hobby, Book, and Music Stores

451110 Sporting Goods Stores
451120 Hobby, Toy, & Game Stores
451130 Sewing, Needlework, & Piece Goods Stores
451140 Musical Instrument & Supplies Stores
451211 Book Stores
451212 News Dealers & Newsstands
451220 Prerecorded Tape, Compact Disc, & Record Stores

General Merchandise Stores

452110 Department stores
452900 Other General Merchandise Stores

Miscellaneous Store Retailers

453110 Florists
453210 Office Supplies & Stationery Stores
453220 Gift, Novelty, & Souvenir Stores
453310 Used Merchandise Stores
453910 Pet & Pet Supplies Stores
453920 Art Dealers
453930 Manufactured (Mobile) Home Dealers
453990 All Other Miscellaneous Store Retailers (including tobacco, candle, & trophy shops)

Nonstore Retailers

454110 Electronic Shopping & Mail-Order Houses
454210 Vending Machine Operators
454311 Heating Oil Dealers
454312 Liquefied Petroleum Gas (Bottled Gas) Dealers
454319 Other Fuel Dealers
454390 Other Direct Selling Establishments (including door-to-door retailing, frozen food plan providers, party plan merchandisers, coffee-break service providers)

Transportation and Warehousing

Air, Rail, and Water Transportation

481000 Air Transportation
482110 Rail Transportation
483000 Water Transportation

Truck Transportation

484110 General Freight Trucking, Local
484120 General Freight Trucking, Long-distance
484200 Specialized Freight Trucking

Transit and Ground Passenger Transportation

485110 Urban Transit Systems
485210 Interurban & Rural Bus Transportation
485310 Taxi Service
485320 Limousine Service
485410 School & Employee Bus Transportation
485510 Charter Bus Industry
485990 Other Transit & Ground Passenger Transportation

Pipeline Transportation

486000 Pipeline Transportation

Scenic & Sightseeing Transportation

487000 Scenic & Sightseeing Transportation

Support Activities for Transportation

488100 Support Activities for Air Transportation
488210 Support Activities for Rail Transportation
488300 Support Activities for Water Transportation
488410 Motor Vehicle Towing
488490 Other Support Activities for Road Transportation
488510 Freight Transportation Arrangement
488990 Other Support Activities for Transportation

Couriers and Messengers

492110 Couriers
492210 Local Messengers & Local Delivery

Warehousing and Storage

493100 Warehousing & Storage (except lessors of miniwarehouses & self-storage units)

Information

Publishing Industries

511110 Newspaper Publishers
511120 Periodical Publishers
511130 Book Publishers
511140 Database & Directory Publishers
511190 Other Publishers
511210 Software Publishers

Motion Picture and Sound Recording Industries

512100 Motion Picture & Video Industries (except video rental)
512200 Sound Recording Industries

Broadcasting and Telecommunications

513100 Radio & Television Broadcasting
513200 Cable Networks & Program Distribution
513300 Telecommunications (including paging, cellular, satellite, & other telecommunications)

Information Services and Data Processing Services

514100 Information Services (including news syndicates, libraries, & on-line information services)
514210 Data Processing Services

Finance and Insurance

Depository Credit Intermediation

522110 Commercial Banking
522120 Savings Institutions
522130 Credit Unions
522190 Other Depository Credit Intermediation

Nondepository Credit Intermediation

522210 Credit Card Issuing
522220 Sales Financing
522291 Consumer Lending
522292 Real Estate Credit (including mortgage bankers & originators)
522293 International Trade Financing
522294 Secondary Market Financing
522298 All Other Nondepository Credit Intermediation

Activities Related to Credit Intermediation

522300 Activities Related to Credit Intermediation (including loan brokers)

Securities, Commodity Contracts, and Other Financial Investments and Related Activities

523110 Investment Banking & Securities Dealing
523120 Securities Brokerage
523130 Commodity Contracts Dealing
523140 Commodity Contracts Brokerage

523210 Securities & Commodity Exchanges
523900 Other Financial Investment Activities (including portfolio management & investment advice)

Insurance Carriers and Related Activities

524140 Direct Life, Health, & Medical Insurance & Reinsurance Carriers
524150 Direct Insurance & Reinsurance (except Life, Health & Medical) Carriers
524210 Insurance Agencies & Brokerages
524290 Other Insurance Related Activities

Funds, Trusts, and Other Financial Vehicles

525100 Insurance & Employee Benefit Funds
525910 Open-End Investment Funds (Form 1120-RIC)
525920 Trusts, Estates, & Agency Accounts
525930 Real Estate Investment Trusts (Form 1120-REIT)
525990 Other Financial Vehicles

Real Estate and Rental and Leasing

Real Estate

531110 Lessors of Residential Buildings & Dwellings
531120 Lessors of Nonresidential Buildings (except Miniwarehouses)
531130 Lessors of Miniwarehouses & Self-Storage Units
531190 Lessors of Other Real Estate Property
531210 Offices of Real Estate Agents & Brokers
531310 Real Estate Property Managers
531320 Offices of Real Estate Appraisers
531390 Other Activities Related to Real Estate

Rental and Leasing Services

532100 Automotive Equipment Rental & Leasing
532210 Consumer Electronics & Appliances Rental
532220 Formal Wear & Costume Rental
532230 Video Tape & Disc Rental
532290 Other Consumer Goods Rental
532310 General Rental Centers
532400 Commercial & Industrial Machinery & Equipment Rental & Leasing

Lessors of Nonfinancial Intangible Assets (except copyrighted works)

533110 Lessors of Nonfinancial Intangible Assets (except copyrighted works)

Professional, Scientific, and Technical Services

Legal Services

541110 Offices of Lawyers
541190 Other Legal Services

Accounting, Tax Preparation, Bookkeeping, and Payroll Services

541211 Offices of Certified Public Accountants
541213 Tax Preparation Services
541214 Payroll Services
541219 Other Accounting Services

Architectural, Engineering, and Related Services

541310 Architectural Services
541320 Landscape Architecture Services
541330 Engineering Services
541340 Drafting Services
541350 Building Inspection Services

Instructions for Form 1120S

Page 27

Code		Code		Code		Code	
541360	Geophysical Surveying & Mapping Services	561500	Travel Arrangement & Reservation Services	**Other Ambulatory Health Care Services**		**Food Services and Drinking Places**	
541370	Surveying & Mapping (except Geophysical) Services	561600	Investigation & Security Services	621900	Other Ambulatory Health Care Services (including ambulance services & blood & organ banks)	722110	Full-Service Restaurants
541380	Testing Laboratories	561710	Exterminating & Pest Control Services			722210	Limited-Service Eating Places
Specialized Design Services		561720	Janitorial Services	**Hospitals**		722300	Special Food Services (including food service contractors & caterers)
541400	Specialized Design Services (including interior, industrial, graphic, & fashion design)	561730	Landscaping Services	622000	Hospitals	722410	Drinking Places (Alcoholic Beverages)
		561740	Carpet & Upholstery Cleaning Services	**Nursing and Residential Care Facilities**			
Computer Systems Design and Related Services		561790	Other Services to Buildings & Dwellings	623000	Nursing & Residential Care Facilities	**Other Services**	
541511	Custom Computer Programming Services	561900	Other Support Services (including packaging & labeling services, & convention & trade show organizers)	**Social Assistance**		**Repair and Maintenance**	
541512	Computer Systems Design Services			624100	Individual & Family Services	811110	Automotive Mechanical & Electrical Repair & Maintenance
541513	Computer Facilities Management Services			624200	Community Food & Housing, & Emergency & Other Relief Services	811120	Automotive Body, Paint, Interior, & Glass Repair
541519	Other Computer Related Services	**Waste Management and Remediation Services**		624310	Vocational Rehabilitation Services	811190	Other Automotive Repair & Maintenance (including oil change & lubrication shops & car washes)
Other Professional, Scientific, and Technical Services		562000	Waste Management & Remediation Services	624410	Child Day Care Services	811210	Electronic & Precision Equipment Repair & Maintenance
541600	Management, Scientific, & Technical Consulting Services	**Educational Services**		**Arts, Entertainment, and Recreation**		811310	Commercial & Industrial Machinery & Equipment (except Automotive & Electronic) Repair & Maintenance
541700	Scientific Research & Development Services	611000	Educational Services (including schools, colleges, & universities)	**Performing Arts, Spectator Sports, and Related Industries**			
541800	Advertising & Related Services			711100	Performing Arts Companies	811410	Home & Garden Equipment & Appliance Repair & Maintenance
541910	Marketing Research & Public Opinion Polling	**Health Care and Social Assistance**		711210	Spectator Sports (including sports clubs & racetracks)	811420	Reupholstery & Furniture Repair
541920	Photographic Services	**Offices of Physicians and Dentists**		711300	Promoters of Performing Arts, Sports, & Similar Events	811430	Footwear & Leather Goods Repair
541930	Translation & Interpretation Services	621111	Offices of Physicians (except mental health specialists)	711410	Agents & Managers for Artists, Athletes, Entertainers, & Other Public Figures	811490	Other Personal & Household Goods Repair & Maintenance
541940	Veterinary Services	621112	Offices of Physicians, Mental Health Specialists	711510	Independent Artists, Writers, & Performers	**Personal and Laundry Services**	
541990	All Other Professional, Scientific, & Technical Services	621210	Offices of Dentists	**Museums, Historical Sites, and Similar Institutions**		812111	Barber Shops
		Offices of Other Health Practitioners		712100	Museums, Historical Sites, & Similar Institutions	812112	Beauty Salons
Management of Companies (Holding Companies)		621310	Offices of Chiropractors			812113	Nail Salons
		621320	Offices of Optometrists	**Amusement, Gambling, and Recreation Industries**		812190	Other Personal Care Services (including diet & weight reducing centers)
551111	Offices of Bank Holding Companies	621330	Offices of Mental Health Practitioners (except Physicians)	713100	Amusement Parks & Arcades	812210	Funeral Homes & Funeral Services
551112	Offices of Other Holding Companies	621340	Offices of Physical, Occupational & Speech Therapists, & Audiologists	713200	Gambling Industries	812220	Cemeteries & Crematories
				713900	Other Amusement & Recreation Industries (including golf courses, skiing facilities, marinas, fitness centers, & bowling centers)	812310	Coin-Operated Laundries & Drycleaners
Administrative and Support and Waste Management and Remediation Services		621391	Offices of Podiatrists			812320	Drycleaning & Laundry Services (except Coin-Operated)
		621399	Offices of All Other Miscellaneous Health Practitioners			812330	Linen & Uniform Supply
Administrative and Support Services		**Outpatient Care Centers**		**Accommodation and Food Services**		812910	Pet Care (except Veterinary) Services
561110	Office Administrative Services	621410	Family Planning Centers			812920	Photofinishing
561210	Facilities Support Services	621420	Outpatient Mental Health & Substance Abuse Centers	**Accommodation**		812930	Parking Lots & Garages
561300	Employment Services	621491	HMO Medical Centers	721110	Hotels (except casino hotels) & Motels	812990	All Other Personal Services
561410	Document Preparation Services	621492	Kidney Dialysis Centers	721120	Casino Hotels	**Religious, Grantmaking, Civic, Professional, and Similar Organizations**	
561420	Telephone Call Centers	621493	Freestanding Ambulatory Surgical & Emergency Centers	721191	Bed & Breakfast Inns		
561430	Business Service Centers (including private mail centers & copy shops)	621498	All Other Outpatient Care Centers	721199	All Other Traveler Accommodation	813000	Religious, Grantmaking, Civic, Professional, & Similiar Organizations
561440	Collection Agencies	**Medical and Diagnostic Laboratories**		721210	RV (Recreational Vehicle) Parks & Recreational Camps		
561450	Credit Bureaus	621510	Medical & Diagnostic Laboratories	721310	Rooming & Boarding Houses		
561490	Other Business Support Services (including repossession services, court reporting, & stenotype services)	**Home Health Care Services**					
		621610	Home Health Care Services				

Form **1120S**

Department of the Treasury
Internal Revenue Service

U.S. Income Tax Return for an S Corporation

▶ Do not file this form unless the corporation has timely filed
Form 2553 to elect to be an S corporation.
▶ See separate instructions.

OMB No. 1545-0130

19**98**

For calendar year 1998, or tax year beginning   , 1998, and ending   , 19

A Effective date of election as an S corporation	Use IRS label. Other-wise, please print or type.	Name	**C** Employer identification number
B NEW bus. code no. (see pages 26–28)		Number, street, and room or suite no. (If a P.O. box, see page 10 of the instructions.)	**D** Date incorporated
		City or town, state, and ZIP code	**E** Total assets (see page 10) $

F Check applicable boxes: (1) ☐ Initial return   (2) ☐ Final return   (3) ☐ Change in address   (4) ☐ Amended return
G Enter number of shareholders in the corporation at end of the tax year . . . . ▶

Caution: *Include only trade or business income and expenses on lines 1a through 21. See the instructions for more information.*

Income

1a	Gross receipts or sales	**b** Less returns and allowances	**c** Bal ▶	**1c**	
2	Cost of goods sold (Schedule A, line 8)	**2**	
3	Gross profit. Subtract line 2 from line 1c	**3**	
4	Net gain (loss) from Form 4797, Part II, line 18 *(attach Form 4797)*	**4**	
5	Other income (loss) *(attach schedule)*	**5**	
6	**Total income (loss).** Combine lines 3 through 5 . . . . ▶	**6**	

Deductions (see page 11 of the instructions for limitations)

7	Compensation of officers	**7**	
8	Salaries and wages (less employment credits)	**8**	
9	Repairs and maintenance.	**9**	
10	Bad debts	**10**	
11	Rents	**11**	
12	Taxes and licenses.	**12**	
13	Interest	**13**	
14a	Depreciation *(if required, attach Form 4562)*	**14a**	
b	Depreciation claimed on Schedule A and elsewhere on return . .	**14b**	
c	Subtract line 14b from line 14a	**14c**	
15	Depletion **(Do not deduct oil and gas depletion.)**	**15**	
16	Advertising	**16**	
17	Pension, profit-sharing, etc., plans	**17**	
18	Employee benefit programs	**18**	
19	Other deductions *(attach schedule)*	**19**	
20	**Total deductions.** Add the amounts shown in the far right column for lines 7 through 19 . ▶	**20**	
21	Ordinary income (loss) from trade or business activities. Subtract line 20 from line 6	**21**	

Tax and Payments

22	**Tax: a** Excess net passive income tax *(attach schedule)*. . .	**22a**		
b	Tax from Schedule D (Form 1120S)	**22b**		
c	Add lines 22a and 22b (see page 14 of the instructions for additional taxes)	**22c**	
23	**Payments: a** 1998 estimated tax payments and amount applied from 1997 return	**23a**		
b	Tax deposited with Form 7004	**23b**		
c	Credit for Federal tax paid on fuels *(attach Form 4136)* . . .	**23c**		
d	Add lines 23a through 23c	**23d**	
24	Estimated tax penalty. Check if Form 2220 is attached . . . . ▶☐	**24**	
25	**Tax due.** If the total of lines 22c and 24 is larger than line 23d, enter amount owed. See page 4 of the instructions for depository method of payment . . . . ▶	**25**	
26	**Overpayment.** If line 23d is larger than the total of lines 22c and 24, enter amount overpaid ▶	**26**	
27	Enter amount of line 26 you want: **Credited to 1999 estimated tax** ▶ Refunded ▶	**27**	

Please Sign Here

Under penalties of perjury, I declare that I have examined this return, including accompanying schedules and statements, and to the best of my knowledge and belief, it is true, correct, and complete. Declaration of preparer (other than taxpayer) is based on all information of which preparer has any knowledge.

▶ _____   _____   ▶ _____
    Signature of officer   Date   Title

Paid Preparer's Use Only

Preparer's signature ▶	Date	Check if self-employed ▶ ☐	Preparer's social security number
Firm's name (or yours if self-employed) and address ▶		EIN ▶	
		ZIP code ▶	

For Paperwork Reduction Act Notice, see the separate instructions.   Cat. No. 11510H   Form **1120S** (1998)

Schedule A   **Cost of Goods Sold** (see page 15 of the instructions)

1	Inventory at beginning of year	**1**	
2	Purchases	**2**	
3	Cost of labor	**3**	
4	Additional section 263A costs *(attach schedule)*	**4**	
5	Other costs *(attach schedule)*	**5**	
6	**Total.** Add lines 1 through 5	**6**	
7	Inventory at end of year	**7**	
8	**Cost of goods sold.** Subtract line 7 from line 6. Enter here and on page 1, line 2	**8**	

9a Check all methods used for valuing closing inventory:
  (i) ☐ Cost as described in Regulations section 1.471-3
  (ii) ☐ Lower of cost or market as described in Regulations section 1.471-4
  (iii) ☐ Other (specify method used and attach explanation) ▶ ---
 b Check if there was a writedown of "subnormal" goods as described in Regulations section 1.471-2(c) . . . . . . ▶ ☐
 c Check if the LIFO inventory method was adopted this tax year for any goods *(if checked, attach Form 970)* . . . . . ▶ ☐
 d If the LIFO inventory method was used for this tax year, enter percentage (or amounts) of closing inventory computed under LIFO . . . . **9d** |
 e Do the rules of section 263A (for property produced or acquired for resale) apply to the corporation? . . . . . ☐ Yes ☐ No
 f Was there any change in determining quantities, cost, or valuations between opening and closing inventory? . . ☐ Yes ☐ No
   If "Yes," attach explanation.

Schedule B   **Other Information**

		Yes	No
1	Check method of accounting: **(a)** ☐ Cash **(b)** ☐ Accrual **(c)** ☐ Other (specify) ▶ ----------------------------		
2	Refer to the list on pages 26 through 28 of the instructions and state the corporation's principal: **(a)** Business activity ▶ ------------------------------ **(b)** Product or service ▶ -----------------------------		
3	Did the corporation at the end of the tax year own, directly or indirectly, 50% or more of the voting stock of a domestic corporation? (For rules of attribution, see section 267(c).) If "Yes," attach a schedule showing: **(a)** name, address, and employer identification number and **(b)** percentage owned.		
4	Was the corporation a member of a controlled group subject to the provisions of section 1561?		
5	At any time during calendar year 1998, did the corporation have an interest in or a signature or other authority over a financial account in a foreign country (such as a bank account, securities account, or other financial account)? (See page 15 of the instructions for exceptions and filing requirements for Form TD F 90-22.1.) . . . . If "Yes," enter the name of the foreign country ▶ -------------------------------------		
6	During the tax year, did the corporation receive a distribution from, or was it the grantor of, or transferor to, a foreign trust? If "Yes," the corporation may have to file Form 3520. See page 15 of the instructions.		
7	Check this box if the corporation has filed or is required to file **Form 8264,** Application for Registration of a Tax Shelter . . . . ▶ ☐		
8	Check this box if the corporation issued publicly offered debt instruments with original issue discount . . ▶ ☐ If so, the corporation may have to file **Form 8281,** Information Return for Publicly Offered Original Issue Discount Instruments.		
9	If the corporation: **(a)** filed its election to be an S corporation after 1986, **(b)** was a C corporation before it elected to be an S corporation **or** the corporation acquired an asset with a basis determined by reference to its basis (or the basis of any other property) in the hands of a C corporation, and **(c)** has net unrealized built-in gain (defined in section 1374(d)(1)) in excess of the net recognized built-in gain from prior years, enter the net unrealized built-in gain reduced by net recognized built-in gain from prior years (see page 16 of the instructions) . . . . . ▶ $ ---------------		
10	Check this box if the corporation had accumulated earnings and profits at the close of the tax year (see page 16 of the instructions) . . . . ▶ ☐		

| Schedule K | Shareholders' Shares of Income, Credits, Deductions, etc. | | |

	(a) Pro rata share items		(b) Total amount	
Income (Loss)	**1** Ordinary income (loss) from trade or business activities (page 1, line 21)	**1**		
	2 Net income (loss) from rental real estate activities *(attach Form 8825)*	**2**		
	3a Gross income from other rental activities	**3a**		
	b Expenses from other rental activities *(attach schedule)*. .	**3b**		
	c Net income (loss) from other rental activities. Subtract line 3b from line 3a	**3c**		
	4 Portfolio income (loss):			
	a Interest income	**4a**		
	b Ordinary dividends	**4b**		
	c Royalty income	**4c**		
	d Net short-term capital gain (loss) *(attach Schedule D (Form 1120S))*	**4d**		
	e Net long-term capital gain (loss) *(attach Schedule D (Form 1120S))*:			
	(1) 28% rate gain (loss) ▶ .... (2) Total for year ▶	**4e(2)**		
	f Other portfolio income (loss) *(attach schedule)*	**4f**		
	5 Net section 1231 gain (loss) (other than due to casualty or theft) *(attach Form 4797)* . .	**5**		
	6 Other income (loss) *(attach schedule)*	**6**		
Deductions	**7** Charitable contributions *(attach schedule)*	**7**		
	8 Section 179 expense deduction *(attach Form 4562)*.	**8**		
	9 Deductions related to portfolio income (loss) (itemize)	**9**		
	10 Other deductions *(attach schedule)*	**10**		
Investment Interest	**11a** Interest expense on investment debts	**11a**		
	b (1) Investment income included on lines 4a, 4b, 4c, and 4f above	**11b(1)**		
	(2) Investment expenses included on line 9 above	**11b(2)**		
Credits	**12a** Credit for alcohol used as a fuel *(attach Form 6478)*	**12a**		
	b Low-income housing credit:			
	(1) From partnerships to which section 42(j)(5) applies for property placed in service before 1990	**12b(1)**		
	(2) Other than on line 12b(1) for property placed in service before 1990.	**12b(2)**		
	(3) From partnerships to which section 42(j)(5) applies for property placed in service after 1989	**12b(3)**		
	(4) Other than on line 12b(3) for property placed in service after 1989	**12b(4)**		
	c Qualified rehabilitation expenditures related to rental real estate activities *(attach Form 3468)* .	**12c**		
	d Credits (other than credits shown on lines 12b and 12c) related to rental real estate activities	**12d**		
	e Credits related to other rental activities	**12e**		
	13 Other credits	**13**		
Adjustments and Tax Preference Items	**14a** Depreciation adjustment on property placed in service after 1986	**14a**		
	b Adjusted gain or loss	**14b**		
	c Depletion (other than oil and gas)	**14c**		
	d (1) Gross income from oil, gas, or geothermal properties	**14d(1)**		
	(2) Deductions allocable to oil, gas, or geothermal properties	**14d(2)**		
	e Other adjustments and tax preference items *(attach schedule)*	**14e**		
Foreign Taxes	**15a** Type of income ▶...			
	b Name of foreign country or U.S. possession			
	c Total gross income from sources outside the United States *(attach schedule)*	**15c**		
	d Total applicable deductions and losses *(attach schedule)*	**15d**		
	e Total foreign taxes (check one): ▶ ☐ Paid ☐ Accrued	**15e**		
	f Reduction in taxes available for credit *(attach schedule)*	**15f**		
	g Other foreign tax information *(attach schedule)*	**15g**		
Other	**16** Section 59(e)(2) expenditures: **a** Type ▶.................................... **b** Amount ▶	**16b**		
	17 Tax-exempt interest income	**17**		
	18 Other tax-exempt income	**18**		
	19 Nondeductible expenses	**19**		
	20 Total property distributions (including cash) other than dividends reported on line 22 below	**20**		
	21 Other items and amounts required to be reported separately to shareholders *(attach schedule)*			
	22 Total dividend distributions paid from accumulated earnings and profits	**22**		
	23 **Income (loss).** (Required only if Schedule M-1 must be completed.) Combine lines 1 through 6 in column (b). From the result, subtract the sum of lines 7 through 11a, 15e, and 16b	**23**		

Schedule L	**Balance Sheets per Books**	Beginning of tax year		End of tax year	
	Assets	**(a)**	**(b)**	**(c)**	**(d)**
1	Cash				
2a	Trade notes and accounts receivable . .				
b	Less allowance for bad debts				
3	Inventories				
4	U.S. Government obligations				
5	Tax-exempt securities				
6	Other current assets *(attach schedule)* .				
7	Loans to shareholders				
8	Mortgage and real estate loans				
9	Other investments *(attach schedule)* . .				
10a	Buildings and other depreciable assets .				
b	Less accumulated depreciation				
11a	Depletable assets				
b	Less accumulated depletion				
12	Land (net of any amortization)				
13a	Intangible assets (amortizable only) . . .				
b	Less accumulated amortization				
14	Other assets *(attach schedule)*				
15	Total assets				
	Liabilities and Shareholders' Equity				
16	Accounts payable				
17	Mortgages, notes, bonds payable in less than 1 year				
18	Other current liabilities *(attach schedule)*				
19	Loans from shareholders				
20	Mortgages, notes, bonds payable in 1 year or more				
21	Other liabilities *(attach schedule)* . . .				
22	Capital stock				
23	Additional paid-in capital				
24	Retained earnings				
25	Adjustments to shareholders' equity *(attach schedule)* .				
26	Less cost of treasury stock		( )		( )
27	Total liabilities and shareholders' equity .				

Schedule M-1	**Reconciliation of Income (Loss) per Books With Income (Loss) per Return** (You are not required to complete this schedule if the total assets on line 15, column (d), of Schedule L are less than $25,000.)		
1	Net income (loss) per books		5 Income recorded on books this year not included on Schedule K, lines 1 through 6 (itemize):
2	Income included on Schedule K, lines 1 through 6, not recorded on books this year (itemize):		a Tax-exempt interest $ ....
	....		6 Deductions included on Schedule K, lines 1 through 11a, 15e, and 16b, not charged against book income this year (itemize):
3	Expenses recorded on books this year not included on Schedule K, lines 1 through 11a, 15e, and 16b (itemize):		a Depreciation $ ....
a	Depreciation $		....
b	Travel and entertainment $		7 Add lines 5 and 6 . . . .
4	Add lines 1 through 3		8 Income (loss) (Schedule K, line 23). Line 4 less line 7 . . . .

Schedule M-2	**Analysis of Accumulated Adjustments Account, Other Adjustments Account, and Shareholders' Undistributed Taxable Income Previously Taxed** (see page 24 of the instructions)		
		(a) Accumulated adjustments account	**(b)** Other adjustments account	**(c)** Shareholders' undistributed taxable income previously taxed
1	Balance at beginning of tax year . . .			
2	Ordinary income from page 1, line 21 . .			
3	Other additions			
4	Loss from page 1, line 21	( )		
5	Other reductions	( )	( )	
6	Combine lines 1 through 5			
7	Distributions other than dividend distributions .			
8	Balance at end of tax year. Subtract line 7 from line 6			

SCHEDULE K-1	**Shareholder's Share of Income, Credits, Deductions, etc.**	OMB No. 1545-0130
(Form 1120S)	▶ See separate instructions.	**1998**
Department of the Treasury Internal Revenue Service	For calendar year 1998 or tax year beginning , 1998, and ending , 19	

Shareholder's identifying number ▶   **Corporation's identifying number ▶**

Shareholder's name, address, and ZIP code   Corporation's name, address, and ZIP code

A   Shareholder's percentage of stock ownership for tax year (see instructions for Schedule K-1) . . . . ▶ .... %
B   Internal Revenue Service Center where corporation filed its return ▶ ....
C   Tax shelter registration number (see instructions for Schedule K-1) . . . . ▶ ....
D   Check applicable boxes: **(1)** ☐ Final K-1   **(2)** ☐ Amended K-1

		(a) Pro rata share items		**(b)** Amount	**(c)** Form 1040 filers enter the amount in column (b) on:
Income (Loss)	1	Ordinary income (loss) from trade or business activities . . .	**1**		See pages 4 and 5 of the Shareholder's Instructions for Schedule K-1 (Form 1120S).
	2	Net income (loss) from rental real estate activities	**2**		
	3	Net income (loss) from other rental activities	**3**		
	4	Portfolio income (loss):			
	a	Interest	**4a**		Sch. B, Part I, line 1
	b	Ordinary dividends	**4b**		Sch. B, Part II, line 5
	c	Royalties	**4c**		Sch. E, Part I, line 4
	d	Net short-term capital gain (loss)	**4d**		Sch. D, line 5, col. (f)
	e	Net long-term capital gain (loss):			
		(1) 28% rate gain (loss)	**e(1)**		Sch. D, line 12, col. (g)
		(2) Total for year	**e(2)**		Sch. D, line 12, col. (f)
	f	Other portfolio income (loss) *(attach schedule)*	**4f**		*(Enter on applicable line of your return.)*
	5	Net section 1231 gain (loss) (other than due to casualty or theft)	**5**		See Shareholder's Instructions for Schedule K-1 (Form 1120S).
	6	Other income (loss) *(attach schedule)*	**6**		*(Enter on applicable line of your return.)*
Deductions	7	Charitable contributions *(attach schedule)*	**7**		Sch. A, line 15 or 16
	8	Section 179 expense deduction	**8**		See page 6 of the Shareholder's Instructions for Schedule K-1 (Form 1120S).
	9	Deductions related to portfolio income (loss) *(attach schedule)* .	**9**		
	10	Other deductions *(attach schedule)*	**10**		
Investment Interest	11a	Interest expense on investment debts	**11a**		Form 4952, line 1
	b	**(1)** Investment income included on lines 4a, 4b, 4c, and 4f above	**b(1)**		See Shareholder's Instructions for Schedule K-1 (Form 1120S).
		(2) Investment expenses included on line 9 above	**b(2)**		
Credits	12a	Credit for alcohol used as fuel	**12a**		Form 6478, line 10
	b	Low-income housing credit:			
		(1) From section 42(j)(5) partnerships for property placed in service before 1990 .	**b(1)**		
		(2) Other than on line 12b(1) for property placed in service before 1990	**b(2)**		
		(3) From section 42(j)(5) partnerships for property placed in service after 1989 .	**b(3)**		Form 8586, line 5
		(4) Other than on line 12b(3) for property placed in service after 1989	**b(4)**		
	c	Qualified rehabilitation expenditures related to rental real estate activities	**12c**		
	d	Credits (other than credits shown on lines 12b and 12c) related to rental real estate activities	**12d**		See page 7 of the Shareholder's Instructions for Schedule K-1 (Form 1120S).
	e	Credits related to other rental activities	**12e**		
	13	Other credits	**13**		

For Paperwork Reduction Act Notice, see the Instructions for Form 1120S.   Cat. No. 11520D   **Schedule K-1 (Form 1120S) 1998**

(a) Pro rata share items		(b) Amount	(c) Form 1040 filers enter the amount in column (b) on:

Adjustments and Tax Preference Items

	(a) Pro rata share items		(b) Amount	(c)
14a	Depreciation adjustment on property placed in service after 1986	14a		See page 7 of the Shareholder's Instructions for Schedule K-1 (Form 1120S) and Instructions for Form 6251
b	Adjusted gain or loss	14b		
c	Depletion (other than oil and gas)	14c		
d	(1) Gross income from oil, gas, or geothermal properties	d(1)		
	(2) Deductions allocable to oil, gas, or geothermal properties	d(2)		
e	Other adjustments and tax preference items *(attach schedule)*	14e		

Foreign Taxes

15a	Type of income ▶			Form 1116, Check boxes
b	Name of foreign country or U.S. possession ▶			
c	Total gross income from sources outside the United States *(attach schedule)*	15c		} Form 1116, Part I
d	Total applicable deductions and losses *(attach schedule)*	15d		
e	Total foreign taxes (check one): ▶ ☐ Paid ☐ Accrued	15e		Form 1116, Part II
f	Reduction in taxes available for credit *(attach schedule)*	15f		Form 1116, Part III
g	Other foreign tax information *(attach schedule)*	15g		See Instructions for Form 1116

Other

16	Section 59(e)(2) expenditures: **a** Type ▶			See Shareholder's Instructions for Schedule K-1 (Form 1120S).
b	Amount	16b		
17	Tax-exempt interest income	17		Form 1040, line 8b
18	Other tax-exempt income	18		See pages 7 and 8 of the Shareholder's Instructions for Schedule K-1 (Form 1120S).
19	Nondeductible expenses	19		
20	Property distributions (including cash) other than dividend distributions reported to you on Form 1099-DIV	20		
21	Amount of loan repayments for "Loans From Shareholders"	21		
22	Recapture of low-income housing credit:			
a	From section 42(j)(5) partnerships	22a		} Form 8611, line 8
b	Other than on line 22a	22b		

Supplemental Information

23 Supplemental information required to be reported separately to each shareholder *(attach additional schedules if more space is needed)*:

_____

_____

_____

_____

_____

_____

_____

_____

_____

_____

_____

_____

_____

_____

_____

_____

✲

IRS Schedules D and E

Capital Gains and Losses and Supplemental Income and Loss

**Department of the Treasury
Internal Revenue Service**

1998

Instructions for Schedule D (Form 1120S)

Capital Gains and Losses and Built-In Gains

Section references are to the Internal Revenue Code unless otherwise noted.

General Instructions

Changes To Note

● For sales, exchanges, and conversions after 1997, property held for more than 1 year (instead of more than 18 months) generally is eligible for the 10%, 20%, and 25% maximum capital gains rates at the shareholder level (for individuals, estates, and trusts). This rule also applies to installment payments received after 1997. Therefore, the corporation should include in Part II, column (g) of Schedule D **only** collectibles gains and losses and certain pre-1998 gains from fiscal year pass-through entities.

● The corporation may be able to postpone gain on the sale of qualified small business stock. For details, see **Rollover of gain from qualified stock** on page 2.

Purpose of Schedule

Schedule D is used by all S corporations to report:

● Sales or exchanges of capital assets.

● Gains on distributions to shareholders of appreciated capital assets (referred to here as distributions).

● Nonbusiness bad debts.

If the corporation filed its election to be an S corporation before 1987 (or filed its election during 1987 or 1988 and qualifies for the transitional relief from the built-in gains tax described in Part IV on page 3), and had net capital gain (line 16) of more than $25,000, it may be liable for a capital gains tax on the gain in excess of $25,000. The tax is figured in Part III of Schedule D.

Generally, if the corporation filed an election to be an S corporation after 1986, was a C corporation at the time it made the election, **and** has net recognized built-in gain as defined in section 1374(d)(2), **it is liable** for the built-in gains tax. The tax is figured in Part IV of Schedule D.

Other Forms That May Be Required

Use **Form 4797**, Sales of Business Property, to report:

● Sales, exchanges, and distributions of property other than capital assets, including property used in a trade or business.

● Involuntary conversions (other than from casualties or thefts).

● Gain from the disposition of an interest in oil, gas, or geothermal property.

Use **Form 4684**, Casualties and Thefts, to report involuntary conversions of property due to casualty or theft.

Use **Form 6781**, Gains and Losses From Section 1256 Contracts and Straddles, to report gains and losses from section 1256 contracts and straddles.

Use **Form 8824**, Like-Kind Exchanges, if the corporation made one or more like-kind exchange. A "like-kind exchange" occurs when business or investment property is exchanged for property of a like kind. For exchanges of capital assets, enter the gain or loss from Form 8824, if any, on line 3 or line 9 in column (f), and in column (g) if required.

Capital Asset

Each item of property the corporation held (whether or not connected with its trade or business) is a capital asset **except:**

1. Assets that can be inventoried or property held mainly for sale to customers.

2. Depreciable or real property used in a trade or business.

3. Certain copyrights; literary, musical, or artistic compositions; letters or memorandums; or similar property.

4. Accounts or notes receivable acquired in the ordinary course of trade or business for services rendered or from the sale of property described in **1** above.

5. U.S. Government publications, including the Congressional Record, that the corporation received from the Government, other than by purchase at the normal sales price, or that the corporation got from another taxpayer who had received it in a similar way, if the corporation's basis is determined by reference to the previous owner.

Items for Special Treatment

Note: *For more information, see Pub. 544, Sales and Other Dispositions of Assets.*

Loss from a sale or exchange between the corporation and a related person. Except for distributions in complete liquidation of a corporation, no loss is allowed from the sale or exchange of property between the corporation and certain related persons. See section 267 for details.

Loss from a wash sale. The corporation cannot deduct a loss from a wash sale of stock or securities (including contracts or options to acquire or sell stock or securities) unless the corporation is a dealer in stock or securities and the loss was sustained in a transaction made in the ordinary course of the corporation's trade or business. A wash sale occurs if the corporation acquires (by purchase or exchange), or has a contract or option to acquire, substantially identical stock or securities within 30 days before or after the date of the sale or exchange. See section 1091 for more information.

Gain on distribution of appreciated property. Generally, gain (but not loss) is recognized on a nonliquidating distribution of appreciated property to the extent that the property's fair market value exceeds its adjusted basis. See section 311 for details.

Gain or loss on distribution of property in complete liquidation. Generally, gain or loss is recognized by a corporation upon the liquidating distribution of property as if it had sold the property at its fair market value. See section 336 for details and exceptions.

Gain or loss on certain short-term Federal, state, and municipal obligations are treated as capital assets in determining gain or loss. On any gain realized, a portion is treated as ordinary income and the balance is considered as a short-term capital gain. See section 1271.

Gain from installment sales. If a corporation has a gain this year from the sale of real property or a casual sale of personal property other than inventory and is to receive any payment in a later year, it must use the installment method (unless it elects not to) and file **Form 6252**, Installment Sale Income. Also use Form 6252 if a payment is received this year from a sale made in an earlier year on the installment basis.

The corporation may elect out of the installment method by reporting the full amount of the gain on a timely filed return (including extensions).

The installment method may not be used for sales of stock or securities (or certain other property described in the regulations) traded on an established securities market. See section 453(k).

Gain or loss on an option to buy or sell property. See sections 1032 and 1234 for the rules that apply to a purchaser or grantor of an option.

Gain or loss from a short sale of property. Report the gain or loss to the extent that the property used to close the short sale is considered a capital asset in the hands of the taxpayer.

Loss from securities that are capital assets that become worthless during the year. Except for securities held by a bank, treat the loss as a capital loss as of the last day of the tax year. See section 582 for the rules on the treatment of securities held by a bank.

Nonrecognition of gain on sale of stock to an employee stock ownership plan (ESOP) or an eligible cooperative. See section 1042 and Temporary Regulations section 1.1042-1T for rules under which a taxpayer may elect not to recognize gain from the sale of certain stock to an ESOP or an eligible cooperative.

Disposition of market discount bonds. See section 1276 for rules on the disposition of any market discount bonds.

Cat. No. 64419L

Capital gain distributions. Report the **total** capital gain distributions as long-term capital gain on line 7, column (f), regardless of how long the corporation held the investment. Enter on line 7, column (g), the total amounts reported as the 28% rate gain portion of your total capital gain distributions.

Nonbusiness bad debts. A nonbusiness bad debt must be treated as a short-term capital loss and can be deducted only in the year the debt becomes totally worthless. For each bad debt, enter the name of the debtor and "schedule attached" in column (a) of line 1 and the amount of the bad debt as a loss in column (f). Also attach a statement of facts to support each bad debt deduction.

Real estate subdivided for sale. Certain lots or parcels that are part of a tract of real estate subdivided for sale may be treated as capital assets. See section 1237.

Constructive sales treatment for certain appreciated positions. Generally, the corporation must recognize gain (but not loss) on the date it enters into a constructive sale of any appreciated interest in stock, a partnership interest, or certain debt instruments as if the position were disposed of at fair market value on that date.

The corporation is treated as making a constructive sale of an appreciated position if it (or a related person, in some cases) does **one** of the following:

● Enters into a short sale of the same or substantially identical property (i.e., a "short sale against the box").

● Enters into an offsetting notional principal contract relating to the same or substantially identical property.

● Enters into a futures or forward contract to deliver the same or substantially identical property.

● Acquires the same or substantially identical property (if the appreciated position is a short sale, offsetting notional principal contract, or a futures or forward contract).

Exception. Generally, constructive sales treatment **does not** apply if:

● The transaction was closed before the end of the 30th day after the end of the year in which it was entered into,

● The appreciated position to which the transaction relates was held throughout the 60-day period starting on the date the transaction was closed, **and**

● At no time during that 60-day period was the corporation's risk of loss reduced by holding certain other positions.

For details and other exceptions to these rules, see **Pub. 550**, Investment Income and Expenses.

Rollover of gain from qualified stock. If the corporation sold qualified small business stock (defined below) that it held for more than 6 months, it may postpone gain if it purchased other qualified small business stock during the 60-day period that began on the date of the sale. The corporation must recognize gain to the extent the sale proceeds exceed the cost of the replacement stock. Reduce the basis of the replacement stock by any postponed gain.

If the corporation chooses to postpone gain, report the entire gain realized on the sale on line 1 or 7. Directly below the line on which the corporation reported the gain, enter in column (a) "Section 1045 Rollover" and enter as a (loss) in column (f) the amount of the postponed gain.

Caution: *The corporation also must separately state the amount of the gain rolled over on qualified stock under section 1045 on Form 1120S, Schedule K, line 6, because each shareholder must determine if he or she qualifies for the rollover at the shareholder level. Also, the corporation must include on Schedule D, line 1 or 7 (and on Form 1120S, Schedule K, line 6), any gain that could qualify for the section 1045 rollover at the shareholder level instead of the corporate level (because a shareholder was entitled to purchase replacement stock). If the corporation had a gain on qualified stock that could qualify for the 50% exclusion under section 1202, report that gain on Schedule D, line 7 (and on Form 1120S, Schedule K, line 6).*

To be **qualified small business stock**, the stock must meet **all** of the following tests:

● It must be stock in a C corporation.

● It must have been originally issued after August 10, 1993.

● As of the date the stock was issued, the C corporation was a qualified small business. A qualified small business is a domestic C corporation with total gross assets of $50 million or less **(a)** at all times after August 9, 1993, and before the stock was issued, and **(b)** immediately after the stock was issued. Gross assets include those of any predecessor of the corporation. All corporations that are members of the same parent-subsidiary controlled group are treated as one corporation.

● The corporation must have acquired the stock at its original issue (either directly or through an underwriter), either in exchange for money or other property or as pay for services (other than as an underwriter) to the corporation. In certain cases, the corporation may meet the test if it acquired the stock from another person who met this test (such as by gift or inheritance) or through a conversion or exchange of qualified small business stock held by the corporation.

● During substantially all the time the corporation held the stock:

   1. The issuer was a C corporation,

   2. At least 80% of the value of the issuer's assets were used in the active conduct of one or more qualified businesses (defined below), and

   3. The issuing corporation **was not** a foreign corporation, DISC, former DISC, corporation that has made (or that has a subsidiary that has made) a section 936 election, regulated investment company, real estate investment trust, REMIC, FASIT, or cooperative.

Note: *A specialized small business investment company (SSBIC) is treated as having met tests **2** and **3** above.*

A **qualified business** is any business **other than** the following:

● One involving services performed in the fields of health, law, engineering, architecture, accounting, actuarial science, performing arts, consulting, athletics, financial services, or brokerage services.

● One whose principal asset is the reputation or skill of one or more employees.

● Any banking, insurance, financing, leasing, investing, or similar business.

● Any farming business (including the raising or harvesting of trees).

● Any business involving the production of products for which percentage depletion can be claimed.

● Any business of operating a hotel, motel, restaurant, or similar business.

Specific Instructions

Parts I and II

Generally, report sales or exchanges (including like-kind exchanges) even if there is no gain or loss. In Part I, report the sale, exchange, or distribution of capital assets held 1 year or less. In Part II, report the sale, exchange, or distribution of capital assets held more than 1 year. Use the trade dates for the dates of acquisition and sale of stocks and bonds on an exchange or over-the-counter market.

Column (e)—Cost or other basis. In determining gain or loss, the basis of property is generally its cost (see section 1012 and related regulations). The exceptions to the general rule are provided in sections contained in subchapters C, K, O, and P of the Code. For example, if the corporation acquired the property by dividend, liquidation of another corporation, transfer from a shareholder, reorganization, bequest, contribution or gift, tax-free exchange, involuntary conversion, certain asset acquisitions, or wash sale of stock, see sections 301 (or 1059), 334, 362 (or 358), 1014, 1015, 1031, 1033, 1060, and 1091, respectively. Attach an explanation if you use a basis other than actual cash cost of the property.

If the corporation is allowed a charitable contribution deduction because it sold property to a charitable organization, figure the adjusted basis for determining gain from the sale by dividing the amount realized by the fair market value and multiplying that result by the adjusted basis.

See section 852(f) for the treatment of certain load charges incurred in acquiring stock in a mutual fund with a reinvestment right.

Before making an entry in column (e), increase the cost or other basis by any expense of sale, such as broker's fees, commissions, option premiums, and state and local transfer taxes, unless the net sales price was reported in column (d).

Column (f)—Gain or (loss). Make a separate entry in this column for each transaction reported on lines 1 and 7 and any other line(s) that apply to the corporation. For lines 1 and 7, subtract the amount in column (e) from the amount in column (d). Enter negative amounts in parentheses.

Column (g)—28% rate gain or (loss). Enter the amount, if any, from Part II, column (f), that is from collectibles gains and losses. A **collectibles gain or loss** is any long-term gain or loss from the sale or exchange of a collectible that is a capital asset.

Collectibles include works of art, rugs, antiques, metals (such as gold, silver, and platinum bullion), gems, stamps, coins, alcoholic beverages, and certain other tangible property.

Also include gain from the sale of an interest in a partnership or trust attributable to unrealized appreciation of collectibles.

Part III—Capital Gains Tax

If the net long-term capital gain is more than the net short-term capital loss, there is a net capital gain. If this gain exceeds $25,000, **and** the corporation elected to be an S corporation before 1987 (or filed its election during 1987 or 1988 and qualifies for the transitional relief from the built-in gains tax described in Part IV on page 3), the corporation may be liable for income tax on the gain.

Determine if the corporation is liable for the tax by answering questions A, B, and C below. If all the answers are "Yes," the tax applies and Part III of Schedule D must be completed. Otherwise, the corporation is not liable for the tax.

If net capital gain is more than $25,000, and the corporation is not liable for the tax, attach the Part III instructions to Schedule D with questions A, B, and C answered to show why the tax does not apply.

A. Is net capital gain (line 16, Schedule D) more than $25,000, and more than 50% of taxable income (see the instructions for line 20, Schedule D)? . . . . . ☐ Yes ☐ No

B. Is taxable income (see the instructions for line 20, Schedule D) more than $25,000? . . . . ☐ Yes ☐ No

C. Does any long-term capital gain (line 15, Schedule D) represent gain from substituted basis property (defined below)? . . . . . ☐ Yes ☐ No

For purposes of the capital gains tax, **substituted basis property** is property that:
• Was acquired by the S corporation during the period that began 36 months before the first day of the tax year and ended on the last day of the tax year, and
• Has a basis determined by reference to the basis of any property in the hands of another corporation, if the other corporation was **not** an S corporation throughout the period that, **began** the later of:

   1. 36 months before the first day of the tax year, or
   2. The time the other corporation came into existence,

and **ended** on the date the other corporation transferred the property used to determine the basis of the property acquired by the S corporation.

Line 16. If the corporation is liable for the tax on excess net passive income (line 22a, page 1, Form 1120S) or the built-in gains tax (see Part IV below), and capital gain or loss was included in the computation of either tax, figure the amount to enter on line 16 as follows:

   Step 1. Refigure lines 1 through 3, 7 through 9 in column (f), and 14 of Schedule D by:
• Excluding the portion of any recognized built-in capital gain or loss that does not qualify for transitional relief, and
• Reducing any capital gain taken into account in determining passive investment income (line 2 of the worksheet for line 22a, page 1 of Form 1120S) by the portion of excess net passive income attributable to such gain. The attributable portion is figured by multiplying excess net passive income by a fraction, the numerator of which is the capital gain (less any expenses attributable to such gain), and the denominator of which is net passive income.

   Step 2. Refigure lines 4, 10, 15, and 16 of Schedule D using the amounts determined in step 1.

Line 20. Figure taxable income by completing lines 1 through 28 of **Form 1120,** U.S. Corporation Income Tax Return. Follow the instructions for Form 1120. Enter the amount from line 28 of Form 1120 on line 20 of Schedule D. Attach to Schedule D the Form 1120 computation or other worksheet used to figure taxable income.

Line 21. Figure the tax under section 11 on the taxable income shown on line 20 as if the corporation were not an S corporation. You may use Schedule J of Form 1120 to figure the tax. Attach the tax computation to Schedule D.

Line 22. Figure the excess of the net long-term capital gain over the net short-term capital loss from substituted basis property (defined above). Reduce this amount by any excess net passive income attributable to this gain (see the instructions for line 16). Attach to Schedule D your computation of the line 22 amount.

Part IV—Built-In Gains Tax

Section 1374 provides for a tax on built-in gains that applies to certain corporations that made the election to be an S corporation after 1986. This tax does not apply to any corporation that has been an S corporation for each of its tax years, unless the corporation acquired an asset with a basis determined by reference to its basis (or the basis of any other property) in the hands of a C corporation.

Transitional relief from built-in gains tax. Section 633(d)(8) of the Tax Reform Act of 1986 provides special transitional relief from the built-in gains tax for qualified corporations that elected to be S corporations during 1987 or 1988. A qualified corporation is any corporation, the stock of which:
• Was more than 50% owned (by value) by a qualified group (defined below) on August 1, 1986, and at all times thereafter before the corporation is completely liquidated, and
• Had a fair market value of less than $10 million on both the date the corporation made a valid S election and on August 1, 1986. However, if the fair market value of the stock on either date was between $5 million and $10 million, the corporation is given only partial relief from the built-in gains tax. The portion of the built-in gain **not** eligible for relief is a fraction, the numerator of which is the amount by which the fair market value of the corporation on the date it made a valid S election (or on August 1, 1986, if higher) exceeds $5 million and the denominator of which is $5 million.

A qualified group is a group of 10 or fewer qualified persons. A qualified person is:
• An individual,
• An estate, or
• A trust described in section 1361(c)(2)(A)(ii) or (iii).

For any corporation that elected to be an S corporation after March 30, 1988, the qualified group must have owned (or be treated as having owned) more than 50% (by value) of the corporation's stock at all times during the 5-year period ending on the date of adoption of a plan of complete liquidation.

Transitional relief **does not** apply to:
• Ordinary gains or losses (determined without regard to section 1239),
• Gains or losses from the disposition of capital assets held for 6 months or less, and
• Gains from the disposition of any asset acquired by the corporation with a substituted basis, if a principal purpose for acquiring the asset was to secure transitional relief from the built-in gains tax.

Line 25. Enter the amount that would be the taxable income of the corporation for the tax year if only recognized built-in gains (including any carryover of gain under section 1374(d)(2)(B)) and recognized built-in losses were taken into account.

Section 1374(d)(3) defines a **recognized built-in gain** as any gain recognized during the recognition period (the 10-year period beginning on the first day of the first tax year for which the corporation is an S corporation, or beginning the date the asset was acquired by the S corporation, for an asset with a basis determined by reference to its basis (or the basis of any other property) in the hands of a C corporation) on the sale or distribution (disposition) of any asset, except to the extent the corporation establishes that—
• The asset was not held by the corporation as of the beginning of the first tax year the corporation was an S corporation (except this does not apply to an asset acquired by the S corporation with a basis determined by reference to its basis (or the basis of any other property) in the hands of a C corporation), or
• The gain exceeds the excess of the fair market value of the asset as of the start of the first tax year (or as of the date the asset was acquired by the S corporation, for an asset with a basis determined by reference to its basis (or the basis of any other property) in the hands of a C corporation) over the adjusted basis of the asset at that time.

Section 1374(d)(4) defines a **recognized built-in loss** as any loss recognized during the recognition period (stated above) on the disposition of any asset to the extent the corporation establishes that—
• The asset was held by the corporation as of the beginning of the first tax year the corporation was an S corporation (except that this does not apply to an asset acquired by the S corporation with a basis determined by reference to its basis (or the basis of any other property) in the hands of a C corporation), and
• The loss does not exceed the excess of the adjusted basis of the asset as of the beginning of the first tax year (or as of the date the asset was acquired by the S corporation, for an asset with a basis determined by reference to its basis (or the basis of any other property) in the hands of a C corporation), over the fair market value of the asset as of that time.

A qualified corporation must show on an attachment to Schedule D its total net recognized built-in gain and also list separately the gain or loss that is from these:
• Capital assets held 6 months or less, and
• Assets for which the disposition results in ordinary income or loss.

A nonqualified corporation must show on an attachment its total net recognized built-in gain and list separately any capital gain or loss and ordinary gain or loss.

Line 26. Figure taxable income by completing lines 1 through 28 of Form 1120. Follow the instructions for Form 1120. Enter the amount from line 28 of Form 1120 on line 26 of Schedule D. Attach to Schedule D the Form 1120 computation or other worksheet used to figure taxable income.

Line 27. If for any tax year the amount on line 25 exceeds the taxable income on line 26, the excess is treated as a recognized built-in gain in the succeeding tax year. This carryover provision applies only in the case of an S corporation that made its election to be an S corporation after March 30, 1988. See section 1374(d)(2)(B).

Line 28. Enter the section 1374(b)(2) deduction. Generally, this is any net operating loss carryforward or capital loss carryforward (to the extent of net capital gain included in recognized built-in gain for the tax year) arising in tax years for which the corporation was a C corporation. See section 1374(b)(2) for details.

Instructions for Schedule D (Form 1120S)

Page 3

SCHEDULE D (Form 1120S) Department of the Treasury Internal Revenue Service	**Capital Gains and Losses and Built-In Gains** ▶ Attach to Form 1120S. ▶ See separate instructions.	OMB No. 1545-0130 **1998**

Name	Employer identification number

Part I Short-Term Capital Gains and Losses—Assets Held One Year or Less

(a) Description of property (Example, 100 shares of "Z" Co.)	(b) Date acquired (mo., day, yr.)	(c) Date sold (mo., day, yr.)	(d) Sales price	(e) Cost or other basis (see instructions)	(f) Gain or (loss) ((d) minus (e))	
1						

2	Short-term capital gain from installment sales from Form 6252, line 26 or 37	2	
3	Short-term capital gain or (loss) from like-kind exchanges from Form 8824	3	
4	Combine lines 1 through 3 in column (f) and enter here	4	
5	Tax on short-term capital gain included on line 32 below	5 (	)
6	**Net short-term capital gain or (loss).** Combine lines 4 and 5. Enter here and on Form 1120S, Schedule K, line 4d or 6	6	

Part II Long-Term Capital Gains and Losses—Assets Held More Than One Year

(a) Description of property (Example, 100 shares of "Z" Co.)	(b) Date acquired (mo., day, yr.)	(c) Date sold (mo., day, yr.)	(d) Sales price	(e) Cost or other basis (see instructions)	(f) Gain or (loss) ((d) minus (e))	(g) 28% rate gain or (loss) * (see instr. below)
7						

8	Long-term capital gain from installment sales from Form 6252, line 26 or 37	8		
9	Long-term capital gain or (loss) from like-kind exchanges from Form 8824	9		
10	Combine lines 7 through 9 in column (f) and enter here	10		
11	Tax on long-term capital gain included on lines 24 and 32 below	11 (	)(	)
12	Combine lines 7 through 11 in column (g). Enter here and on Form 1120S, Schedule K, line 4e(1) or 6	12		
13	**Net long-term capital gain or (loss).** Combine lines 10 and 11 in column (f). Enter here and on Form 1120S, Schedule K, line 4e(2) or 6	13		

* **28% rate gain or (loss)** includes **ALL** "collectibles gains and losses" (as defined in the instructions).

Part III Capital Gains Tax (See instructions **before** completing this part.)

14	Enter section 1231 gain from Form 4797, line 9, column (g)	14	
15	Net long-term capital gain or (loss). Combine lines 10 and 14	15	
	Note: If the corporation is liable for the excess net passive income tax (Form 1120S, page 1, line 22a) or the built-in gains tax (Part IV below), see the line 16 instructions before completing line 16.		
16	Net capital gain. Enter excess of net long-term capital gain (line 15) over net short-term capital loss (line 4)	16	
17	Statutory minimum	17	$25,000
18	Subtract line 17 from line 16	18	
19	Enter 34% of line 18	19	
20	Taxable income (attach computation schedule)	20	
21	Enter tax on line 20 amount (attach computation schedule)	21	
22	Net capital gain from substituted basis property (attach computation schedule)	22	
23	Enter 35% of line 22	23	
24	**Tax.** Enter the smallest of line 19, 21, or 23 here and on Form 1120S, page 1, line 22b	24	

Part IV Built-In Gains Tax (See instructions **before** completing this part.)

25	Excess of recognized built-in gains over recognized built-in losses (attach computation schedule)	25	
26	Taxable income (attach computation schedule)	26	
27	Net recognized built-in gain. Enter the smallest of line 25, line 26, or line 9 of Schedule B	27	
28	Section 1374(b)(2) deduction	28	
29	Subtract line 28 from line 27. If zero or less, enter -0- here and on line 32	29	
30	Enter 35% of line 29	30	
31	Business credit and minimum tax credit carryforwards under section 1374(b)(3) from C corporation years	31	
32	**Tax.** Subtract line 31 from line 30 (if zero or less, enter -0-). Enter here and on Form 1120S, page 1, line 22b	32	

For Paperwork Reduction Act Notice, see the Instructions for Form 1120S.   Cat. No. 11516V   Schedule D (Form 1120S) 1998

SCHEDULE E
(Form 1040)

Department of the Treasury
Internal Revenue Service   (99)

Supplemental Income and Loss

(From rental real estate, royalties, partnerships,
S corporations, estates, trusts, REMICs, etc.)

▶ **Attach to Form 1040 or Form 1041.**   ▶ **See Instructions for Schedule E (Form 1040).**

OMB No. 1545-0074

19**98**

Attachment
Sequence No. **13**

Name(s) shown on return

Your social security number

Part I   **Income or Loss From Rental Real Estate and Royalties**   **Note:** *Report income and expenses from your business of renting personal property on* **Schedule C** *or* **C-EZ** *(see page E-1). Report farm rental income or loss from* **Form 4835** *on page 2, line 39.*

1 Show the kind and location of each **rental real estate property:**

A ....

B ....

C ....

2 For each rental real estate property listed on line 1, did you or your family use it during the tax year for personal purposes for more than the greater of:
  • 14 days, **or**
  • 10% of the total days rented at fair rental value?
   (See page E-1.)

	Yes	No
A		
B		
C		

Income:

		Properties			Totals
		A	**B**	**C**	(Add columns A, B, and C.)
3 Rents received	**3**				**3**
4 Royalties received	**4**				**4**

Expenses:

5 Advertising	**5**				
6 Auto and travel (see page E-2) .	**6**				
7 Cleaning and maintenance . . .	**7**				
8 Commissions	**8**				
9 Insurance	**9**				
10 Legal and other professional fees	**10**				
11 Management fees	**11**				
12 Mortgage interest paid to banks, etc. (see page E-2)	**12**				**12**
13 Other interest	**13**				
14 Repairs	**14**				
15 Supplies	**15**				
16 Taxes	**16**				
17 Utilities	**17**				
18 Other (list) ▶	**18**				
19 Add lines 5 through 18	**19**				**19**
20 Depreciation expense or depletion (see page E-3)	**20**				**20**
21 Total expenses. Add lines 19 and 20	**21**				
22 Income or (loss) from rental real estate or royalty properties. Subtract line 21 from line 3 (rents) or line 4 (royalties). If the result is a (loss), see page E-3 to find out if you must file **Form 6198** . .	**22**				
23 Deductible rental real estate loss. **Caution:** *Your rental real estate loss on line 22 may be limited. See page E-3 to find out if you must file* **Form 8582.** *Real estate professionals must complete line 42 on page 2*	**23**	( )(	)(	)(	)

24 **Income.** Add positive amounts shown on line 22. **Do not** include any losses . . . . | **24** | |

25 **Losses.** Add royalty losses from line 22 and rental real estate losses from line 23. Enter total losses here | **25** | ( ) |

26 Total rental real estate and royalty income or (loss). Combine lines 24 and 25. Enter the result here. If Parts II, III, IV, and line 39 on page 2 do not apply to you, also enter this amount on Form 1040, line 17. Otherwise, include this amount in the total on line 40 on page 2 . . . . | **26** | |

For Paperwork Reduction Act Notice, see Form 1040 instructions.   Cat. No. 11344L   Schedule E (Form 1040) 1998

Name(s) shown on return. Do not enter name and social security number if shown on other side.

Your social security number

Note: *If you report amounts from farming or fishing on Schedule E, you must enter your gross income from those activities on line 41 below. Real estate professionals must complete line 42 below.*

Part II   Income or Loss From Partnerships and S Corporations   Note: *If you report a loss from an at-risk activity, you MUST check either column (e) or (f) on line 27 to describe your investment in the activity. See page E-5. If you check column (f), you must attach Form 6198.*

27	(a) Name	(b) Enter **P** for partnership; **S** for S corporation	(c) Check if foreign partnership	(d) Employer identification number	Investment At Risk?	
					(e) All is at risk	(f) Some is not at risk
A						
B						
C						
D						
E						

	Passive Income and Loss		Nonpassive Income and Loss		
	(g) Passive loss allowed (attach **Form 8582** if required)	(h) Passive income from **Schedule K–1**	(i) Nonpassive loss from **Schedule K–1**	(j) Section 179 expense deduction from **Form 4562**	(k) Nonpassive income from **Schedule K–1**
A					
B					
C					
D					
E					
28a Totals					
b Totals					

29	Add columns (h) and (k) of line 28a	29	
30	Add columns (g), (i), and (j) of line 28b	30 (	)
31	Total partnership and S corporation income or (loss). Combine lines 29 and 30. Enter the result here and include in the total on line 40 below	31	

Part III   Income or Loss From Estates and Trusts

32	(a) Name	(b) Employer identification number
A		
B		

	Passive Income and Loss		Nonpassive Income and Loss	
	(c) Passive deduction or loss allowed (attach **Form 8582** if required)	(d) Passive income from **Schedule K–1**	(e) Deduction or loss from **Schedule K–1**	(f) Other income from **Schedule K–1**
A				
B				
33a Totals				
b Totals				

34	Add columns (d) and (f) of line 33a	34	
35	Add columns (c) and (e) of line 33b	35 (	)
36	Total estate and trust income or (loss). Combine lines 34 and 35. Enter the result here and include in the total on line 40 below	36	

Part IV   Income or Loss From Real Estate Mortgage Investment Conduits (REMICs)—Residual Holder

37	(a) Name	(b) Employer identification number	(c) Excess inclusion from **Schedules Q**, line 2c (see page E-6)	(d) Taxable income (net loss) from **Schedules Q**, line 1b	(e) Income from **Schedules Q**, line 3b

38	Combine columns (d) and (e) only. Enter the result here and include in the total on line 40 below	38	

Part V   Summary

39	Net farm rental income or (loss) from **Form 4835**. Also, complete line 41 below	39	
40	**TOTAL** income or (loss). Combine lines 26, 31, 36, 38, and 39. Enter the result here and on Form 1040, line 17 ▶	40	

41	**Reconciliation of Farming and Fishing Income.** Enter your **gross** farming and fishing income reported on Form 4835, line 7; Schedule K-1 (Form 1065), line 15b; Schedule K-1 (Form 1120S), line 23; and Schedule K-1 (Form 1041), line 14 (see page E-6)	41	

42	**Reconciliation for Real Estate Professionals.** If you were a real estate professional (see page E-4), enter the net income or (loss) you reported anywhere on Form 1040 from all rental real estate activities in which you materially participated under the passive activity loss rules . . .	42	

✱

C

IRS Form 4562
Depreciation and Amortization

Instructions for Form 4562

Depreciation and Amortization
(Including Information on Listed Property)

Section references are to the Internal Revenue Code unless otherwise noted.

Changes To Note

• For tax years beginning in 1998, the maximum section 179 expense deduction has been increased to $18,500 ($38,500 for enterprise zone businesses).

• If you elect under section 168(b)(5) to depreciate property placed in service after 1998 using the 150% declining balance method, the GDS recovery period is used instead of the ADS recovery period. For more details, see the instructions for line 15, column (d) on page 4.

General Instructions

Purpose of Form

Use Form 4562 to:

• Claim your deduction for depreciation and amortization;

• Make the election to expense certain tangible property (section 179); and

• Provide information on the business/investment use of automobiles and other listed property.

Who Must File

Except as otherwise noted, complete and file Form 4562 if you are claiming any of the following.

• Depreciation for property placed in service during the 1998 tax year.

• A section 179 expense deduction (which may include a carryover from a previous year).

• Depreciation on any vehicle or other listed property (regardless of when it was placed in service).

• A deduction for any vehicle reported on a form other than **Schedule C (Form 1040),** Profit or Loss From Business, or **Schedule C-EZ (Form 1040),** Net Profit From Business.

• Any depreciation on a corporate income tax return (other than Form 1120S).

• Amortization of costs that begins during the 1998 tax year.

However, **do not** file Form 4562 to report depreciation and information on the use of vehicles if you are an employee deducting job-related vehicle expenses using either the standard mileage rate or actual expenses. Instead, use **Form 2106,** Employee Business Expenses, or **Form 2106-EZ,** Unreimbursed Employee Business Expenses, for this purpose.

Submit a separate Form 4562 for each business or activity on your return. If you need more space, attach additional sheets. However, complete only one Part I in its entirety when computing your allowable section 179 expense deduction.

Definitions

Depreciation

Depreciation is the annual deduction allowed to recover the cost or other basis of business or income-producing property with a determinable useful life of more than 1 year. However, land is not depreciable.

Depreciation starts when you first use the property in your business or for the production of income. It ends when you take the property out of service, deduct all your depreciable cost or other basis, or no longer use the property in your business or for the production of income.

Amortization

Amortization is similar to the straight line method of depreciation in that an annual deduction is allowed to recover certain costs over a fixed time period. You can amortize such items as the costs of starting a business, goodwill and certain other intangibles, reforestation, and pollution control facilities. For additional information, get **Pub. 535,** Business Expenses.

Listed Property

Listed property generally includes:

• Passenger automobiles weighing 6,000 pounds or less.

• Any other property used for transportation if the nature of the property lends itself to personal use, such as motorcycles, pick-up trucks, etc.

• Any property used for entertainment or recreational purposes (such as photographic, phonographic, communication, and video recording equipment).

• Cellular telephones (or other similar telecommunications equipment).

• Computers or peripheral equipment.

Exception. Listed property does not include **(a)** photographic, phonographic, communication, or video equipment used exclusively in a taxpayer's trade or business or at the taxpayer's regular business establishment; **(b)** any computer or peripheral equipment used exclusively at a regular business establishment and owned or leased by the person operating the establishment; or **(c)** an ambulance, hearse, or vehicle used for transporting persons or property for hire. For purposes of the preceding sentence, a portion of the taxpayer's home is treated as a regular business establishment only if that portion meets the requirements under section 280A(c)(1) for deducting expenses attributable to the business use of a home. However, for any property listed under **(a)** above, the regular business establishment of an employee is his or her employer's regular business establishment.

Recordkeeping

Except for Part V (relating to listed property), the IRS does not require you to submit detailed information with your return on the depreciation of assets placed in service in previous tax years. However, the information needed to compute your depreciation deduction (basis, method, etc.) must be part of your permanent records.

Cat. No. 12907Y

Because Form 4562 does not provide for permanent recordkeeping, you may use the depreciation worksheet on page 12 to assist you in maintaining depreciation records. However, the worksheet is designed only for Federal income tax purposes. You may need to keep additional records for accounting and state income tax purposes.

Specific Instructions

Part I

Caution: *An estate or trust cannot make this election.*

You may elect to expense part of the cost of certain tangible personal property used in your trade or business and certain other property described in section 1245(a)(3). To do so, you must have:

• Purchased the property (as defined in section 179(d)(2)) and

• Placed it in service during the 1998 tax year.

You must make the election with:

1. The original return you file for the tax year the property was placed in service (whether or not you file your return on time), or

2. An amended return filed no later than the due date (including extensions) for your return for the tax year the property was placed in service.

Once made, the election (and the selection of the property you elect to expense) may not be revoked without IRS consent.

If you elect this deduction, reduce the amount on which you figure your depreciation or amortization deduction by the section 179 expense deduction.

Section 179 property does **not** include:

1. Property used 50% or less in your trade or business.

2. Property held for investment (section 212 property).

3. Property you lease to others as a noncorporate lessor **unless (a)** you manufactured or produced the property or **(b)** the term of the lease is less than 50% of the property's class life, and for the first 12 months after the property is transferred to the lessee, the sum of the deductions related to the property that are allowed to you **solely** under section

162 (except rents and reimbursed amounts) is more than 15% of the rental income from the property.

4. Property used mainly outside the United States (except for property described in section 168(g)(4)).

5. Property used for lodging or for furnishing the lodging (except as provided in section 50(b)(2)).

6. Property used by a tax-exempt organization (other than a section 521 farmers' cooperative) unless the property is used mainly in a taxable unrelated trade or business.

7. Property used by a governmental unit or foreign person or entity (except for property used under a lease with a term of less than 6 months).

8. Air conditioning or heating units.

The section 179 expense deduction is subject to two separate limitations: a dollar limitation and a taxable income limitation. Both limitations are figured in Part I.

For a partnership, these limitations apply to the partnership and each partner, but for an electing large partnership (as defined in section 775), the limitations apply only to the partnership. For an S corporation, these limitations apply to the S corporation and each shareholder. For a controlled group, all component members are treated as one taxpayer.

For more details on the section 179 expense deduction, see **Pub. 946,** How To Depreciate Property.

Line 1

For an enterprise zone business, the maximum section 179 expense deduction of $18,500 is increased by the **smaller** of:

• $20,000 or

• The cost of section 179 property that is also qualified zone property (including such property placed in service by your spouse, even if you are filing a separate return).

Cross out the preprinted entry on line 1 and enter in the margin the larger amount if your business is an enterprise zone business. For the definitions of enterprise zone business and qualified zone property, see sections 1397B and 1397C.

Recapture Rule: *If any qualified zone property placed in service during the current year ceases to be used in an empowerment zone by an enterprise zone business in a later*

year, the benefit of the increased section 179 expense deduction must be reported as "other income" on your return.

Line 2

Enter the cost of all section 179 property placed in service during the tax year. Include amounts from any listed property from Part V. Also include any section 179 property placed in service by your spouse, even if you are filing a separate return.

For an enterprise zone business, include on this line only 50% of the cost of section 179 property that is also qualified zone property.

Line 5

If line 5 is zero, you cannot elect to expense any property. Skip lines 6 through 11, enter zero on line 12, and enter the carryover of any disallowed deduction from 1997 on line 13.

If you are married filing separately, you and your spouse must allocate the dollar limitation for the tax year. To do so, multiply the total limitation that you would otherwise enter on line 5 by 50%, unless you both elect a different allocation. If you both elect a different allocation, multiply the total limitation by the percentage elected. The sum of the percentages you and your spouse elect must equal 100%. **Do not** enter on line 5 more than your share of the total dollar limitation.

Line 6

Caution: *Do not* include any listed property on line 6.

Column (a). Enter a brief description of the property for which you are making the election (e.g., truck, office furniture, etc.).

Column (b). Enter the cost of the property. If you acquired the property through a trade-in, **do not** include any undepreciated basis of the assets you traded in. See **Pub. 551,** Basis of Assets, for more details.

Column (c). Enter the amount you elect to expense. You do not have to expense the entire cost of the property. You can depreciate the amount you do not expense. See the line 15 and line 16 instructions.

To report your share of a section 179 expense deduction from a partnership or an S corporation, write "from Schedule K-1 (Form 1065)" or "from Schedule K-1 (Form 1120S)" across columns (a) and (b).

Line 10

The carryover of disallowed deduction from 1997 is the amount of section 179 property, if any, you elected to expense in previous years, but not allowed as a deduction due to the business income limitation. If you filed Form 4562 for 1997, enter the amount from line 13 of your 1997 Form 4562. For additional details, see Pub. 946.

Line 11

The section 179 expense deduction is further limited to the "business income" limitation under section 179(b)(3).

For purposes of the rules that follow:

• If you have to apply another Code section that has a limitation based on taxable income, see Regulations section 1.179-2(c)(5) for rules on how to apply the business income limitation under section 179 in such a case.

• You are considered to **actively conduct** a trade or business if you meaningfully participate in its management or operations. A mere passive investor is not considered to actively conduct a trade or business.

Individuals. Enter the smaller of line 5 or the aggregate taxable income from any trade or business you actively conducted, computed without regard to any section 179 expense deduction, the deduction for one-half of self-employment taxes under section 164(f), or any net operating loss deduction. Include in aggregate taxable income the wages, salaries, tips, and other compensation you earned as an employee (not reduced by unreimbursed employee business expenses). If you are married filing a joint return, combine the aggregate taxable incomes for you and your spouse.

Partnerships. Enter the smaller of line 5 or the aggregate of the partnership's items of income and expense described in section 702(a) from any trade or business the partnership actively conducted (other than credits, tax-exempt income, the section 179 expense deduction, and guaranteed payments under section 707(c)).

S corporations. Enter the smaller of line 5 or the aggregate of the corporation's items of income and expense described in section 1366(a) from any trade or business the

corporation actively conducted (other than credits, tax-exempt income, the section 179 expense deduction, and the deduction for compensation paid to the corporation's shareholder-employees).

Corporations other than S corporations. Enter the smaller of line 5 or the corporation's taxable income before the section 179 expense deduction, net operating loss deduction, and special deductions (excluding items not derived from a trade or business actively conducted by the corporation).

Line 12

The limitations on lines 5 and 11 apply to the taxpayer, and not to each separate business or activity. Therefore, if you have more than one business or activity, you may allocate your allowable section 179 expense deduction among them.

To do so, write "Summary" at the top of Part I of the separate Form 4562 you are completing for the aggregate amounts from all businesses or activities. **Do not** complete the rest of that form. On line 12 of the Form 4562 you prepare for each separate business or activity, enter the amount allocated to the business or activity from the "Summary." No other entry is required in Part I of the separate Form 4562 prepared for each business or activity.

Part II

The term "Modified Accelerated Cost Recovery System" (MACRS) includes the General Depreciation System and the Alternative Depreciation System. Generally, MACRS is used to depreciate any tangible property placed in service after 1986. However, MACRS does not apply to films, videotapes, and sound recordings. See section 168(f) for other exceptions. For more details on MACRS, see Pub. 946. For information on other methods of depreciation, see **Pub. 534,** Depreciating Property Placed in Service Before 1987.

Depreciation may be an adjustment for alternative minimum tax purposes. For details, see **Form 4626,** Alternative Minimum Tax—Corporations; **Form 6251,** Alternative Minimum Tax—Individuals; or Schedule I of **Form 1041,** U.S. Income Tax Return for Estates and Trusts.

Section A

Line 14

To simplify the computation of MACRS depreciation, you may elect to group assets into one or more general asset accounts under section 168(i)(4). The assets in each general asset account are depreciated as a single asset.

Each account must include only assets that were placed in service during the same tax year with the same asset class (if any), depreciation method, recovery period, and convention. However, an asset cannot be included in a general asset account if the asset is used both for personal purposes and business/investment purposes.

When an asset in an account is disposed of, the amount realized generally must be recognized as ordinary income. The unadjusted depreciable basis and depreciation reserve of the general asset account are not affected as a result of a disposition.

Special rules apply to passenger automobiles, assets generating foreign source income, assets converted to personal use, and certain asset dispositions. For more details, see Regulations section 1.168(i)-1.

To make the election, check the box on line 14. You must make the election on your return filed no later than the due date (including extensions) for the tax year in which the assets included in the general asset account were placed in service. Once made, the election is irrevocable and applies to the tax year for which the election is made and all later tax years.

Section B

Lines 15a Through 15i

Use lines 15a through 15i only for assets placed in service during the tax year beginning in 1998 and depreciated under the General Depreciation System (GDS), except for automobiles and other listed property (which are reported in Part V).

Column (a). Determine which property you acquired and placed in service during the tax year beginning in 1998. Then, sort that property according to its classification (3-year property, 5-year property, etc.) as shown in column (a) of lines 15a through 15i. The classifications for

Page 3

some property are shown below. For property not shown, see **Determining the classification** on this page.

3-year property includes:
- A race horse that is more than 2 years old at the time it is placed in service.
- Any horse (other than a race horse) that is more than 12 years old at the time it is placed in service.
- Any qualified rent-to-own property (as defined in section 168(i)(14)).

5-year property includes:
- Automobiles.
- Light general purpose trucks.
- Typewriters, calculators, copiers, and duplicating equipment.
- Any semi-conductor manufacturing equipment.
- Any computer or peripheral equipment.
- Any section 1245 property used in connection with research and experimentation.
- Certain energy property specified in section 168(e)(3)(B)(vi).

7-year property includes:
- Office furniture and equipment.
- Appliances, carpets, furniture, etc., used in residential rental property.
- Railroad track.
- Any property that does not have a class life and is not otherwise classified.

10-year property includes:
- Vessels, barges, tugs, and similar water transportation equipment.
- Any single purpose agricultural or horticultural structure (see section 168(i)(13)).
- Any tree or vine bearing fruit or nuts.

15-year property includes:
- Any municipal wastewater treatment plant.
- Any telephone distribution plant and comparable equipment used for 2-way exchange of voice and data communications.
- Any section 1250 property that is a retail motor fuels outlet (whether or not food or other convenience items are sold there).

20-year property includes:
- Farm buildings (other than single purpose agricultural or horticultural structures).
- Municipal sewers not classified as 25-year property.

25-year property is water utility property, which is:

- Property that is an integral part of the gathering, treatment, or commercial distribution of water, that, without regard to this classification, would be 20-year property.
- Municipal sewers. This classification applies to property placed in service after June 12, 1996, except for property placed in service under a binding contract in effect at all times since June 9, 1996.

Residential rental property is a building in which 80% or more of the total rent is from dwelling units.

Nonresidential real property is any real property that is neither residential rental property nor property with a class life of less than 27.5 years.

50-year property includes any improvements necessary to construct or improve a roadbed or right-of-way for railroad track that qualifies as a railroad grading or tunnel bore under section 168(e)(4).

There is no separate line to report 50-year property. Therefore, attach a statement showing the same information as required in columns (a) through (g). Include the deduction in the line 21 "Total" and write "See attachment" in the bottom margin of the form.

Determining the classification. If your depreciable property is **not** listed above, determine the classification as follows.

1. Find the property's class life. See the Table of Class Lives and Recovery Periods in Pub. 946.

2. Use the following table to find the classification in column (b) that corresponds to the class life of the property in column (a).

(a) Class life (in years) (See Pub. 946)	(b) Classification
4 or less	3-year property
More than 4 but less than 10.	5-year property
10 or more but less than 16..	7-year property
16 or more but less than 20 ..	10-year property
20 or more but less than 25 ..	15-year property
25 or more	20-year property

Column (b). For lines 15h and 15i, enter the month and year you placed the property in service. If you converted property held for personal use to use in a trade or business or for the production of income, treat the property as being placed in service on the conversion date.

Column (c). To find the basis for depreciation, multiply the cost or other basis of the property by the percentage of business/investment

use. From that result, subtract any section 179 expense deduction, deduction for removal of barriers to the disabled and the elderly, disabled access credit, and enhanced oil recovery credit. See section 50(c) to determine the basis adjustment for investment credit property.

Column (d). Determine the recovery period from the table below, unless either **1** or **2** below applies.

1. You make an irrevocable election to use the 150% declining balance method of depreciation for 3-, 5-, 7-, or 10-year property (excluding any tree or vine bearing fruit or nuts). The election applies to all property within the classification for which it is made that was placed in service during the tax year. If you elect this method for property placed in service **before 1999**, you must use the recovery period under the Alternative Depreciation System (ADS) discussed in the line 16 instructions. For property placed in service **after 1998**, use the GDS recovery period (shown in the table below). You will not have an adjustment for alternative minimum tax purposes on the property for which you make this election.

2. You acquired qualified Indian reservation property (as defined in section 168(j)(4)). Qualified Indian reservation property does not include property placed in service to conduct class I, II, or III gaming activities. See Pub. 946 for the table for qualified Indian reservation property.

Recovery Period for Most Property

In the case of:	The recovery period is:
3-year property	3 yrs.
5-year property	5 yrs.
7-year property	7 yrs.
10-year property	10 yrs.
15-year property	15 yrs.
20-year property	20 yrs.
25-year property	25 yrs.
Residential rental property	27.5 yrs.
Nonresidential real property placed in service before May 13, 1993	31.5 yrs.
Nonresidential real property placed in service after May 12, 1993	* 39 yrs.
Railroad gradings and tunnel bores	50 yrs.

* The recovery period is 31.5 years for property you placed in service before 1994, if you started construction on the property before May 13, 1993, or you had a binding written contract to buy or build it before that date.

Column (e). The applicable convention determines the portion of the tax year for which depreciation is allowable during a year property is either placed in service or disposed of. There are three types of conventions. To select the correct convention, you must know when you placed the property in service and the type of property.

Half-year convention (HY). This convention applies to all property reported on lines 15a through 15g, unless the mid-quarter convention applies. It does not apply to residential rental property, nonresidential real property, and railroad gradings and tunnel bores. It treats all property placed in service (or disposed of) during any tax year as placed in service (or disposed of) on the midpoint of that tax year.

Mid-quarter convention (MQ). If the aggregate bases of property subject to depreciation under section 168 and placed in service during the last 3 months of your tax year exceed 40% of the aggregate bases of property subject to depreciation under section 168 and placed in service during the entire tax year, the mid-quarter, instead of the half-year, convention applies.

In determining whether the mid-quarter convention applies, **do not** take into account the following:
- Property that is being depreciated under the pre-1987 rules.
- Any residential rental property, nonresidential real property, or railroad gradings and tunnel bores.
- Property that is placed in service and disposed of within the same tax year.

The mid-quarter convention treats all property placed in service (or disposed of) during any quarter as placed in service (or disposed of) on the midpoint of that quarter. However, no depreciation is allowed under this convention for property that is placed in service and disposed of within the same tax year.

Mid-month convention (MM). This convention applies ONLY to residential rental property, nonresidential real property (lines 15h or 15i), and railroad gradings and tunnel bores. It treats all property placed in service (or disposed of) during any month as placed in service (or disposed of) on the midpoint of that month.

Enter "HY" for half-year, "MQ" for mid-quarter, or "MM" for mid-month convention.

Column (f). Applicable depreciation methods are prescribed for each classification of property. Except as otherwise stated below, the applicable method for 3-, 5-, 7-, and 10-year property is the 200% declining balance method, switching to the straight line method in the first tax year that maximizes the depreciation allowance.

For 15- and 20-year property, property used in a farming business, and property for which you elected to use the 150% declining balance method, the applicable method is the 150% declining balance method, switching to the straight line method in the first tax year that maximizes the depreciation allowance.

For water utility property, residential rental property, nonresidential real property, any railroad grading or tunnel bore, or any tree or vine bearing fruit or nuts, the only applicable method is the straight line method.

You may also make an irrevocable election to use the straight line method for all property within a classification that is placed in service during the tax year.

Enter "200 DB" for 200% declining balance, "150 DB" for 150% declining balance, or "S/L" for straight line.

Column (g). To compute the depreciation deduction you may use optional Tables A through E, starting on page 10. To do this, multiply the applicable rate from the appropriate table by the property's **unadjusted** basis (column (c)). See Pub. 946 for complete tables. If you disposed of the property during the current tax year, multiply the result by the applicable decimal amount from the tables in step 3 below. Or you may compute the deduction yourself by completing the following steps.

Step 1. Determine the depreciation rate as follows.
- If you are using the 200% or 150% declining balance method in column (f), divide the declining balance rate (use 2.00 for 200 DB or 1.50 for 150 DB) by the number of years in the recovery period in column (d). For example, for property depreciated using the 200 DB method over a recovery period of 5 years, divide 2.00 by 5 for a rate of 40%.

You must switch to the straight line rate in the first year that the straight line rate exceeds the declining balance rate.
- If you are using the straight line method, divide 1.00 by the remaining number of years in the recovery period as of the beginning of the tax year (but not less than one). For example, if there are 6½ years remaining in the recovery period as of the beginning of the year, divide 1.00 by 6.5 for a rate of 15.38%.

Step 2. Multiply the percentage rate determined in Step 1 by the property's unrecovered basis (basis for depreciation (as defined in column (c)) reduced by all prior year's depreciation).

Step 3. For property placed in service or disposed of during the current tax year, multiply the result from Step 2 by the applicable decimal amount from the tables below (based on the convention shown in column (e)).

Half-year (HY) convention	0.5

Mid-quarter (MQ) convention

Placed in service (or disposed of) during the:	Placed in service	Disposed of
1st quarter	0.875	0.125
2nd quarter	0.625	0.375
3rd quarter	0.375	0.625
4th quarter	0.125	0.875

Mid-month (MM) convention

Placed in service (or disposed of) during the:	Placed in service	Disposed of
1st month...................	0.9583	0.0417
2nd month	0.8750	0.1250
3rd month	0.7917	0.2083
4th month	0.7083	0.2917
5th month	0.6250	0.3750
6th month	0.5417	0.4583
7th month	0.4583	0.5417
8th month	0.3750	0.6250
9th month	0.2917	0.7083
10th month	0.2083	0.7917
11th month	0.1250	0.8750
12th month	0.0417	0.9583

Short tax years. See Pub. 946 for rules on how to compute the depreciation deduction for property placed in service in a short tax year.

Section C

Lines 16a Through 16c

Complete lines 16a through 16c for assets, other than automobiles and other listed property, placed in service ONLY during the tax year beginning in 1998 and depreciated under the Alternative Depreciation System. Report on line 17 depreciation on assets placed in service in prior years.

Under ADS, use the applicable depreciation method, the applicable recovery period, and the applicable convention to compute depreciation.

The following types of property **must** be depreciated under ADS:

Page 5

- Tangible property used predominantly outside the United States.
- Tax-exempt use property.
- Tax-exempt bond financed property.
- Imported property covered by an executive order of the President of the United States.
- Property used predominantly in a farming business and placed in service during any tax year in which you made an election under section 263A(d)(3).

Instead of depreciating property under GDS (line 15), you may make an irrevocable election with respect to any classification of property for any tax year to use ADS. For residential rental and nonresidential real property, you may make this election separately for each property.

Column (a). Use the following rules to determine the classification of the property under ADS.

Class life. Under ADS, the depreciation deduction for most property is based on the property's class life. See the Table of Class Lives and Recovery Periods in Pub. 946. Use line 16a for all property depreciated under ADS, except property that does not have a class life, residential rental and nonresidential real property, water utility property, and railroad gradings and tunnel bores.

See section 168(g)(3) for special rules for determining the class life for certain property.

12-year property. Use line 16b for property that does not have a class life.

40-year property. Use line 16c for residential rental and nonresidential real property.

Water utility property and railroad gradings and tunnel bores. These assets are 50-year property under ADS. There is no separate line to report 50-year property. Therefore, attach a statement showing the same information required in columns (a) through (g). Include the deduction in the line 21 "Total" and write "See attachment" in the bottom margin of the form.

Column (b). For 40-year property, enter the month and year placed in service or converted to use in a trade or business or for the production of income.

Column (c). See the instructions for line 15, column (c).

Column (d). On line 16a, enter the property's class life.

Column (e). Under ADS, the applicable conventions are the same as those used under GDS. See the instructions for line 15, column (e).

Column (g). Compute the depreciation deduction in the same manner as under GDS, except use the straight line method over the ADS recovery period and use the applicable convention.

Part III

Do not use Part III for automobiles and other listed property. Instead, report this property in Part V on page 2 of Form 4562.

Line 17

For tangible property placed in service in tax years beginning before 1998 and depreciated under MACRS, enter the GDS and ADS deductions for the current year. To compute the deductions, see the instructions for column (g), line 15.

Line 18

Report property that you elect, under section 168(f)(1), to depreciate under the unit-of-production method or any other method not based on a term of years (other than the retirement-replacement-betterment method).

Attach a separate sheet showing:
- A description of the property and the depreciation method you elect that excludes the property from ACRS or MACRS.
- The depreciable basis (cost or other basis reduced, if applicable, by salvage value, any section 179 expense deduction, deduction for removal of barriers to the disabled and the elderly, disabled access credit, and enhanced oil recovery credit).

See section 50(c) to determine the basis adjustment for investment credit property.

Line 19

Enter the total depreciation you are claiming for the following types of property (except listed property and property subject to a section 168(f)(1) election):
- Accelerated cost recovery system (ACRS) property (pre-1987 rules). See Pub. 534.
- Property placed in service before 1981.

- Certain public utility property, which does not meet certain normalization requirements.
- Certain property acquired from related persons.
- Property acquired in certain nonrecognition transactions.
- Certain sound recordings, movies, and videotapes.
- Property depreciated under the income forecast method. The use of the income forecast method is limited to motion picture films, videotapes, sound recordings, copyrights, books, and patents. You cannot use this method to depreciate any amortizable section 197 intangible. See page 9 for more details on section 197 intangibles.

Note: *If you use the income forecast method for any property placed in service after September 13, 1995, you may owe or be entitled to a refund for the 3rd and 10th tax years beginning after the tax year the property was placed in service. For more details, get **Form 8866,** Interest Computation Under the Look-Back Method for Property Depreciated Under the Income Forecast Method.*

- Intangible property, other than section 197 intangibles, including:
  1. Computer software. Use the straight line method over 36 months.
  2. Any right to receive tangible property or services under a contract or granted by a governmental unit (not acquired as part of a business).
  3. Any interest in a patent or copyright not acquired as part of a business.
  4. Residential mortgage servicing rights. Use the straight line method over 108 months.

See section 167(f) for more details.

Prior years' depreciation, plus current year's depreciation, can never exceed the depreciable basis of the property.

The basis and amounts claimed for depreciation should be part of your permanent books and records. **No attachment is necessary.**

Part IV

Line 21

A partnership (other than an electing large partnership) or S corporation does not include any section 179 expense deduction (line 12) on this line. Instead, any section 179 expense deduction is passed through separately to the partners and shareholders on the appropriate line of their Schedules K-1.

Line 22

If you are subject to the uniform capitalization rules of section 263A, enter the increase in basis from costs you must capitalize. For a detailed discussion of who is subject to these rules, which costs must be capitalized, and allocation of costs among activities, see Regulations section 1.263A-1.

Part V

If you claim the standard mileage rate, actual vehicle expenses (including depreciation), or depreciation on other listed property, you must provide the information requested in Part V, regardless of the tax year the property was placed in service. However, if you file Form 2106, 2106-EZ, or Schedule C-EZ (Form 1040), report this information on that form and not in Part V. Also, if you file Schedule C (Form 1040) and are claiming the standard mileage rate or actual vehicle expenses (except depreciation), and you are not required to file Form 4562 for any other reason, report vehicle information in Part IV of Schedule C and not on Form 4562.

Section A

Lines 24 and 25

Qualified business use. To determine whether to use line 24 or line 25 to report your listed property, you must first determine the percentage of qualified business use for each property. Generally, a qualified business use is any use in your trade or business. However, it does not include any of the following:

- Investment use.
- Leasing the property to a 5% owner or related person.
- The use of the property as compensation for services performed by a 5% owner or related person.
- The use of the property as compensation for services performed by any person (who is not a 5% owner or related person), unless an amount is included in that person's income for the use of the property and, if required, income tax was withheld on that amount.

Exception. If at least 25% of the total use of any aircraft during the tax year is for a qualified business use, the leasing or compensatory use of

the aircraft by a 5% owner or related person is treated as a qualified business use.

Determine your percentage of qualified business use similar to the method used to figure the business/investment use percentage in column (c). Your percentage of qualified business use may be smaller than the business/investment use percentage.

For more information, see Pub. 946.

Column (a). List on a property-by-property basis all your listed property in the following order:

1. Automobiles and other vehicles; and

2. Other listed property (computers and peripheral equipment, etc.).

In column (a), list the make and model of automobiles, and give a general description of other listed property.

If you have more than five vehicles used 100% for business/investment purposes, you may group them by tax year. Otherwise, list each vehicle separately.

Column (b). Enter the date the property was placed in service. If property held for personal use is converted to business/investment use, treat the property as placed in service on the date of conversion.

Column (c). Enter the percentage of business/investment use. For automobiles and other vehicles, determine this percentage by dividing the number of miles the vehicle is driven for trade or business purposes or for the production of income during the year (not to include any commuting mileage) by the total number of miles the vehicle is driven for all purposes. Treat vehicles used by employees as being used 100% for business/investment purposes if the value of personal use is included in the employees' gross income, or the employees reimburse the employer for the personal use.

Employers who report the amount of personal use of the vehicle in the employee's gross income, and withhold the appropriate taxes, should enter "100%" for the percentage of business/investment use. For more information, see **Pub. 463,** Travel, Entertainment, Gift, and Car Expenses.

For listed property (such as computers or video equipment), allocate the use based on the most appropriate unit of time the property

is actually used. See Temporary Regulations section 1.280F-6T.

If during the tax year you convert property used solely for personal purposes to business/investment use, figure the percentage of business/investment use only for the number of months you use the property in your business or for the production of income. Multiply that percentage by the number of months you use the property in your business or for the production of income, and divide the result by 12.

Column (d). Enter the property's actual cost (including sales tax) or other basis (unadjusted for prior years' depreciation). If you traded in old property, your basis is the adjusted basis of the old property (figured as if 100% of the property's use had been for business/investment purposes) plus any additional amount you paid for the new property.

For a vehicle, reduce your basis by any diesel-powered highway vehicle credit, qualified electric vehicle credit, or deduction for clean-fuel vehicles you claimed.

If you converted the property from personal use to business/investment use, your basis for depreciation is the smaller of the property's adjusted basis or its fair market value on the date of conversion.

Column (e). Multiply column (d) by the percentage in column (c). From that result, subtract any section 179 expense deduction and half of any investment credit taken before 1986 (unless you took the reduced credit). For automobiles and other listed property placed in service after 1985 (i.e., transition property), reduce the depreciable basis by the entire investment credit.

Column (f). Enter the recovery period. For property placed in service after 1986 and used more than 50% in a qualified business use, use the table in the line 15, column (d) instructions. For property placed in service after 1986 and used 50% or less in a qualified business use, depreciate the property using the straight line method over its ADS recovery period. The ADS recovery period is 5 years for automobiles and computers.

Column (g). Enter the method and convention used to figure your depreciation deduction. See the instructions for line 15, columns (e) and (f). Write "200 DB," "150 DB," or "S/L," for the depreciation method, and "HY," "MM," or "MQ," for

Page 7

half-year, mid-month, or mid-quarter conventions, respectively. For property placed in service before 1987, write "PRE" if you used the prescribed percentages under ACRS. If you elected an alternate percentage, enter "S/L."

Column (h). See **Limits for passenger automobiles** below before entering an amount in column (h).

For property used more than 50% in a qualified business use (line 24) and placed in service after 1986, figure column (h) by following the instructions for line 15, column (g). If placed in service before 1987, multiply column (e) by the applicable percentage given in Pub. 534 for ACRS property. If the recovery period for an automobile ended before your tax year beginning in 1998, enter your unrecovered basis, if any, in column (h).

For property used 50% or less in a qualified business use (line 25) and placed in service after 1986, figure column (h) by dividing column (e) by column (f) and using the same conventions as discussed in the instructions for line 15, column (e). The amount in column (h) cannot exceed the property's unrecovered basis. If the recovery period for an automobile ended before your tax year beginning in 1998, enter your unrecovered basis, if any, incolumn (h). For computers placed in service in a tax year beginning in 1986, multiply column (e) by 4.167%.

For property placed in service before 1987 that was disposed of during the year, enter zero.

Limits for passenger automobiles. The depreciation deduction plus section 179 expense deduction for passenger automobiles is limited for any tax year.

Definition. "Passenger automobiles" are 4-wheeled vehicles manufactured primarily for use on public roads that are rated at 6,000 pounds unloaded gross vehicle weight or less. For a truck or van, gross vehicle weight is substituted for unloaded gross vehicle weight.

Exception. The following vehicles are not considered passenger automobiles:
• An ambulance, hearse, or combination ambulance-hearse used in your trade or business.
• A vehicle used in your trade or business of transporting persons or property for compensation or hire.

For any passenger automobile you list on line 24 or line 25, the total of columns (h) and (i) for that automobile cannot exceed the limit shown in the tables below. The limit is further reduced when the business/investment use percentage is less than 100%.

Example. If an automobile placed in service in 1998 is used 60% for business/investment purposes, the limit generally is figured as follows: $3,160 × 60% = $1,896. However, the $3,160 limit is increased for certain clean-fuel and electric vehicles. See the footnote below.

Limits for Passenger Automobiles Placed in Service Before 1995

IF you placed your automobile in service:	THEN the limit on your depreciation and section 179 expense deduction is:
June 19–Dec. 31, 1984	$6,000
Jan. 1–Apr. 2, 1985	$6,200
Apr. 3, 1985–Dec. 31, 1986	$4,800
Jan. 1, 1987–Dec. 31, 1990	$1,475
Jan. 1, 1991–Dec. 31, 1992	$1,575
Jan. 1, 1993–Dec. 31, 1994	$1,675

Limits for Passenger Automobiles Placed in Service After 1994

IF you placed your automobile in service:	AND the number of tax years in which this automobile has been in service is:	THEN the limit on your depreciation and section 179 expense deduction is:
Jan. 1, 1995–Dec. 31, 1996	3	$2,950
	4 or more	$1,775
Jan. 1 – Dec. 31, 1997	2	$5,000 *
	3	$3,050 *
Jan. 1 – Dec. 31, 1998	1	$3,160 *
	2	$5,000 *
After Dec. 31, 1998	1	*, **

*For vehicles placed in service after August 5, 1997:
• This limit does not apply to the cost of any qualified clean-fuel vehicle property (such as retrofit parts and components) installed on a vehicle for the purpose of permitting that vehicle to run on a clean-burning fuel. See section 179A for definitions.
• The limit for vehicles produced by an original equipment manufacturer and designed to run primarily on electricity is as follows:
 (a) Vehicles placed in service during calendar year 1997 — $15,100 for the 2nd tax year; $9,050 for the 3rd tax year.
 (b) Vehicles placed in service during calendar year 1998 — $9,380 for the 1st tax year; $15,000 for the 2nd tax year.
**The limit for automobiles placed in service after Dec. 31, 1998, will be published in the Internal Revenue Bulletin. This amount was not available at the time these instructions were printed.

Column (i). Enter the amount you choose to expense for section 179 property used more than 50% in a qualified business use (subject to the limits for passenger automobiles noted above). Refer to the Part I instructions to determine if the property qualifies under section 179. Be sure to include the total cost of such property (50% of the cost if qualified zone property placed in service by an enterprise zone business) on line 2, page 1.

Recapture of depreciation and section 179 expense deduction. For listed property used more than 50% in a qualified business use in the year placed in service and used 50% or less in a later year, you may have to recapture in the later year part of the depreciation and section 179 expense deduction. Use **Form 4797,** Sales of Business Property, to figure the recapture amount.

Section B

Except as noted below, you must complete items 28 through 34 for each vehicle identified in Section A. Employees must provide their employers with the information requested in items 28 through 34 for each automobile or vehicle provided for their use.

Exception. Employers are not required to complete items 28 through 34 for vehicles used by employees who are not more than 5% owners or related persons and for which question 35, 36, 37, 38, or 39 is answered "Yes."

Section C

For employers providing vehicles to their employees, two types of written policy statements will satisfy the employer's substantiation requirements under section 274(d):
• A policy statement that prohibits personal use including commuting, and
• A policy statement that prohibits personal use except for commuting.

An employee does not need to keep a separate set of records for any vehicle that satisfies these written policy statement rules.

Line 35

A policy statement that prohibits personal use (including commuting) must meet **all** of the following conditions:
• The employer owns or leases the vehicle and provides it to one or more

employees for use in the employer's trade or business.

● When the vehicle is not used in the employer's trade or business, it is kept on the employer's business premises, unless it is temporarily located elsewhere (e.g., for maintenance or because of a mechanical failure).

● No employee using the vehicle lives at the employer's business premises.

● No employee may use the vehicle for personal purposes, other than de minimis personal use (e.g., a stop for lunch between two business deliveries).

● Except for de minimis use, the employer reasonably believes that no employee uses the vehicle for any personal purpose.

Line 36

A policy statement that prohibits personal use (except for commuting) is **not** available if the commuting employee is an officer, director, or 1% or more owner. This policy must meet **all** of the following conditions:

● The employer owns or leases the vehicle and provides it to one or more employees for use in the employer's trade or business, and it is used in the employer's trade or business.

● For bona fide noncompensatory business reasons, the employer requires the employee to commute to and/or from work in the vehicle.

● The employer establishes a written policy under which the employee may not use the vehicle for personal purposes, other than commuting or de minimis personal use (e.g., a stop for a personal errand between a business delivery and the employee's home).

● Except for de minimis use, the employer reasonably believes that the employee does not use the vehicle for any personal purpose other than commuting.

● The employer accounts for the commuting use by including an appropriate amount in the employee's gross income.

For both written policy statements, there must be evidence that would enable the IRS to determine whether use of the vehicle meets the conditions stated above.

Line 38

An employer that provides more than five vehicles to its employees who are not 5% owners or related persons need not complete Section B for such vehicles. Instead, the employer must obtain the information from its employees and retain the information received.

Line 39

An automobile meets the requirements for qualified demonstration use if the employer maintains a written policy statement that:

● Prohibits its use by individuals other than full-time automobile salespersons.

● Prohibits its use for personal vacation trips.

● Prohibits storage of personal possessions in the automobile.

● Limits the total mileage outside the salesperson's normal working hours.

Part VI

Each year you may elect to deduct part of certain capital costs over a fixed period. If you amortize property, the part you amortize does not qualify for the election to expense certain tangible property or for depreciation.

For individuals reporting amortization of bond premium for bonds acquired before October 23, 1986, **do not** report the deduction here. See the instructions for Schedule A (Form 1040), line 27.

For taxpayers (other than corporations) claiming a deduction for amortization of bond premium for bonds acquired after October 22, 1986, but before January 1, 1988, the deduction is treated as interest expense and is subject to the investment interest limitations. Use **Form 4952,** Investment Interest Expense Deduction, to compute the allowable deduction.

For taxable bonds acquired after 1987, the amortization offsets the interest income. See **Pub. 550,** Investment Income and Expenses.

Line 40

Complete line 40 only for those costs for which the amortization period begins during your tax year beginning in 1998.

Column (a). Describe the costs you are amortizing. You may amortize:

● Pollution control facilities (section 169, limited by section 291 for corporations).

● Certain bond premiums (section 171).

● Research and experimental expenditures (section 174).

● The cost of acquiring a lease (section 178).

● Qualified forestation and reforestation costs (section 194).

● Business start-up expenditures (section 195).

● Organizational expenditures for a corporation (section 248) or partnership (section 709).

● Optional write-off of certain tax preferences over the period specified in section 59(e).

● Certain section 197 intangibles, which generally include the following:

  1. Goodwill.

  2. Going concern value.

  3. Workforce in place.

  4. Business books and records, operating systems, or any other information base.

  5. Any patent, copyright, formula, process, design, pattern, knowhow, format, or similar item.

  6. Any customer-based intangible (e.g., composition of market or market share).

  7. Any supplier-based intangible.

  8. Any license, permit, or other right granted by a governmental unit.

  9. Any covenant not to compete entered into in connection with the acquisition of a business.

  10. Any franchise (other than a sports franchise), trademark, or trade name.

Section 197 intangibles must be amortized over 15 years starting with the month the intangibles were acquired.

Column (b). Enter the date the amortization period begins under the applicable Code section.

Column (c). Enter the total amount you are amortizing. See the applicable Code section for limits on the amortizable amount.

Column (d). Enter the Code section under which you amortize the costs.

Column (f). Compute the amortization deduction by:

  1. Dividing column (c) by the number of months over which the costs are to be amortized, and multiplying the result by the number of months in the amortization period included in your tax year beginning in 1998; or

  2. Multiplying column (c) by the percentage in column (e).

Attach any other information the Code and regulations may require to make a valid election. See Pub. 535 for more information.

Table A—General Depreciation System
Method: 200% declining balance switching to straight line
Convention: Half-year

Year	If the recovery period is:			
	3 years	5 years	7 years	10 years
1	33.33%	20.00%	14.29%	10.00%
2	44.45%	32.00%	24.49%	18.00%
3	14.81%	19.20%	17.49%	14.40%
4	7.41%	11.52%	12.49%	11.52%
5		11.52%	8.93%	9.22%
6		5.76%	8.92%	7.37%
7			8.93%	6.55%
8			4.46%	6.55%
9				6.56%
10				6.55%
11				3.28%

Table B—General and Alternative Depreciation System
Method: 150% declining balance switching to straight line
Convention: Half-year

Year	If the recovery period is:					
	5 years	7 years	10 years	12 years	15 years	20 years
1	15.00%	10.71%	7.50%	6.25%	5.00%	3.750%
2	25.50%	19.13%	13.88%	11.72%	9.50%	7.219%
3	17.85%	15.03%	11.79%	10.25%	8.55%	6.677%
4	16.66%	12.25%	10.02%	8.97%	7.70%	6.177%
5	16.66%	12.25%	8.74%	7.85%	6.93%	5.713%
6	8.33%	12.25%	8.74%	7.33%	6.23%	5.285%
7		12.25%	8.74%	7.33%	5.90%	4.888%
8		6.13%	8.74%	7.33%	5.90%	4.522%
9			8.74%	7.33%	5.91%	4.462%
10			8.74%	7.33%	5.90%	4.461%
11			4.37%	7.32%	5.91%	4.462%
12				7.33%	5.90%	4.461%
13				3.66%	5.91%	4.462%

Page 10

Table C—General Depreciation System
Method: Straight line
Convention: Mid-month
Recovery period: 27.5 years

	The month in the 1st recovery year the property is placed in service:											
Year	1	2	3	4	5	6	7	8	9	10	11	12
1	3.485%	3.182%	2.879%	2.576%	2.273%	1.970%	1.667%	1.364%	1.061%	0.758%	0.455%	0.152%
2–9	3.636%	3.636%	3.636%	3.636%	3.636%	3.636%	3.636%	3.636%	3.636%	3.636%	3.636%	3.636%
10, 12	3.637%	3.637%	3.637%	3.637%	3.637%	3.637%	3.636%	3.636%	3.636%	3.636%	3.636%	3.636%
11, 13	3.636%	3.636%	3.636%	3.636%	3.636%	3.636%	3.637%	3.637%	3.637%	3.637%	3.637%	3.637%

Table D—General Depreciation System
Method: Straight line
Convention: Mid-month
Recovery period: 31.5 years

	The month in the 1st recovery year the property is placed in service:											
Year	1	2	3	4	5	6	7	8	9	10	11	12
4–7	3.175%	3.175%	3.175%	3.175%	3.175%	3.175%	3.175%	3.175%	3.175%	3.175%	3.175%	3.175%
8	3.175%	3.174%	3.175%	3.174%	3.175%	3.174%	3.175%	3.175%	3.175%	3.175%	3.175%	3.175%
9, 11, 13	3.174%	3.175%	3.174%	3.175%	3.174%	3.175%	3.174%	3.175%	3.174%	3.175%	3.174%	3.175%
10, 12	3.175%	3.174%	3.175%	3.174%	3.175%	3.174%	3.175%	3.174%	3.175%	3.174%	3.175%	3.174%

Table E—General Depreciation System
Method: Straight line
Convention: Mid-month
Recovery period: 39 years

	The month in the 1st recovery year the property is placed in service:											
Year	1	2	3	4	5	6	7	8	9	10	11	12
1	2.461%	2.247%	2.033%	1.819%	1.605%	1.391%	1.177%	0.963%	0.749%	0.535%	0.321%	0.107%
2–39	2.564%	2.564%	2.564%	2.564%	2.564%	2.564%	2.564%	2.564%	2.564%	2.564%	2.564%	2.564%

Page 11

Depreciation Worksheet

Description of Property	Date Placed in Service	Cost or Other Basis	Business/ Investment Use %	Section 179 Deduction	Depreciation Prior Years	Basis for Depreciation	Method/ Convention	Recovery Period	Rate or Table %	Depreciation Deduction

Form **4562**

Department of the Treasury
Internal Revenue Service   (99)

Depreciation and Amortization
(Including Information on Listed Property)

► **See separate instructions.** ► **Attach this form to your return.**

Name(s) shown on return	Business or activity to which this form relates	Identifying number

Part I Election To Expense Certain Tangible Property (Section 179) (Note: *If you have any "listed property," complete Part V before you complete Part I.*)

1	Maximum dollar limitation. If an enterprise zone business, see page 2 of the instructions . .	**1**	$18,500
2	Total cost of section 179 property placed in service. See page 2 of the instructions	**2**	
3	Threshold cost of section 179 property before reduction in limitation	**3**	$200,000
4	Reduction in limitation. Subtract line 3 from line 2. If zero or less, enter -0-	**4**	
5	Dollar limitation for tax year. Subtract line 4 from line 1. If zero or less, enter -0-. If married filing separately, see page 2 of the instructions	**5**	

(a) Description of property	(b) Cost (business use only)	(c) Elected cost
6		

7	Listed property. Enter amount from line 27	**7**	
8	Total elected cost of section 179 property. Add amounts in column (c), lines 6 and 7 . . .	**8**	
9	Tentative deduction. Enter the smaller of line 5 or line 8	**9**	
10	Carryover of disallowed deduction from 1997. See page 3 of the instructions	**10**	
11	Business income limitation. Enter the smaller of business income (not less than zero) or line 5 (see instructions)	**11**	
12	Section 179 expense deduction. Add lines 9 and 10, but do not enter more than line 11 . .	**12**	
13	Carryover of disallowed deduction to 1999. Add lines 9 and 10, less line 12 ►	**13**	

Note: *Do not use Part II or Part III below for listed property (automobiles, certain other vehicles, cellular telephones, certain computers, or property used for entertainment, recreation, or amusement). Instead, use Part V for listed property.*

Part II MACRS Depreciation For Assets Placed in Service ONLY During Your 1998 Tax Year (Do Not Include Listed Property.)

Section A—General Asset Account Election

14 If you are making the election under section 168(i)(4) to group any assets placed in service during the tax year into one or more general asset accounts, check this box. See page 3 of the instructions . . . . ► ☐

Section B—General Depreciation System (GDS) (See page 3 of the instructions.)

(a) Classification of property	(b) Month and year placed in service	(c) Basis for depreciation (business/investment use only—see instructions)	(d) Recovery period	(e) Convention	(f) Method	(g) Depreciation deduction
15a 3-year property						
b 5-year property						
c 7-year property						
d 10-year property						
e 15-year property						
f 20-year property						
g 25-year property			25 yrs.		S/L	
h Residential rental property			27.5 yrs.	MM	S/L	
			27.5 yrs.	MM	S/L	
i Nonresidential real property			39 yrs.	MM	S/L	
				MM	S/L	

Section C—Alternative Depreciation System (ADS) (See page 5 of the instructions.)

16a Class life					S/L	
b 12-year			12 yrs.		S/L	
c 40-year			40 yrs.	MM	S/L	

Part III Other Depreciation (Do Not Include Listed Property.) (See page 6 of the instructions.)

17	GDS and ADS deductions for assets placed in service in tax years beginning before 1998	**17**	
18	Property subject to section 168(f)(1) election	**18**	
19	ACRS and other depreciation	**19**	

Part IV Summary (See page 6 of the instructions.)

20	Listed property. Enter amount from line 26	**20**	
21	**Total.** Add deductions on line 12, lines 15 and 16 in column (g), and lines 17 through 20. Enter here and on the appropriate lines of your return. Partnerships and S corporations—see instructions . .	**21**	
22	For assets shown above and placed in service during the current year, enter the portion of the basis attributable to section 263A costs	**22**	

For Paperwork Reduction Act Notice, see the separate instructions.   Cat. No. 12906N   Form **4562** (1998)

Part V **Listed Property—Automobiles, Certain Other Vehicles, Cellular Telephones, Certain Computers, and Property Used for Entertainment, Recreation, or Amusement**

Note: *For any vehicle for which you are using the standard mileage rate or deducting lease expense, complete **only** 23a, 23b, columns (a) through (c) of Section A, all of Section B, and Section C if applicable.*

Section A—Depreciation and Other Information (Caution: *See page 8 of the instructions for limits for passenger automobiles.***)**

23a Do you have evidence to support the business/investment use claimed? ☐ **Yes** ☐ **No**   **23b** If "Yes," is the evidence written? ☐ **Yes** ☐ **No**

(a) Type of property (list vehicles first)	(b) Date placed in service	(c) Business/ investment use percentage	(d) Cost or other basis	(e) Basis for depreciation (business/investment use only)	(f) Recovery period	(g) Method/ Convention	(h) Depreciation deduction	(i) Elected section 179 cost
24 Property used more than 50% in a qualified business use (See page 7 of the instructions.):								
		%						
		%						
		%						
25 Property used 50% or less in a qualified business use (See page 7 of the instructions.):								
		%			S/L –			
		%			S/L –			
		%			S/L –			

26 Add amounts in column (h). Enter the total here and on line 20, page 1 . . . . . **26**

27 Add amounts in column (i). Enter the total here and on line 7, page 1 . . . . **27**

Section B—Information on Use of Vehicles

Complete this section for vehicles used by a sole proprietor, partner, or other "more than 5% owner," or related person.

If you provided vehicles to your employees, first answer the questions in Section C to see if you meet an exception to completing this section for those vehicles.

		(a) Vehicle 1		(b) Vehicle 2		(c) Vehicle 3		(d) Vehicle 4		(e) Vehicle 5		(f) Vehicle 6	
28	Total business/investment miles driven during the year (DO NOT include commuting miles)												
29	Total commuting miles driven during the year												
30	Total other personal (noncommuting) miles driven												
31	Total miles driven during the year. Add lines 28 through 30.												
		Yes	No	Yes	No	Yes	No	Yes	No	Yes	No	Yes	No
32	Was the vehicle available for personal use during off-duty hours?												
33	Was the vehicle used primarily by a more than 5% owner or related person?												
34	Is another vehicle available for personal use?												

Section C—Questions for Employers Who Provide Vehicles for Use by Their Employees

*Answer these questions to determine if you meet an exception to completing Section B for vehicles used by employees who **are not** more than 5% owners or related persons.*

		Yes	No
35	Do you maintain a written policy statement that prohibits all personal use of vehicles, including commuting, by your employees?		
36	Do you maintain a written policy statement that prohibits personal use of vehicles, except commuting, by your employees? See page 9 of the instructions for vehicles used by corporate officers, directors, or 1% or more owners		
37	Do you treat all use of vehicles by employees as personal use?		
38	Do you provide more than five vehicles to your employees, obtain information from your employees about the use of the vehicles, and retain the information received?		
39	Do you meet the requirements concerning qualified automobile demonstration use? See page 9 of the instructions . .		

Note: *If your answer to 35, 36, 37, 38, or 39 is "Yes," you need not complete Section B for the covered vehicles.*

Part VI **Amortization**

(a) Description of costs	(b) Date amortization begins	(c) Amortizable amount	(d) Code section	(e) Amortization period or percentage	(f) Amortization for this year
40 Amortization of costs that begins during your 1998 tax year:					

41 Amortization of costs that began before 1998 . . . . **41**

42 **Total.** Enter here and on "Other Deductions" or "Other Expenses" line of your return . . . **42**

✦

D

IRS Form 4797

Sales of Business Property

Instructions for Form 4797

Sales of Business Property
(Also Involuntary Conversions and Recapture Amounts Under Sections 179 and 280F(b)(2))

Section references are to the Internal Revenue Code unless otherwise noted.

General Instructions

A Change To Note

The IRS Restructuring and Reform Act of 1998 changed the definition of 28% rate gain (or loss) for sales, exchanges, and conversions (including installment payments received) after 1997. As a result, column (h) in Part I of Form 4797 should be used only to report pre-1998 28% rate gain (or loss) from a 1997-98 fiscal year partnership or S corporation.

Purpose of Form

Use Form 4797 to report:
● The sale or exchange of property used in your trade or business; depreciable and amortizable property; oil, gas, geothermal, or other mineral properties; and section 126 property.
● The involuntary conversion (from other than casualty or theft) of property used in your trade or business and capital assets held in connection with a trade or business or a transaction entered into for profit.
● The disposition of noncapital assets (other than inventory or property held primarily for sale to customers in the ordinary course of your trade or business).
● The recapture of section 179 expense deductions for partners and S corporation shareholders from property dispositions by partnerships and S corporations.
● The computation of recapture amounts under sections 179 and 280F(b)(2), when the business use of section 179 or listed property drops to 50% or less.

Other Forms To Use

● Use **Form 4684,** Casualties and Thefts, to report involuntary conversions from casualties and thefts.
● Use **Form 8824,** Like-Kind Exchanges, for each exchange of qualifying business or investment property for property of a like kind. For exchanges of property used in a trade or business (and other noncapital assets), enter the gain or (loss) from Form 8824, if any, on line 5 or 16.
● If you sold property on which you claimed investment credit, see **Form 4255,** Recapture of Investment Credit, to find out if you must recapture some or all of the credit.

Special Rules

At-risk rules. If you report a loss on an asset used in an activity for which you are not at risk, in whole or in part, see the instructions for **Form 6198,** At-Risk Limitations. Also, see **Pub. 925,** Passive Activity and At-Risk Rules. Losses from passive activities are first subject to the at-risk rules and then to the passive activity rules.

Depreciable property and other property disposed of in the same transaction. If you disposed of both depreciable property and other property (e.g., a building and land) in the same transaction and realized a gain, you must allocate the amount realized between the two types of property based on their respective fair market values to figure the part of the gain to be recaptured as ordinary income because of depreciation. The disposition of each type of property is reported separately in the appropriate part of Form 4797 (e.g., for property held more than 1 year, report the sale of a building in Part III and land in Part I).

Disposition of assets that constitute a trade or business. For such a disposition, the buyer and seller must allocate the total purchase price using the residual method and file **Form 8594,** Asset Acquisition Statement.

Installment sales. If you sold property at a gain and you will receive a payment in a tax year after the year of sale, you generally must report the sale on the installment method unless you elect not to do so.

Use **Form 6252,** Installment Sale Income, to report the sale on the installment method. Also use Form 6252 to report any payment received in 1998 from a sale made in an earlier year that you reported on the installment method.

To elect out of the installment method, report the full amount of the gain on a timely filed return (including extensions).

See **Pub. 537,** Installment Sales, for more details.

Involuntary conversion of property. You may not have to pay tax on a gain from an involuntary or compulsory conversion of property. See **Pub. 544,** Sales and Other Dispositions of Assets, for details.

Exclusion of gain on sale of a home used for business. If the property sold was used as your home for 2 or more years during the 5-year period ending on the date of the sale, you may be able to exclude part or all of the gain figured on Form 4797. For details on the exclusion (and to figure the exclusion), see **Pub. 523,** Selling Your Home.

If the property was held more than 1 year, complete Part III to figure the gain. **Do not** take the exclusion into account when figuring the gain on line 24. If line 22 includes depreciation for periods after May 6, 1997, you **cannot** exclude gain to the extent of that depreciation. On line 2 of Form 4797, write "Section 121 exclusion" and enter the amount of gain excluded as a (loss) in column (g).

If the property was held for 1 year or less, report the sale and the amount of gain excluded in a similar manner on line 10 of Form 4797.

Passive loss limitations. If you have an overall loss from passive activities, and you report a loss on an asset used in a passive activity, use **Form 8582,** Passive Activity Loss

Where To Make First Entry for Certain Items Reported on This Form

	(a) Type of property	(b) Held 1 year or less	(c) Held more than 1 year
1	Depreciable trade or business property:		
a	Sold or exchanged at a gain	Part II	Part III (1245, 1250)
b	Sold or exchanged at a loss	Part II	Part I
2	Depreciable residential rental property:		
a	Sold or exchanged at a gain	Part II	Part III (1250)
b	Sold or exchanged at a loss	Part II	Part I
3	Farmland held less than 10 years upon which soil, water, or land clearing expenses were deducted:		
a	Sold at a gain	Part II	Part III (1252)
b	Sold at a loss	Part II	Part I
4	Disposition of cost-sharing payment property described in section 126	Part II	Part III (1255)
5	Cattle and horses used in a trade or business for draft, breeding, dairy, or sporting purposes:	**Held less than 24 months**	**Held 24 months or more**
a	Sold at a gain	Part II	Part III (1245)
b	Sold at a loss	Part II	Part I
c	Raised cattle and horses sold at a gain	Part II	Part I
6	Livestock other than cattle and horses used in a trade or business for draft, breeding, dairy, or sporting purposes:	**Held less than 12 months**	**Held 12 months or more**
a	Sold at a gain	Part II	Part III (1245)
b	Sold at a loss	Part II	Part I
c	Raised livestock sold at a gain	Part II	Part I

Cat. No. 13087T

Limitations, to see how much loss is allowed before entering it on Form 4797.

You cannot claim unused passive activity credits when you dispose of your interest in an activity. However, if you dispose of your entire interest in an activity, you may elect to increase the basis of the credit property by the original basis reduction of the property to the extent that the credit has not been allowed because of the passive activity rules. Make the election on **Form 8582-CR,** Passive Activity Credit Limitations, or **Form 8810,** Corporate Passive Activity Loss and Credit Limitations. No basis adjustment may be elected on a partial disposition of your interest in an activity.

Recapture of preproductive expenses. If you elected out of the uniform capitalization rules of section 263A, any plant that you produce is treated as section 1245 property. For dispositions of plants reportable on Form 4797, enter the recapture amount taxed as ordinary income on line 22 of Form 4797. See **Pub. 225,** Farmer's Tax Guide, for details.

Section 197(f)(9)(B)(ii) election. If you elected under section 197(f)(9)(B)(ii) to recognize gain on the disposition of a section 197 intangible and to pay a tax on that gain at the highest tax rate, include the additional tax on Form 1040, line 40 (or the appropriate line of other income tax returns). On the dotted line next to that line, write "197." The additional tax is the amount that, when added to any other income tax on the gain, equals the gain multiplied by the highest tax rate.

Specific Instructions

To show losses, enclose figures in (parentheses).

Part I

Section 1231 transactions are:
- Sales or exchanges of real or depreciable property used in a trade or business and held for more than 1 year. To figure the holding period, begin counting on the day after you received the property and include the day you disposed of it.
- Cutting of timber that the taxpayer elects to treat as a sale or exchange under section 631(a).
- Disposal of timber with a retained economic interest that is treated as a sale under section 631(b).
- Disposal of coal (including lignite) or domestic iron ore with a retained economic interest that is treated as a sale under section 631(c).
- Sales or exchanges of cattle and horses, regardless of age, used in a trade or business by the taxpayer for draft, breeding, dairy, or sporting purposes and held for 24 months or more from acquisition date.
- Sales or exchanges of livestock other than cattle and horses, regardless of age, used by the taxpayer for draft, breeding, dairy, or sporting purposes and held for 12 months or more from acquisition date.

Note: Livestock does not include poultry, chickens, turkeys, pigeons, geese, other birds, fish, frogs, reptiles, etc.
- Sales or exchanges of unharvested crops. See section 1231(b)(4).
- Involuntary conversions of trade or business property or capital assets held more than 1 year in connection with a trade or business or a transaction entered into for profit.

These conversions may result from **(a)** part or total destruction, **(b)** theft or seizure, or **(c)** requisition or condemnation (whether threatened or carried out). If any recognized losses were from involuntary conversions from fire, storm, shipwreck, or other casualty, or from theft, and they exceed the recognized gains from the conversions, do not include them when figuring your net section 1231 losses.

Section 1231 transactions **do not** include sales or exchanges of:
- Inventory or property held primarily for sale to customers.
- Copyrights, literary, musical, or artistic compositions, letters or memoranda, or similar property **(a)** created by your personal efforts, **(b)** prepared or produced for you (in the case of letters, memoranda, or similar property), or **(c)** received from someone who created them or for whom they were created, as mentioned in **(a)** or **(b),** in a way that entitled you to the basis of the previous owner (such as by gift).
- U.S. Government publications, including the Congressional Record, that you received from the Government, other than by purchase at the normal sales price, or that you got from someone who had received it in a similar way, if your basis is determined by reference to the previous owner's basis.

Lines 2 through 6, column (g). You must make a separate entry in this column for each transaction reported on line 2 and any other line(s) that apply to you.

Tip: If you are required to complete column (h), complete column (g) before you begin column (h).

Line 8, column (g). Part or all of your section 1231 gains on line 7, column (g) may be taxed as ordinary income instead of receiving long-term capital gain treatment. These net section 1231 gains are treated as ordinary income to the extent of the "nonrecaptured section 1231 losses." The nonrecaptured losses are net section 1231 losses deducted during the 5 preceding tax years that have not yet been applied against any net section 1231 gain for determining how much gain is ordinary income under these rules.

Example. If you had net section 1231 losses of $4,000 and $6,000 in 1993 and 1994 and net section 1231 gains of $3,000 and $2,000 in 1997 and 1998, line 7, column (g) would show the 1998 gain of $2,000, and line 8, column (g) would show nonrecaptured net section 1231 losses of $7,000 ($10,000 net section 1231 losses minus the $3,000 that was recaptured because of the 1997 gain). The $2,000 gain on line 7, column (g) is all ordinary income and would be entered on line 12 of Form 4797. For recordkeeping purposes, the $4,000 loss from 1993 is all recaptured ($3,000 in 1997 and $1,000 in 1998) and you have $5,000 left to recapture from 1994 ($6,000 minus the $1,000 recaptured this year).

Figuring the prior year losses. You had a net section 1231 loss if section 1231 losses exceeded section 1231 gains. Gains are included only to the extent taken into account in figuring gross income. Losses are included only to the extent taken into account in figuring taxable income except that the limitation on capital losses does not apply.

Line 8, column (h). Make an entry on line 8, column (h) **only** if line 9, column (g) is more than zero. Figure the amount to enter as follows:
- If line 7, column (h) is zero or less, enter zero on line 8, column (h).
- If line 7, column (h) is more than zero, enter on line 8, column (h) the **smaller** of line 7, column (h) or line 8, column (g).

Line 9, column (g). For recordkeeping purposes, if line 9, column (g) is zero, the amount on line 7, column (g) is the amount of net section 1231 loss recaptured in 1998. If line 9, column (g) is more than zero, you have recaptured in 1998 all your net section 1231 losses from prior years.

Part II

If a transaction is not reportable in Part I or Part III and the property is not a capital asset reportable on Schedule D, report the transaction in Part II.

If you receive ordinary income from a sale or other disposition of your interest in a partnership, see **Pub. 541,** Partnerships.

Line 10. Report other ordinary gains and losses, including property held 1 year or less, on this line.

Small business investment company stock. Report on line 10 ordinary losses from the sale or exchange (including worthlessness) of stock in a small business investment company operating under the Small Business Investment Act of 1958. See section 1242.

Section 1244 (small business) stock. Individuals report ordinary losses from the sale or exchange (including worthlessness) of section 1244 (small business) stock on line 10.

To qualify as section 1244 stock, all of the following requirements must be met:

1. You acquired the stock after June 30, 1958, upon original issuance from a domestic corporation (or the stock was acquired by a partnership in which you were a partner continuously from the date the stock was issued until the time of the loss).

2. If the stock was issued before November 7, 1978, it was issued under a written plan that met the requirements of Regulations section 1.1244(c)-1(f), and when that plan was adopted, the corporation was treated as a small business corporation under Regulations section 1.1244(c)-2(c).

3. If the stock was issued after November 6, 1978, the corporation was treated as a small business corporation, at the time the stock was issued, under Regulations section 1.1244(c)-2(b). To be treated as a small business corporation, the total amount of money and other property received by the corporation for its stock as a contribution to capital and paid-in surplus generally may not exceed $1 million.

4. The stock was issued for money or other property (excluding stock or securities).

5. The corporation, for its 5 most recent tax years ending before the loss, derived more than 50% of its gross receipts from sources **other than** royalties, rents, dividends, interest, annuities, and gains from sales and exchanges of stocks or securities. (If the corporation was in existence for at least 1 tax year but fewer than 5 tax years ending before the loss, the 50% test applies for the tax years ending before the loss. If the corporation was not in existence for at least 1 tax year ending before the loss, the 50% test applies for the entire period ending before the loss.) However, the 50% test does not apply if the corporation's deductions (other than the net operating loss and dividends-received deductions) exceeded its gross income during that period.

6. If the stock was issued before July 19, 1984, it must have been common stock.

The maximum amount that may be treated as an ordinary loss is $50,000 ($100,000 if married filing jointly). Special rules may limit the amount of your ordinary loss if **(a)** you received section 1244 stock in exchange for property with a basis in excess of its fair market value or **(b)** your stock basis increased from contributions to capital or otherwise. See **Pub. 550,** Investment Income and Expenses, for more details. Report on Schedule D losses in excess of the maximum amount that may be

Page 2

treated as an ordinary loss (and gains from the sale or exchange of section 1244 stock).

Keep adequate records to distinguish section 1244 stock from any other stock owned in the same corporation.

Line 17. Enter any recapture of section 179 expense deduction included on Schedule K-1 (Form 1065), line 25, and on Schedule K-1 (Form 1120S), line 23, but only if it is due to a disposition. Include it only to the extent that you took a deduction for it in an earlier year. See the instructions for Part IV if you have section 179 recapture when the business use percentage of the property dropped to 50% or less.

Line 18b(1). You must complete this line if there is a gain on Form 4797, line 3, column (g); a loss on Form 4797, line 11; **and** a loss on Form 4684, line 35, column (b)(ii). Enter on this line the **smaller** of the loss on Form 4797, line 11; or the loss on Form 4684, line 35, column (b)(ii). To figure which loss is smaller, treat both losses as positive numbers. Enter the part of the loss from income-producing property on Schedule A (Form 1040), line 27, and the part of the loss from property used as an employee on Schedule A (Form 1040), line 22.

Part III

Generally, **do not** complete Part III for property held 1 year or less; use Part III instead. For exceptions, see the chart on page 1.

Part III is used to figure recapture of depreciation and certain other items that must be reported as ordinary income on the disposition of property. Fill out lines 19 through 24 to determine the gain on the disposition of the property. If you have more than four properties to report, use additional forms. For more details on depreciation recapture, see Pub. 544.

Note: *If the property was sold on the installment sale basis, see the Instructions for Form 6252 before completing this part. Also, if you have both installment sales and noninstallment sales, you may want to use a separate Form 4797, Part III, for each installment sale and one Form 4797, Part III, for the noninstallment sales.*

Line 20. The gross sales price includes money, the fair market value of other property received, and any existing mortgage or other debt the buyer assumes or takes the property subject to. For casualty or theft gains, include insurance or other reimbursement you received or expect to receive for each item. Include on this line your insurance coverage, whether or not you are submitting a claim for reimbursement.

For section 1255 property disposed of in a sale, exchange, or involuntary conversion, enter the amount realized. For section 1255 property disposed of in any other way, enter the fair market value.

Line 21. Reduce the cost or other basis of the property by the amount of any diesel-powered highway vehicle credit, enhanced oil recovery credit, or disabled access credit.

However, **do not** reduce the cost or other basis on this line by any of the following amounts:

1. Deductions allowed or allowable for depreciation, amortization, depletion, or preproductive expenses;

2. The section 179 expense deduction;

3. The downward basis adjustment under section 50(c) (or the corresponding provision of prior law);

4. The deduction for qualified clean-fuel vehicle property or refueling property;

5. Deductions claimed under section 190, 193, or 1253(d)(2) or (3) (as in effect before the enactment of P.L. 103-66); or

6. The basis reduction for the qualified electric vehicle credit.

Instead, include these amounts on line 22. They will be used to determine the property's adjusted basis on line 23.

Line 22. For a taxpayer other than a partnership or an S corporation, complete the following steps to figure the amount to enter on line 22:

Step 1. **Add** the following amounts:

1. Deductions allowed or allowable for depreciation, amortization, depletion, or preproductive expenses;

2. The section 179 expense deduction;

3. The downward basis adjustment under section 50(c) (or the corresponding provision of prior law);

4. The deduction for qualified clean-fuel vehicle property or refueling property;

5. Deductions claimed under section 190, 193, or 1253(d)(2) or (3) (as in effect before the enactment of P.L. 103-66); and

6. The basis reduction for the qualified electric vehicle credit.

Step 2. From the step 1 total, **subtract** the following amounts:

1. Any investment credit recapture amount if the basis of the property was reduced for the tax year the property was placed in service under section 50(c)(1) (or the corresponding provision of prior law). See section 50(c)(2) (or the corresponding provision of prior law).

2. Any section 179 or 280F(b)(2) recapture amount included in gross income in a prior tax year because the business use of the property dropped to 50% or less.

3. Any qualified clean-fuel vehicle property or refueling property deduction you were required to recapture because the property ceased to be eligible for the deduction.

4. Any basis increase for qualified electric vehicle credit recapture.

You may have to include depreciation allowed or allowable on another asset (and refigure the basis amount for line 21) if you use its adjusted basis in determining the adjusted basis of the property described on line 19. An example is property acquired by a trade-in. See Regulations section 1.1245-2(a)(4).

Partnerships should enter the deductions allowed or allowable for depreciation, amortization, or depletion on line 22. Enter the section 179 expense deduction on Form 1065, Schedule K, line 24 (unless the partnership is an electing large partnership). Partnerships should make the basis adjustment required under section 50(c) (or the corresponding provision of prior law). Partners adjust the basis of their interest in the partnership to take into account the basis adjustments made at the partnership level.

S corporations should enter the deductions allowed or allowable for depreciation, amortization, or depletion on line 22. Enter the section 179 expense deduction on Form 1120S, Schedule K, line 21, but only if the corporation disposed of property acquired in a tax year beginning after 1982. S corporations should make the basis adjustment required under section 50(c) (or the corresponding provision of prior law). Shareholders adjust the basis in their stock in the corporation to take into account the basis adjustments made at the S corporation level under section 50(c) (or the corresponding provision of prior law).

Line 23. For section 1255 property, enter the adjusted basis of the section 126 property disposed of.

Line 25. Section 1245 property is depreciable (or amortizable under section 185 (repealed), 197, or 1253(d)(2) or (3) (as in effect before the enactment of P.L. 103-66)) and is one of the following:

• Personal property.

• Elevators and escalators placed in service before 1987.

• Real property (other than property described under tangible real property below) subject to amortization or deductions under section 169, 179, 185 (repealed), 188 (repealed), 190, 193, or 194.

• Tangible real property (except buildings and their structural components) if it is used in any of the following ways:

1. As an integral part of manufacturing, production, extraction, or furnishing transportation, communications, or certain public utility services.

2. As a research facility in these activities.

3. For the bulk storage of fungible commodities (including commodities in a liquid or gaseous state) used in these activities.

• A single purpose agricultural or horticultural structure (as defined in section 168(i)(13)).

• A storage facility (not including a building or its structural components) used in connection with the distribution of petroleum or any primary petroleum product.

• Any railroad grading or tunnel bore (as defined in section 168(e)(4)).

See section 1245(b) for exceptions and limits involving:

• Gifts.

• Transfers at death.

• Certain tax-free transactions.

• Certain like-kind exchanges, involuntary conversions, etc.

• Exchanges to comply with SEC orders.

• Property distributed by a partnership to a partner.

• Transfers to tax-exempt organizations where the property will be used in an unrelated business.

• Timber property.

See the following sections for special rules:

• Section 1245(a)(4) for player contracts and section 1056(c) for information required from the transferor of a franchise of any sports enterprise if the sale or exchange involves the transfer of player contracts.

• Section 1245(a)(5) (repealed) for property placed in service before 1987, when only a portion of a building is section 1245 recovery property.

• Section 1245(a)(6) (repealed) for qualified leased property placed in service before 1987.

Line 26. Section 1250 property is depreciable real property (other than section 1245 property). Section 1250 recapture applies when an accelerated depreciation method was used.

Section 1250 recapture does not apply to dispositions of the following property placed in service after 1986 (or after July 31, 1986, if elected):

1. 27.5-year (or 40-year, if elected) residential rental property.

2. 22-, 31.5-, or 39-year (or 40-year, if elected) nonresidential real property.

Real property depreciable under ACRS (pre-1987 rules) is subject to recapture under section 1245, except for the following, which are treated as section 1250 property:

• 15-, 18-, or 19-year real property and low-income housing that is residential rental property.

• 15-, 18-, or 19-year real property and low-income housing that is used mostly outside the United States.

Page 3

- 15-, 18-, or 19-year real property and low-income housing for which a straight line election was made.
- Low-income rental housing described in clause (i), (ii), (iii), or (iv) of section 1250(a)(1)(B). See instructions for line 26b.

See section 1250(d) for exceptions and limits involving:
- Gifts.
- Transfers at death.
- Certain tax-free transactions.
- Certain like-kind exchanges, involuntary conversions, etc.
- Exchanges to comply with SEC orders.
- Property distributed by a partnership to a partner.
- Disposition of qualified low-income housing.
- Transfers of property to tax-exempt organizations where the property will be used in an unrelated business.
- Dispositions of property as a result of foreclosure proceedings.

Special rules:
- For additional depreciation attributable to rehabilitation expenditures, see section 1250(b)(4).
- If substantial improvements have been made, see section 1250(f).

Line 26a. Enter the additional depreciation for the period after 1975. **Additional depreciation** is the excess of actual depreciation over depreciation figured using the straight line method. For this purpose, do not reduce the basis under section 50(c)(1) (or the corresponding provision of prior law) in figuring straight line depreciation.

Line 26b. Use 100% as the percentage for this line, except for low-income rental housing described in clause (i), (ii), (iii), or (iv) of section 1250(a)(1)(B). For this type of low-income rental housing, see section 1250(a)(1)(B) for the percentage to use.

Line 26d. Enter the additional depreciation after 1969 and before 1976. If straight line depreciation exceeds the actual depreciation for the period after 1975, reduce line 26d by the excess. Do not enter less than zero on line 26d.

Line 26f. The amount the corporation treats as ordinary income under section 291 is 20% of the excess, if any, of the amount that would be treated as ordinary income if such property were section 1245 property, over the amount treated as ordinary income under section 1250. If the corporation used the straight line method of depreciation, the ordinary income under section 291 is 20% of the amount figured under section 1245.

Line 27. Partnerships (other than electing large partnerships) should skip this section. Partners should enter on the applicable lines of Part III amounts subject to section 1252 according to instructions from the partnership.

You may have ordinary income on the disposition of certain farmland held more than 1 year but less than 10 years.

Refer to section 1252 to determine if there is ordinary income on the disposition of certain farmland for which deductions were allowed under sections 175 (soil and water conservation) and 182 (land clearing) (repealed). Skip line 27 if you dispose of such farmland during the 10th or later year after you acquired it.

Gain from disposition of certain farmland is subject to ordinary income rules under section 1252 before being considered under section 1231 (Part I).

When filling out line 27b, enter 100% of line 27a on line 27b, except as follows:
- 80% if the farmland was disposed of within the 6th year after it was acquired.
- 60% if disposed of within the 7th year.
- 40% if disposed of within the 8th year.
- 20% if disposed of within the 9th year.

Line 28. If you had a gain on the disposition of oil, gas, or geothermal property placed in service before 1987, you must treat all or part of the gain as ordinary income. Include on line 22 of Form 4797 any depletion allowed (or allowable) in determining the adjusted basis of the property.

If you had a gain on the disposition of oil, gas, geothermal, or other mineral properties (section 1254 property) placed in service after 1986, you must recapture all expenses that were deducted as intangible drilling costs, depletion, mine exploration costs, and development costs, under sections 263, 616, and 617.

Exception. Property placed in service after 1986 and acquired under a written contract entered into before September 26, 1985, and binding at all times thereafter is treated as placed in service before 1987.

Note: *In the case of a corporation that is an integrated oil company, amounts amortized under section 291(b)(2) are treated as a deduction under section 263(c) when completing line 28a.*

Line 28a. If the property was placed in service before 1987, enter the total expenses after 1975 that:
- Were deducted by the taxpayer or any other person as intangible drilling and development costs under section 263(c). (Previously expensed mining costs that have been included in income upon reaching the producing state are not taken into account in determining recapture.); and
- Would have been reflected in the adjusted basis of the property if they had not been deducted.

If the property was placed in service after 1986, enter the total expenses that:
- Were deducted under section 263, 616, or 617 by the taxpayer or any other person;
- Which, but for such deduction, would have been included in the basis of the property; plus
- The deduction under section 611 that reduced the adjusted basis of such property.

If you disposed of a portion of section 1254 property or an undivided interest in it, see section 1254(a)(2).

Line 29a. Use 100% if the property is disposed of less than 10 years after receipt of payments excluded from income. Use 100% minus 10% for each year, or part of a year, that the property was held over 10 years after receipt of the excluded payments. Use zero if 20 years or more.

Line 29b. If any part of the gain shown on line 24 is treated as ordinary income under sections 1231 through 1254 (e.g., section 1252), enter the smaller of **(a)** line 24 reduced by the part of the gain treated as ordinary income under the other provision or **(b)** line 29a.

Part IV

Column (a). If you took a section 179 expense deduction for property placed in service after 1986 (other than listed property, as defined in section 280F(d)(4)), and the business use of the property was reduced to 50% or less this year, complete column (a) of lines 33 through 35 to figure the recapture amount.

Column (b). If you have listed property that you placed in service in a prior year and the business use dropped to 50% or less this year, figure the amount to be recaptured under section 280F(b)(2). Complete column (b), lines 33 through 35. See **Pub. 463,** Travel, Entertainment, Gift, and Car Expenses, for more details on recapture of excess depreciation.

Note: *If you have more than one property subject to the recapture rules, use separate statements to figure the recapture amounts and attach the statements to your tax return.*

Line 33. In column (a), enter the section 179 expense deduction claimed when the property was placed in service. In column (b), enter the depreciation allowable on the property in prior tax years. Include any section 179 expense deduction you took as depreciation.

Line 34. In column (a), enter the depreciation that would have been allowable on the section 179 amount from the year it was placed in service through the current year. See **Pub. 946,** How To Depreciate Property. In column (b), enter the depreciation that would have been allowable if the property had not been used more than 50% in a qualified business. Figure the depreciation from the year it was placed in service until the current year. See Pub. 463 and Pub. 946.

Line 35. Subtract line 34 from line 33 and enter the recapture amount as "other income" on the same form or schedule on which you took the deduction. For example, if you took the deduction on Schedule C (Form 1040), report the recapture amount as other income on Schedule C (Form 1040).

Note: *If you filed Schedule C or F (Form 1040) and the property was used in both your trade or business and for the production of income, the portion attributable to your trade or business is subject to self-employment tax. Allocate the amount on line 35 before entering the recapture amount on the appropriate schedule.*

Be sure to increase the basis of the property by the recapture amount.

Form **4797**		**Sales of Business Property**	OMB No. 1545-0184
		(Also Involuntary Conversions and Recapture Amounts Under Sections 179 and 280F(b)(2))	**1998**
Department of the Treasury Internal Revenue Service (99)		▶ Attach to your tax return. ▶ See separate instructions.	Attachment Sequence No. **27**

Name(s) shown on return — Identifying number

1   Enter here the gross proceeds from the sale or exchange of real estate reported to you for 1998 on Form(s) 1099-S (or a substitute statement) that you will be including on line 2, 10, or 20 . . . . | **1** |

Part I   Sales or Exchanges of Property Used in a Trade or Business and Involuntary Conversions From Other Than Casualty or Theft—Property Held More Than 1 Year

(a) Description of property	(b) Date acquired (mo., day, yr.)	(c) Date sold (mo., day, yr.)	(d) Gross sales price	(e) Depreciation allowed or allowable since acquisition	(f) Cost or other basis, plus improvements and expense of sale	(g) GAIN or (LOSS) Subtract (f) from the sum of (d) and (e)	(h) 28% RATE GAIN or (LOSS) * (see instr. below)
2							

3 Gain, if any, from Form 4684, line 39	**3**	
4 Section 1231 gain from installment sales from Form 6252, line 26 or 37	**4**	
5 Section 1231 gain or (loss) from like-kind exchanges from Form 8824	**5**	
6 Gain, if any, from line 32, from other than casualty or theft	**6**	
7 Combine lines 2 through 6 in columns (g) and (h). Enter gain or (loss) here, and on the appropriate line as follows:	**7**	

Partnerships—Report the gain or (loss) following the instructions for Form 1065, Schedule K, line 6. Skip lines 8, 9, 11, and 12 below.

S corporations—Report the gain or (loss) following the instructions for Form 1120S, Schedule K, lines 5 and 6. Skip lines 8, 9, 11, and 12 below, unless line 7, column (g) is a gain and the S corporation is subject to the capital gains tax.

All others—If line 7, column (g) is zero or a loss, enter that amount on line 11 below and skip lines 8 and 9. If line 7, column (g) is a gain and you did not have any prior year section 1231 losses, or they were recaptured in an earlier year, enter the gain or (loss) in each column as a long-term capital gain or (loss) on Schedule D and skip lines 8, 9, and 12 below.

8 Nonrecaptured net section 1231 losses from prior years (see instructions)	**8**	
9 Subtract line 8 from line 7. For column (g) **only,** if the result is zero or less, enter -0-. Enter here and on the appropriate line(s) as follows (see instructions):	**9**	

S corporations—Enter only the gain in column (g) on Schedule D (Form 1120S), line 14, and skip lines 11 and 12 below.

All others—If line 9, column (g) is zero, enter the gain from line 7, column (g) on line 12 below. If line 9, column (g) is more than zero, enter the amount from line 8, column (g) on line 12 below, and enter the gain or (loss) in each column of line 9 as a long-term capital gain or (loss) on Schedule D.

* Corporations (other than S corporations) should not complete column (h). Partnerships and S corporations must complete column (h). All others must complete column (h) only if line 7, column (g), is a gain. Use column (h) only to report pre-1998 28% rate gain (or loss) from a 1997-98 fiscal year partnership or S corporation.

Part II   Ordinary Gains and Losses

10   Ordinary gains and losses not included on lines 11 through 17 (include property held 1 year or less):

11 Loss, if any, from line 7, column (g)	**11** ( )
12 Gain, if any, from line 7, column (g) or amount from line 8, column (g) if applicable	**12**
13 Gain, if any, from line 31	**13**
14 Net gain or (loss) from Form 4684, lines 31 and 38a	**14**
15 Ordinary gain from installment sales from Form 6252, line 25 or 36	**15**
16 Ordinary gain or (loss) from like-kind exchanges from Form 8824	**16**
17 Recapture of section 179 expense deduction for partners and S corporation shareholders from property dispositions by partnerships and S corporations (see instructions)	**17**
18 Combine lines 10 through 17 in column (g). Enter gain or (loss) here, and on the appropriate line as follows:	**18**

a   For all except individual returns: Enter the gain or (loss) from line 18 on the return being filed.

b   For individual returns:

(1)   If the loss on line 11 includes a loss from Form 4684, line 35, column (b)(ii), enter that part of the loss here. Enter the part of the loss from income-producing property on Schedule A (Form 1040), line 27, and the part of the loss from property used as an employee on Schedule A (Form 1040), line 22. Identify as from "Form 4797, line 18b(1)." See instructions . . . | **18b(1)** |

(2)   Redetermine the gain or (loss) on line 18, excluding the loss, if any, on line 18b(1). Enter here and on Form 1040, line 14 . . . . | **18b(2)** |

For Paperwork Reduction Act Notice, see separate instructions.   Cat. No. 13086I   Form **4797** (1998)

Part III   Gain From Disposition of Property Under Sections 1245, 1250, 1252, 1254, and 1255

19	(a) Description of section 1245, 1250, 1252, 1254, or 1255 property:	(b) Date acquired (mo., day, yr.)	(c) Date sold (mo., day, yr.)
A			
B			
C			
D			

These columns relate to the properties on lines 19A through 19D. ▶		Property A	Property B	Property C	Property D
20	Gross sales price (**Note:** See line 1 before completing.) .	**20**				
21	Cost or other basis plus expense of sale	**21**				
22	Depreciation (or depletion) allowed or allowable	**22**				
23	Adjusted basis. Subtract line 22 from line 21	**23**				
24	Total gain. Subtract line 23 from line 20	**24**				
25	**If section 1245 property:**					
a	Depreciation allowed or allowable from line 22	**25a**				
b	Enter the **smaller** of line 24 or 25a	**25b**				
26	**If section 1250 property:** If straight line depreciation was used, enter -0- on line 26g, except for a corporation subject to section 291.					
a	Additional depreciation after 1975 (see instructions) . . .	**26a**				
b	Applicable percentage multiplied by the **smaller** of line 24 or line 26a (see instructions)	**26b**				
c	Subtract line 26a from line 24. If residential rental property or line 24 is not more than line 26a, skip lines 26d and 26e	**26c**				
d	Additional depreciation after 1969 and before 1976 . . .	**26d**				
e	Enter the **smaller** of line 26c or 26d	**26e**				
f	Section 291 amount (corporations only)	**26f**				
g	Add lines 26b, 26e, and 26f	**26g**				
27	**If section 1252 property:** Skip this section if you did not dispose of farmland or if this form is being completed for a partnership (other than an electing large partnership).					
a	Soil, water, and land clearing expenses	**27a**				
b	Line 27a multiplied by applicable percentage (see instructions)	**27b**				
c	Enter the **smaller** of line 24 or 27b	**27c**				
28	**If section 1254 property:**					
a	Intangible drilling and development costs, expenditures for development of mines and other natural deposits, and mining exploration costs (see instructions)	**28a**				
b	Enter the **smaller** of line 24 or 28a	**28b**				
29	**If section 1255 property:**					
a	Applicable percentage of payments excluded from income under section 126 (see instructions)	**29a**				
b	Enter the **smaller** of line 24 or 29a (see instructions) . .	**29b**				

Summary of Part III Gains. Complete property columns A through D through line 29b before going to line 30.

30	Total gains for all properties. Add property columns A through D, line 24	**30**	
31	Add property columns A through D, lines 25b, 26g, 27c, 28b, and 29b. Enter here and on line 13	**31**	
32	Subtract line 31 from line 30. Enter the portion from casualty or theft on Form 4684, line 33. Enter the portion from other than casualty or theft on Form 4797, line 6	**32**	

Part IV   Recapture Amounts Under Sections 179 and 280F(b)(2) When Business Use Drops to 50% or Less
See instructions.

			(a) Section 179	(b) Section 280F(b)(2)
33	Section 179 expense deduction or depreciation allowable in prior years	**33**		
34	Recomputed depreciation. See instructions	**34**		
35	Recapture amount. Subtract line 34 from line 33. See the instructions for where to report . .	**35**		

♲

E

IRS Form 8825

Rental Real Estate Income
and Expenses of a Partnership
or an "S" Corporation

Form 8825

Department of the Treasury
Internal Revenue Service

Rental Real Estate Income and Expenses of a Partnership or an S Corporation
▶ See instuctions on back.
▶ Attach to Form 1065, Form 1065-B, or Form 1120S.

OMB No. 1545-1186

1998

Name

Employer identification number

---

1 Show the kind and location of each property. See page 2 for additional properties.

A ....

B ....

C ....

D ....

Properties

		A		B		C		D	
Rental Real Estate Income									
2 Gross rents	2								
Rental Real Estate Expenses									
3 Advertising	3								
4 Auto and travel	4								
5 Cleaning and maintenance	5								
6 Commissions	6								
7 Insurance	7								
8 Legal and other professional fees	8								
9 Interest	9								
10 Repairs	10								
11 Taxes	11								
12 Utilities	12								
13 Wages and salaries	13								
14 Depreciation (see instructions)	14								
15 Other (list) ▶	15								
16 Total expenses for each property. Add lines 3 through 15	16								

17 Total gross rents. Add gross rents from line 2, columns A through H **17**

18 Total expenses. Add total expenses from line 16, columns A through H . . . . **18** ( )

19 Net gain (loss) from Form 4797, Part II, line 18, from the disposition of property from rental real estate activities **19**

20a Net income (loss) from rental real estate activities from partnerships, estates, and trusts in which this partnership or S corporation is a partner or beneficiary (from Schedule K-1) **20a**

b Identify below the partnerships, estates, or trusts from which net income (loss) is shown on line 20a. Attach a schedule if more space is needed:

   (1) Name   **(2)** Employer identification number

   ....

   ....

   ....

21 Net income (loss) from rental real estate activities. Combine lines 17 through 20a. Enter the result here and on:
• **Form 1065 or 1120S:** Schedule K, line 2, or
• **Form 1065-B:** Part I, line 4 . . . . } **21**

For Paperwork Reduction Act Notice, see back of form.   Cat. No. 10136Z   Form **8825** (1998)

1   Show the kind and location of each property.

E   ....

F   ....

G   ....

H   ....

		Properties							
		E		F		G		H	
Rental Real Estate Income									
2 Gross rents	**2**								
Rental Real Estate Expenses									
3 Advertising	**3**								
4 Auto and travel.	**4**								
5 Cleaning and maintenance . .	**5**								
6 Commissions	**6**								
7 Insurance	**7**								
8 Legal and other professional fees .	**8**								
9 Interest	**9**								
10 Repairs	**10**								
11 Taxes	**11**								
12 Utilities	**12**								
13 Wages and salaries	**13**								
14 Depreciation (see instructions).	**14**								
15 Other (list) ▶................									
....	**15**								
....									
16 Total expenses for each property. Add lines 3 through 15. . . .	**16**								

Instructions

Section references are to the Internal Revenue Code.

Purpose of form. Partnerships and S corporations use Form 8825 to report income and deductible expenses from rental real estate activities, including net income (loss) from rental real estate activities that flow through from partnerships, estates, or trusts.

Before completing this form, be sure to read **Passive Activity Limitations** in the instructions for Form 1065 or Form 1120S, or **Passive Loss Limitation Activities** in the Instructions for Form 1065-B, especially for the definition of "rental activity."

Lines 1 through 21. Form 8825 provides space for up to eight properties. If there are more than eight properties, complete and attach additional Forms 8825.

The number of columns to be used for reporting income and expenses on this form may differ from the number of rental real estate activities the partnership or S corporation has for purposes of the passive activity limitations. For example, a partnership owns two apartment buildings, each located in a different city. For purposes of the passive activity limitations, the partnership grouped both buildings into a single activity. Although the partnership has only one rental real estate activity, it must report the income and deductions for each building in separate columns.

However, if the partnership or S corporation has more than one rental real estate activity,

attach a statement to Schedule K that reports the net income (loss) for each separate activity. Also, attach a statement to each Schedule K-1 that reports each partner's or shareholder's share of the net income (loss) for each separate activity (except for limited partners in an electing large partnership). See **Passive Activity Reporting Requirements** in the instructions for Form 1065, Form 1065-B, or Form 1120S for additional information that must be provided for each activity.

Complete lines 1 through 16 for each property. But complete lines 17 through 21 on only one Form 8825. The figures on lines 17 and 18 should be the combined totals of all forms.

Do not report on Form 8825 any:

● Income or deductions from a trade or business activity or a rental activity other than rental real estate.

● Portfolio income or deductions.

● Section 179 expense deduction.

● Other items that must be reported separately to the partners or shareholders.

Line 1. Show the kind of property rented out (e.g., "apartment building"). Give the street address, city or town, and state.

Line 14. The partnership or S corporation may claim a depreciation deduction each year for rental property (except for land, which is not depreciable). If the partnership or S corporation placed property in service during the current tax year or claimed depreciation on any vehicle or other listed property, complete and attach

Form 4562, Depreciation and Amortization. See Form 4562 and its instructions to figure the depreciation deduction.

Paperwork Reduction Act Notice. We ask for the information on this form to carry out the Internal Revenue laws of the United States. You are required to give us the information. We need it to ensure that you are complying with these laws and to allow us to figure and collect the right amount of tax.

You are not required to provide the information requested on a form that is subject to the Paperwork Reduction Act unless the form displays a valid OMB control number. Books or records relating to a form or its instructions must be retained as long as their contents may become material in the administration of any Internal Revenue law. Generally, tax returns and return information are confidential, as required by section 6103.

The time needed to complete and file this form will vary depending on individual circumstances. The estimated average time is: **Recordkeeping,** 6 hr., 28 min.; **Learning about the law or the form,** 28 min.; **Preparing the form,** 1 hr., 31 min.; **Copying, assembling, and sending the form to the IRS,** 16 min.

If you have comments concerning the accuracy of these time estimates or suggestions for making this form simpler, we would be happy to hear from you. See the instructions for the tax return with which this form is filed.

Index

minimizing, advantages of,
82–84
payment of unreasonable,
80–82
Continuing grantor and
testamentary trusts. 34
Corporate kit, 16–17, 29
Corporation
defined, 8–9
disqualified from owning
shares in "S" corporation,
33

D

Death
and stock basis
determination, 74
of shareholder, 9, 33
of sole proprietor, 8
Debt
determining basis in, 74–75
treated as second class of
stock, 36–37
Delaware incorporation ,
13–15
benefits of, 14–15
close corporation, 17–18, 19
forming without registered
agent, 15–17
registered agents, 18–26
Depreciation of assets, 121,
128
Distribution of shares, 96, 98
Distribution payment, 80, 82
Domestic International Sales
Corporations, 38
Double taxation, 2–3
Drilling costs, 128

E

Eisenhower, Dwight D., 1
Electing small business trust,
34–35, 52–54
Eligibility, and filing, 52
Employee stock ownership
plan, 92
Employer ID Number, 49–50,
63–67
Environmental laws, 9
Equipment purchases, 123
ESBT. *See* Electing small
business trust
Estates, 33
Exchange of shares, 95–97
vs. distribution, 98–99

F

Filing, 49–54
and eligibility, 52
Form 2553, 50–51
relief for late, 52–54
securing employer ID
number, 49–50
shareholder consent, 53–58
Film production company, 124
Fire coverage, 122
Five-year rule, 38–39
Foreign taxes, 128
Form 1120S. *See* Tax return
preparation
(Form 1120S)
Form 2553, 50–51, 59–62
Form 4797, 200–205
Form 8825, 208–9
Fraud, 8
Fringe benefits, 89–91, 128.
See also Compensation

G–H

Grantor trust, 34
HR-10 plan, 92

I

Income. *See also*
Compensation
passive investment, 39, 71,
110
splitting, 85–87
Income tax. *See* Tax return
preparation
(Form 1120S)
Incorporation, need for, 13.
See also Delaware
incorporation
Independent contractors, 96
commissions or fees paid to,
122
Ineligible business activities,
110
Insurance premiums, 122
Interest-free loans, 87–88
Internal Revenue Code
loans and, 87
Section 1244, 77–78
Inventory, 123–24
Investment income, passive,
39, 71
Investment tax credits, 72
Investors, attracting new, 9

IRS Form 2553, 50–51, 59–62

J

Jointly held stock, 32

L

Labor costs, 123
Leases, 121
Legal fees, 122
Liability coverage, 122. *See
also* Personal liability
License, from governmental
authority, 121
Limited liability company,
10–11
Limited partnership, 10
Liquidations, 72
Losses, maximizing benefits
on, 73–78
basis, 74–75
carrying losses forward, 76

M

Mining exploration and
development, 128
Multiple ownership of shares,
81, 110

O

Office stationery, 122

P

Partnership, 8
disqualified from owning
shares in "S" corporation,
33
fringe benefits and, 89
Pension plans, 122
Personal liability
limited partnerships and, 10
partnerships and, 8
"S" corporations and, 12
sole proprietorships and, 7–8
Profit-sharing plans, 122
Promotional expenses, 121–22
Property distributions, 128
Publishers, 124, 128

Q

QSSS. *See* Qualified
subchapter "S"
subsidiary